W9-CDG-815

The Achievement of Thomas Hardy

Also by Phillip Mallett

KIPLING CONSIDERED (*editor*)

RUDYARD KIPLING: *LIMITS AND RENEWALS* (*editor*)

A SPACIOUS VISION: Essays on Thomas Hardy (*editor*)

SATIRE (*editor*)

THOMAS HARDY: *THE MAYOR OF CASTERBRIDGE* (*editor*)

The Achievement of
Thomas Hardy

Edited by

Phillip Mallett

First published in Great Britain 2000 by
MACMILLAN PRESS LTD
Houndmills, Basingstoke, Hampshire RG21 6XS and London
Companies and representatives throughout the world

A catalogue record for this book is available from the British Library.

ISBN 0–333–73702–4

 First published in the United States of America 2000 by
ST. MARTIN'S PRESS, LLC,
Scholarly and Reference Division,
175 Fifth Avenue, New York, N.Y. 10010

ISBN 0–312–23536–4

Library of Congress Cataloging-in-Publication Data
The achievement of Thomas Hardy / edited by Phillip Mallett.
p.   cm.
Includes bibliographical references and index.
ISBN 0–312–23536–4
1. Hardy, Thomas, 1840–1928—Criticism and interpretation. 2. Wessex
(England)—In literature. I. Mallett, Phillip, 1946–

PR4754 .A25   2000
823'.8—dc21

00–036900

Selection, editorial matter and Chapter 10 © Phillip Mallett 2000
Chapters 1–9, 11 © Macmillan Press Ltd 2000

All rights reserved. No reproduction, copy or transmission of this publication may be made
without written permission.

No paragraph of this publication may be reproduced, copied or transmitted save with written
permission or in accordance with the provisions of the Copyright, Designs and Patents Act
1988, or under the terms of any licence permitting limited copying issued by the Copyright
Licensing Agency, 90 Tottenham Court Road, London W1P 0LP.

Any person who does any unauthorised act in relation to this publication may be liable to
criminal prosecution and civil claims for damages.

The authors have asserted their rights to be identified as the authors of this work in accordance
with the Copyright, Designs and Patents Act 1988.

This book is printed on paper suitable for recycling and made from fully managed and sustained
forest sources.

10   9   8   7   6   5   4   3   2   1
09   08   07   06   05   04   03   02   01   00

Printed and bound in Great Britain by
Antony Rowe Ltd, Chippenham, Wiltshire

Dedicated to the memory of Desmond Hawkins

Contents

Preface by Phillip Mallett   viii

Notes on the Contributors   xvi

1   Merely a Good Hand at a Serial?
    from *A Pair of Blue Eyes* to *Far from the Madding Crowd*   1
    Charles P. C. Pettit

2   Geology, Genealogy and Church Restoration
    in Hardy's Writing   22
    Sophie Gilmartin

3   'Gifted, even in November':
    the Meanings of *The Well-Beloved*   41
    Michael Irwin

4   A Feast of Language: Hardy's Allusions   58
    Mary Rimmer

5   'As near to poetry as the conditions would allow':
    the Presence of the Poet in Hardy's Novels   72
    William Morgan

6   Hardy's Architecture:
    a General Perspective and a Personal View   95
    Timothy Hands

7   *Wessex Poems*, 1898   105
    James Gibson

8   The Figure of the Singer in the Poetry of Thomas Hardy   117
    Danny Karlin

9   Thomas Hardy's Narrative Art: the Poems and Short Stories   137
    Douglas Dunn

10 Noticing Things: Hardy and the Nature of 'Nature'   155
    Phillip Mallett

11 Rediscovering Thomas Hardy's 'Facts' Notebook   171
    William Greenslade

Index   187

Preface

The essays and lectures collected in this volume are concerned with both Hardy the novelist and Hardy the poet, and with the relation between his two careers as a writer. Unlike Rudyard Kipling and D. H. Lawrence, the two writers who most obviously compare with him in producing major work in both poetry and prose fiction, Hardy had been known as a novelist for twenty-five years before he made his first public appearance as a poet. The shift from prose to verse signalled by the publication in 1897 of his last novel, *The Well-Beloved*, and in the following year of his first collection of poems, *Wessex Poems*, means that readers new to Hardy's work now find themselves making two different discoveries. Hardy the novelist is usually encountered as the slightly younger contemporary of Trollope, Wilkie Collins and George Eliot. Trollope's Barchester novels, beginning with *The Warden* (1855), may have influenced Hardy's plan to write a series of novels set in Wessex; *Desperate Remedies*, Hardy's first published novel, has numerous similarities with Collins's most successful work, *The Woman in White* (1860); Richard Hutton, reviewing *Far from the Madding Crowd* in the *Spectator*, was not the only critic to invoke George Eliot's name, and to suggest that if this was not another of her novels, then it was the work of her equal.

Hardy the poet, on the other hand, is the older contemporary of the T. S. Eliot of *Prufrock* and *The Waste Land*, if not of *Four Quartets*. Christopher Ricks has shown the similarities between Hardy's poem 'A Spellbound Palace' and Eliot's 'Sweeney Erect', and argues, convincingly but unexpectedly, that if there is a question of influence, 'Eliot is not the borrower but the lender'.[1] Famously, Philip Larkin, until his death the unofficial laureate of post-1945 England, was enabled to shed the influence of Yeats when he fell under the spell of Hardy. In short, few other writers sit so firmly in two ages as Hardy does in the 'Victorian' and the 'Modern'. Wordsworth and Yeats, perhaps: but we remember Wordsworth as a great young poet, and Yeats as a great old one. Hardy became a major novelist in his thirties, and remained a major poet into his eighties.

There is a deeper puzzle to be resolved before we can come to terms with Hardy's achievement in either form. In the 'Apology' which prefaced *Late Lyrics and Earlier* (1922) Hardy looked for an alliance between religion, 'in its essential and undogmatic sense', which had somehow to be preserved, and 'complete rationality', which would come whether it was desired or not, by means of 'the interfusing effect of poetry' – though, characteristically, he noted that this might be only a forlorn hope.[2] The 'Apology' thus takes its place in the line which runs from Wordsworth's Preface to *Lyrical Ballads*, through Arnold's *Essays in Criticism*, on into the launch of *Scrutiny* in 1932, and beyond. But beside this exalted notion of the power of literature, and poetry in particular, to act as a bulwark for the essential values of a civilised society, Hardy's claims for his own work are curiously modest. He wanted, he told Leslie Stephen in 1874, to be 'a good hand at a serial' (though he admitted that later he might have higher aims), and he said of his poems that he hoped to write at least some good enough for an anthology like the *Golden Treasury*. From the first, Hardy has exasperated his critics by seeming not to have the kind of ambition they demanded of him. *Far from the Madding Crowd*, grumbled Henry James – four years Hardy's junior, but contriving to sound a good deal older – was 'singularly inartistic', 'a really curious imitation of something better'.[3] Almost a century later, Donald Davie complained that Hardy's poems, 'instead of transforming . . . the reality of commonsense, are on the contrary just so many glosses on that reality'. Like James, Davie feels that Hardy is somehow less than he ought to be: in Davie's words, he 'sold the vocation short'. And yet Davie is in no doubt that Hardy's is a 'poetic imagination of the first magnitude', and that his influence, even more than that of Pound and Eliot, has been the most far-reaching in British poetry in the twentieth century.[4]

Novelist and poet, Victorian and modern, an inheritor of the high Romantic tradition who insisted on the modesty of his aims – these are some of the paradoxes which meet Hardy's readers, and which are addressed in varying ways by the essays and lectures collected here. Charles Pettit concentrates on *A Pair of Blue Eyes*, Hardy's third published novel, and compares it with *Far from the Madding Crowd*, which followed a year later. These were apprentice novels, and it is clear that Hardy took his apprenticeship seriously. From the first he set himself to explore different narrative strategies, especially in the handling of point of view. For George Eliot this was primarily a moral issue: her famous question – 'but why always Dorothea?'[5] – leads to her insistence that narrator and reader should allow every character a fair hearing, recognising that each has his or her own 'centre of self'; it is because she learns to act in this spirit in the course of the novel that Dorothea becomes its heroine and exemplar. Hardy's concern with point of view is at once more literal and more unsettling. As Pettit shows, one of the lessons Hardy learned from *A Pair of Blue Eyes* was the effect of presenting a scene from the limited perspective of a single observer or participant, fusing dramatic action and psychological interest: Elfride as her actions were seen at that moment by Knight, or by Stephen, Sergeant Troy as he is first glimpsed by Bathsheba, and so on. Technically, this may owe something to Hardy's reading of Browning's dramatic monologues, or even to his studies in the National Gallery. What makes it unsettling is that it allows Hardy to resist what George Eliot so often seeks to create: the supposition that there is some way for characters, readers and narrators to come together in a shared sense of reality. When Hardy insisted that his work dealt with 'unadjusted impressions', he meant to cast doubt on whether consensus, or final adjustment, was ever possible. The narrator's Elfride is not Stephen's, nor Knight's, nor yet the reader's: and what is true about Elfride or Bathsheba in these early novels was to be still more true of Tess, or Sue, in the later ones.

Sophie Gilmartin also discusses *A Pair of Blue Eyes*, which she takes together with *The Well-Beloved* as a means to explore Hardy's fascination with a cluster of linked themes: graveyards, church restoration, geology and genealogy. What unites these interests is the pursuit of origins and continuities, and with those a sense of identity and belonging. In both novels the geological time-span is set against the human one, and the individual life against the repetition of character and experience across the generations. The notion of belonging is in Hardy's work typically a paradoxical one, as in *Tess*: on the one hand, Tess suffers the loss of a sense of belonging, as she becomes a migrant worker, cut off by her education from the values and traditions of her parents and her peers; on the other, she fears being trapped into an identity given by her ancestry, and finding that she is destined to repeat the experiences of her d'Urberville ancestors. As Dr Gilmartin shows, Hardy's major novels explore both the fragility of identity and the disruption of a genealogical line: Eustacia, Henchard, Tess, Jude, Pierston, all die childless.

Michael Irwin's essay concentrates on *The Well-Beloved*. This is a novel which until recently Hardy's critics were content to ignore, or regret, usually with some description of it as objective, abstract or geometrical. It is these things but, as Irwin shows, it is also a deeply-felt novel, which not only returns to many of the themes and concerns of earlier novels – the brevity of life, heredity, the way men and women fall in love – but goes on to explore the nature of the artist within a framework given by those themes. The narrative tells us that 'the ever-bubbling spring of emotion' in Pierston requires a 'conduit into space', which he seeks to discover, more or less indifferently, in women of flesh and blood, or in carved images of them. This inevitably raises the question of the relation between the real woman and the admittedly created one. In following out his argument, Irwin links Hardy with Robert Graves and his White Goddess; but his essay also takes us back not only to *The Well-Beloved*, but to the 'Poems of 1912–13'. Do we, here, see art growing out of love, or used as a means to create it? Does the love flow from the poems, or the poetry from the love? Revising *The Well-Beloved* in 1897, Hardy had no especial reason to pause over the account of Pierston's reaction to the death of the first Avice: 'He loved the woman dead and inaccessible as he had never loved her in life.' For the reader who knows the story of Hardy's marriage, it leaps off the page.

Both Mary Rimmer and William Morgan are interested in Hardy's allusions. Dr Rimmer's chapter suggests two distinct but related lines of inquiry. One is to examine the local effect of a given allusion, or as often as not in Hardy the competing effect of a cluster of allusions. The other is to explore the cultural tradition(s) implied by the allusions taken as a whole. Here Dr Rimmer valuably extends a suggestion made by Dennis Taylor, that 'Hardy resists the urbanity of allusiveness which confirms the high culture of the best that is thought and written.'[6] Hardy reminds his readers that there were more things known and thought in this world than were dreamt of by the guardians of high culture. Here too he seeks to unsettle the consensus, to keep alive the apparently marginal or eccentric – what Matthew Arnold would term the 'provincial'. In their different ways, George Eliot and Arnold were both willing to evoke a consensual and authoritative 'we', who are the owners, or at least the custodians of 'the best'. Hardy – it is one of his great attractions – is stubbornly resistant to such a consensus.

Morgan's essay discusses allusion in relation to Hardy's ambition to keep his novel-writing as close to his interests as a poet as he could. One way was to quote the poets, or to have his characters do so; others were to rework his own as yet unpublished poems as passages of prose, or to write prose which the reader is encouraged to read with the kind of attention to movement and texture that is usually reserved for poetry. Like Rimmer, Morgan finds self-conscious experiment and innovation where earlier critics had assumed clumsiness, and even some more recent scholars have detected a lack of certainty. His discussion of Hardy's chapter on 'Collecting Old Poems and Making New' also serves as a reminder that his dictated biography – cited in this volume as *The Life and Work of Thomas Hardy, by Thomas Hardy* – is a far more cunning and pointed guide to his work than its apparently casual construction at first suggests.

This last point is also borne out by Timothy Hands's essay, which takes its bearings from Hardy's comments in *Life and Work* on the way he carried into his writing the principles he had learned from architecture. The best known of these is what Hardy called 'cunning irregularity', typified by the sudden change of metrical pattern in the last stanza of 'The Voice', or by the changing rhyme patterns in 'Shut Out that Moon' (which allow the word 'love', in the third verse, to remain unrhymed), or – but every reader will have his or her own favourite examples. As Hands points out, adherence to Gothic principles was not without its disadvantages. Victorian Gothic has its triumphs, but there are other buildings which fail to cohere, breaking into a mass of brilliant fragments, and there are moments in Hardy's verse too where all the details seem foregrounded, and the sense of a whole is lost. One might also find a parallel between the eclecticism of Gothic Revival architects – George Gilbert Scott, for example, happily used pointed arches to frame sash windows – and Hardy's readiness, as William Archer put it in his review of *Wessex Poems*, to draw 'from all the words of the dictionary on one plane', so that the archaic and the familiar, the learned and the colloquial, jostle against each other in poem after poem. Here again, however, what one might at first suppose to be clumsiness often proves to be the result of a conscious refusal to adjust discordant impressions. Hardy was the least Parnassian of poets.

James Gibson also touches on Hardy and architecture in his essay on *Wessex Poems*. This is, as Gibson shows, a still more curious volume than it seemed even to its first readers, who had no prevision that Hardy would appear before them as a poet. We can only speculate on why Hardy included the poems he did, and not others, such as 'Wessex Heights', which were written earlier but published later; or why he chose to open the volume with 'The Temporary the All', just about the most likely of all his poems to bemuse his readers; or why he chose to make the volume even stranger to them, by publishing it with illustrations (that there was something of a fashion for this in the 1890s seems hardly explanation enough). As Gibson demonstrates, some of the reviewers were obtuse; but as he also reveals, they had some reason to be puzzled.

Danny Karlin's essay raises a general question, and examines Hardy as a special instance of it: why did poets continue to refer to themselves as singers, and to poetry as song, long after the mass of poetry was being not heard, but read, silently, from a printed page? In addressing this question, Karlin, like Morgan, is led to reflect on the prestige of poetry, not just in relation to the increasing dominance of prose fiction, but in a wider context of cultural change. While this volume was in preparation, one Poet Laureate died, and another was appointed; nobody – not even a novelist – proposed that there should be a comparable role for a writer of prose fiction. But while Karlin's essay reflects on the tradition of the divinely inspired bard, it also suggests how deeply song and singing – profoundly communal arts in Hardy's time, far removed from the modern and essentially solitary activity of listening to recorded music on a personal stereo – were part of Hardy's life, and part of the fabric of his stories and poems, from the first novel, *Desperate Remedies*, in which Aeneas Manston and an increasingly drunken postman make their rounds singing 'Joan's Ale', on to the last poem in *Winter Words*, entitled (it is part of the paradox) 'He Resolves to Say No More'.

Douglas Dunn's essay, on Hardy's narrative art, raises similarly large questions, and in its references to the oral tradition touches on some of the matters raised by Karlin. Dunn draws on Walter Benjamin's important essay on Leskov, 'The Storyteller', included in *Illuminations*. Benjamin discusses the decline of storytelling as an art which depends on 'the epic side of truth, wisdom', and which depends on its closeness to the realm of living speech. Here again, though in a very different form, Hardy had hinted at some of the things his readers and critics ought to know. In *Life and Work*, he recalled his surprise that experienced readers like John Morley and Alexander Macmillan failed to recognise that the events described in his unpublished novel *The Poor Man and the Lady* had no foundation in Hardy's own experience, but owed their 'seeming actuality' to the 'affected simplicity' of Defoe.[7] In *The Hand of Ethelberta*, it is Defoe's style which the heroine seeks to imitate in her public performances as a storyteller. Style, and the relation between seeming and actuality, are central issues in this novel. When Ethelberta recounts her true story, in Chapter 38, her listeners assume it is a fiction; when Christopher Julian stumbles across her in rehearsal he supposes her fictional tale is a true one, and rushes to offer his support. Tales 'of the weird kind', she explains to Julian, 'were made to be told, not written. The action of a teller is wanted to give due effect to all stories of incident' (Chapter 13). Hardy, poised like his heroine between two worlds, one rural and one metropolitan, one marginalised and one privileged, one given to story and song and the other to the printed book, had every reason to be conscious of the cultural implications of his narrative art and style.

The concluding essay in the volume, William Greenslade's account of the compilation of Hardy's 'Facts' notebook, serves to encourage further speculation on Hardy's relation to what Matthew Arnold was teaching his contemporaries to call 'culture'. This is not an account of Hardy the autodidact, if by that ungracious term is meant someone awkwardly mugging up whatever in a given society educated people are supposed to know. Greenslade's research adds weight and substance to Raymond Williams's seminal essay on Hardy in *The Country and the City* (London, 1973). Williams recognised that Hardy's position as a writer required him to be both the educated observer of his community, and a passionate participant in it. Here too, Hardy can be seen to have anticipated what later critics would need to consider. In his account of the writing of *Far from the Madding Crowd*, in *Life and Work*, he teases the reader with a description of his rural solitude, claiming to have written some sentences of the novel on a leaf with wood chips – a task the reader might like to attempt, by way of experiment – before submitting it to his editor, Leslie Stephen, Cambridge and Bloomsbury to the core, for publication in the highbrow *Cornhill Magazine*. As Greenslade shows, the importance of the 'Facts' notebook was that it allowed Hardy to immerse himself as a reader in a world he also knew by report from his family, especially from his mother and grandmother, and to explore his own relation to that world, as he moved back into Dorchester, and began to render the world of 'Wessex' with ever-increasing solidity.

Most of the essays collected in this volume are based on lectures given at the Thirteenth International Conference organised by the Thomas Hardy Society, which took place in Dorchester in the summer of 1998, in the centenary year of *Wessex Poems*. Three of the lectures were not available for publication, and I have replaced these with three others. William Greenslade's essay is a much extended version of a seminar paper; my own essay, 'Noticing Things: Hardy and the Nature of "Nature"', is a version of a lecture given at the British Library in June 1999 at the invitation of the Thomas Hardy Society; while the essay by Michael Irwin was written especially for this volume. None of the essays has appeared in this form before. Dr Hands's lecture was accompanied by a number of slides, and appears here in a format more suitable for publication; it is based on his contribution to the forthcoming *Readers' Companion to Thomas Hardy*, edited for Oxford University Press by Norman Page, and we are grateful to OUP and to Professor Page for their co-operation. Dr Gilmartin's essay overlaps in part with a chapter in her *Ancestry and Narrative in Nineteenth-Century British Fiction*

(Cambridge, 1998), and again we are grateful for permission to use that material here.

Wherever possible, references to the novels are to the relevant World's Classics editions, except for *Desperate Remedies*, where the edition used is that prepared for Penguin Classics by Mary Rimmer (1998). References to the poems are to *The Complete Poems of Thomas Hardy*, edited by James Gibson (Macmillan: London, 1976). References to Hardy's dictated biography are to *The Life and Work of Thomas Hardy, by Thomas Hardy*, edited by Michael Millgate (Macmillan: London, 1984).

While this work was in preparation, the death was announced of Desmond Hawkins, author of (among other works) *Hardy the Novelist, Hardy: Novelist and Poet* and *Concerning Agnes*, and a long-serving Vice-President of the Thomas Hardy Society. In his triple role as scholar, writer and broadcaster, Desmond Hawkins contributed greatly to Thomas Hardy studies over a period of some fifty years. This volume is dedicated to his memory.

Notes

1. Christopher Ricks, *Essays in Appreciation* (Oxford, 1996), p. 242.
2. The 'Apology' is included in *The Complete Poems of Thomas Hardy*, ed. James Gibson (London, 1976), pp. 556–62.
3. In his review of the novel in the *Nation*, 24 December 1874.
4. Donald Davie, *Thomas Hardy and British Poetry* (London, 1973), pp. 62, 6.
5. At the beginning of Chapter 29 of *Middlemarch*. Compare Dorothea's self-questioning in Chapter 80: 'Was she alone in that scene? Was it her event only?'
6. See his *Hardy's Literary Language and Victorian Philology* (Oxford, 1993), p. 293.
7. See *The Life and Work of Thomas Hardy, by Thomas Hardy*, ed. Michael Millgate (London, 1984), pp. 62–3.

Notes on the Contributors

Douglas Dunn is Professor of English and Director of the Scottish Studies Institute at the University of St Andrews. In addition to his work as a critic he is also an award-winning poet. His first volume, *Terry Street*, was published in 1969; his most recent, *Dante's Drum-Kit*, was published in 1993. *Elegies*, published in 1985, won the Whitbread Book of the Year award. He has also published a translation of Racine's *Andromache* (1990), and a volume of short stories, *Secret Villages* (1985).

James Gibson was formerly Head of the English Field at Christ Chruch College, Canterbury, and sometime Chairman of the Thomas Hardy Society. He is the editor of both *The Complete Poems of Thomas Hardy* and of the Variorum edition. His many studies and editions of Hardy include the Casebook volume on the poems, as well as *Thomas Hardy: a Literary Life* (1996), and *Thomas Hardy: Interviews and Recollections* (1999).

Sophie Gilmartin is Lecturer in English at Royal Holloway College, University of London, working mainly in the fields of Victorian literature, art and cultural studies. Her study of *Ancestry and Narrative in Nineteenth-Century British Literature* was published in 1998.

William Greenslade is Lecturer in Literary Studies at the University of the West of England. He has written a number of articles on late Victorian literature and culture, and is the author of *Degeneration, Culture and the Novel* (1994). He is currently preparing an edition of Hardy's 'Facts' notebook.

Timothy Hands is Headmaster of Portsmouth Grammar School. He is the author of a number of studies of Hardy, including *Thomas Hardy: Distracted Preacher?* (1989), the volume *Thomas Hardy* in the series Writers in their Time (1995), and *A Hardy Chronology* (1992).

Michael Irwin is Professor of English at the University of Kent. He is the author of numerous essays and studies, including *Picturing: Description and Illusion in the Nineteenth Century Novel* (1979), as well as of two novels, *Working Orders* (1969) and *Striker* (1985), and of translations of libretti for Kent Opera. His study, *Reading Hardy's Landscapes*, is due to appear in 1999.

Danny Karlin is Professor of English at University College, London. He is the editor (with John Woolford) of *The Poems of Robert Browning* (1991), and author of *The Courtship of Robert Browning and Elizabeth Barrett* (1985). He is also the editor of the *Penguin Book of Victorian Verse* (1997), and of the volume on Kipling in the Oxford Authors series (1999).

Phillip Mallett is Senior Lecturer in English at the University of St Andrews. In addition to chapters and articles on a number of Victorian and earlier writers, he is the editor of several collections of essays, including *Kipling Considered* (1989) and (with Ronald Draper) *A Spacious Vision: Essays on Thomas Hardy* (1994), and of an edition of *The Mayor of Casterbridge* (2000).

William Morgan is Professor of English at Illinois State University, where he teaches courses in Victorian literature, poetry, and English as an academic discipline. He has published essays and articles on Hardy and on others in such journals as *PMLA*, *Victorian Poetry* and *Critical Inquiry*. He has also won awards for his poetry and has published a chapbook of poems, *Trackings: the Body's Memory, the Heart's Fiction* (1998).

Charles P. C. Pettit is Assistant County Librarian for Oxfordshire County Council. The compiler of *A Catalogue of the Works of Thomas Hardy in the Dorchester Reference Library* (1984), he has directed three of the International Thomas Hardy Conferences held under the auspices of the Thomas Hardy Society. He has also edited three collections of essays on Hardy, including *New Perspectives on Hardy* (1994) and most recently *Reading Thomas Hardy* (1998).

Mary Rimmer is Associate Professor of English at the University of New Brunswick, Canada. She is the editor of both *Desperate Remedies* and *The Trumpet-Major*, as well as the author of articles on Canadian and Trinidadian fiction. She is writing a book on allusion in Hardy.

1
Merely a Good Hand at a Serial? from *A Pair of Blue Eyes* to *Far from the Madding Crowd*

Charles P. C. Pettit

It was in a letter to Leslie Stephen during the serialisation of *Far from the Madding Crowd* in the *Cornhill Magazine* that Hardy famously, and perhaps somewhat disingenuously, claimed that he had no higher wish 'for the present' than to be considered 'a good hand at a serial'.[1] There is of course some truth in this claim. He was part-way through the writing of only his second serialised novel, and having recently abandoned architecture, he desperately needed to make a success of his new career as a writer in order to generate a steady income, particularly in view of his forthcoming marriage. He therefore *had* to produce a serial acceptable to both editors and readers, so that more commissions would come his way. But whatever Hardy's conscious aims were (and they may well have been higher than he cared to admit to his editor), *Far from the Madding Crowd* is infinitely more than simply a good serial. It is universally regarded as Hardy's first major achievement, and one of the half-dozen novels on which rests his stature as a major novelist. In contrast, by general critical consent, *A Pair of Blue Eyes* is seen as interesting and enjoyable but slight, an apprentice piece.

There is a similar disparity in achievement between *The Hand of Ethelberta* and *The Return of the Native*, but we know that between those two novels Hardy allowed himself virtually a two-year breathing space, a time he very deliberately used for a period of reading and note-taking. But *A Pair of Blue Eyes* and *Far from the Madding Crowd* were written in remarkably quick succession. The conclusion of *A Pair of Blue Eyes* was sent to Tinsley on 12 March 1873, and in June Hardy sent to Leslie Stephen some chapters and an outline of *Far from the Madding Crowd*. There is no time here for reading, note-taking and reassessing aesthetic aims, or for any other literary activities which might explain the differing stature of the two novels. Is it that in *Far from the Madding Crowd*

1

Hardy chose a subject better suited to his literary gifts? Was there simply a moment at which everything came together, when all the years of preparation gelled? Or can we in fact see the germs of the achievement of *Far from the Madding Crowd* in the earlier novel? Can we watch the emergence of the major novelist from the minor, of the master craftsman from the apprentice? I believe that we can, and this is what I would like to explore in this chapter.

The critical consensus on the relative standing of *A Pair of Blue Eyes* and *Far from the Madding Crowd* which I have referred to is well established, having lasted for the best part of the twentieth century. It found an early and persuasive exponent in Lascelles Abercrombie. Writing in 1912, Abercrombie's view was that 'when all is said, *A Pair of Blue Eyes* is a slight book; slight, that is, compared with the novel which followed it. It is a well-ordered system of charming, pathetic, but unimportant occurrences . . .'. On the other hand, he considers *Far from the Madding Crowd* as one of 'the six great novels which form the main building, in our architectural image, of Hardy's fiction'; it is here that 'his genius has reached full scope'.[2] And the critical view established by such writers as Abercrombie in the early years of the century has in essence been maintained throughout all the intervening years up to the century's end.[3] And yet, it has not always been like this. Listen to these extracts from the reviews which greeted *A Pair of Blue Eyes* on its first publication in 1873. This is the *Pall Mall Gazette*:

> We are very careful how we use the word 'genius'; but we have no hesitation in saying of the author of 'A Pair of Blue Eyes' and 'Under the Greenwood Tree' that he is distinctly a man of genius; there is in these books more inborn strength, more inborn knowledge, more of that fine humour which is the mark and test of genius, than we are able to detect in any living English novelist of our acquaintance: one only excepted.[4]

The next extract comes from the *Spectator*, whose review of *Desperate Remedies* had been so crushing that as he sat on a stile reading it Hardy 'wished that he were dead'.[5] The tone this time is astonishingly different:

> we have a really powerful story, well proportioned in its parts, of varied and deep interest, yet not too harrowing for pleasure, relieved by exquisite touches of word pictures, and supported by characters not too numerous to crowd the stage and divert us from an atten-

tive study of the three central figures. . . . [Elfride's character] is all told, or rather revealed, with such a wonderful insight into a woman's nature, that we are surprised to find as perfect a comprehension of the force and straightforwardness of her lover's [Knight's] utterly different and strictly manly characteristics. . . . And we might devote a second review with ease to [the] admirably true and humorous description of the humble neighbours. The scenes at the mason's where the pig is being killed, and in the church vault where they are enlarging it for the poor countess, are almost worthy of George Eliot. . . . The exquisite little bits of description of natural scenery abound throughout.

The review was indeed so enthusiastic that Hardy wrote out a section of it and sent it to Tinsley in hope that it might make good copy for an advertisement.[6] The *Graphic* was equally enthusiastic:

This book abundantly confirms us in the high estimate of Mr. Hardy's powers which we had formed from his previous stories. . . . There is nothing in it to which we could take exception, or even wish to improve, except the title . . . and an occasional affectation of phrase. . . . [I]n his descriptions of village folk and their talks and ways, Mr. Hardy seems to us to excel every one but George Eliot . . . But we have no space to draw attention to the many perfections of this book, which unquestionably places its author in the first rank of writers of high-class fiction of our day.[7]

My last extract comes from the *Saturday Review*:

It is one of the most artistically constructed among recent novels. And, from considerations affecting higher matters than mere construction, we would assign it a very high place among works of its class.

The distinctive feature of this novel is that out of simple materials there has been evolved a result of really tragic power. . . . The author of *A Pair of Blue Eyes* . . . is a writer who to a singular purity of thought and intention unites great power of imagination, strong enough to sustain interest at a very high point of vitality, without resorting to mere surprises or descending to what is ignoble.[8]

This is a tremendous reception! Could any author wish for more? Even those reviews which are not quite so enthusiastic have plenty of positive points to make. *The Times* talks of the novel's 'good workmanship' and 'carefully drawn' characters; the *Athenaeum* speaks of the 'considerable skill' Hardy shows in enlisting our sympathies for Elfride; *John Bull* describes the novel's 'good mixture of grave and gay, a well-arranged plot, an extraordinary and unparalleled denouement'.[9] And while the reviews of Elfride's novel are characterised as 'significantly short' (Ch. 14), the majority of these are long, and often include lengthy quotations. They are indeed so glowing that they necessitate a modification of the traditional view that it was with *Far from the Madding Crowd* that Hardy made his name.[10] Popularity with the general reading public may indeed have come only with the later novel, but these little-noticed reviews make it clear that it was with *A Pair of Blue Eyes* that Hardy made his real breakthrough with the critics, though of course the positive reviews of *Under the Greenwood Tree* had started the process of critical acceptance.

The reviews of *Far from the Madding Crowd* are much more widely known,[11] so I will not quote extensively from them here. However, if they are compared with the reviews of *A Pair of Blue Eyes* it is remarkable that they are markedly *less* enthusiastic than those of the earlier novel, singling out some of the same areas of praise with rather less of the excitement of discovering a new force in literature, and carping rather more about alleged deficiencies in Hardy's use of language. The reviews may be typified in the touch of weariness in the *Saturday Review*'s comment that: 'There was promise, too, in both these books [*Under the Greenwood Tree* and *A Pair of Blue Eyes*] of something really good being produced in future works. And that promise, though not quite fulfilled, is given again in *Far from the Madding Crowd.*'[12]

It's not just that the initial critical reception of *A Pair of Blue Eyes* was enthusiastic. The novel retained enormous popularity and critical acclaim throughout the remaining years of the nineteenth century. As Hardy himself noted, it was always a 'selling book',[13] and well into the 1890s, many Sampson Low editions of Hardy's novels proclaimed on the title-page that they were by 'Thomas Hardy/author of *Far from the Madding Crowd, A Pair of Blue Eyes* etc.', not mentioning *The Return of the Native* and *The Mayor of Casterbridge* even though these titles (so much more highly regarded today) were published in the same series. W. E. Henley's review of *The Return of the Native* said that it was 'not by any means so good a book as *A Pair of Blue Eyes*'.[14] When a collection of literary extracts was compiled in 1882–83 under the title *Gleanings from Popular Authors, Grave and Gay*,[15] the two Hardy pieces included were 'The Christmas Choir' (from *Under the Greenwood Tree*) and 'Love will Find out the Way', the scene from *A Pair of Blue Eyes* in which Elfride rescues Knight from the Cliff without a Name. The novel also had some well-known enthusiasts in the world of literature. Coventry Patmore wrote to Hardy in March 1875: 'I trust that you will not think I am taking too great a liberty in writing to tell you with what extraordinary pleasure and admiration I have read your novels, especially that called "A Pair of Blue Eyes".' Moreover Patmore, who later described Hardy as 'our first living novelist', maintained his enthusiasm for this novel for the rest of his life. After his death in 1896 his widow wrote to Hardy telling him that Patmore had 'continually' chosen to have *A Pair of Blue Eyes* read to him: 'In illness, when he asked for *A Pair of Blue Eyes* one knew he was able to *enjoy* again.'[16] Tennyson told Hardy that he liked *A Pair of Blue Eyes* the best of his novels.[17] Robert Louis Stevenson cited *A Pair of Blue Eyes* as a 'worthy specimen[s]' of what he termed the 'dramatic novel'.[18] The author of one of the first book-length studies of Hardy, Lionel Johnson, writing in 1892, lists the 'six books, upon which Mr. Hardy's readers love to dwell' as *The Return of the Native, The Woodlanders, Tess of the d'Urbervilles, The Mayor of Casterbridge, Far from The Madding Crowd* and *A Pair of Blue Eyes*.[19] Ironically, one of the few people of this period on record as saying that he did *not* think much of it was its publisher, William Tinsley, who later wrote that it was 'by far the weakest of the three books I published of his'.[20] Did he really think it was far weaker than *Desperate Remedies*?

We also know that Hardy himself had a particular interest in this book: he wrote in 1877 that he had reasons for wanting to reissue it 'even at the expense of profit'; he suggested to Elgar that he set it to music; and it was the only title in the Mellstock edition for which he supplied a quantity of amendments and read proofs.[21] This is generally, and I think correctly, taken to mean that he had a personal interest in the novel because of its association with his Cornish romance. But, added to all the other evidences of the novel's public and critical popularity in the last century, it does raise the question: is the traditional twentieth-century view wrong? Are we missing something vital in our assessment of this novel? Or is it simply that *A Pair of Blue Eyes* contains particular qualities which appealed to Victorian literary tastes and sensibilities – particularly for those people who discovered Hardy through this novel – and not to those of today? I will have to leave this last question hanging in the air – an exploration of the particular characteristics shared by successful Victorian literary fiction is a major subject in its own right. But accepting that in any popularly acclaimed artistic work there is likely to be something which reflects the mood and tastes of the times, this alone cannot account for such universal and long-standing critical enthusiasm. What I believe those early readers saw clearly, through all the flaws of the book, was something tremendous: the emergence of a 'genius', of a new author in 'the first rank of high-class fiction', to quote those early reviews. In other words, the kind of literary event that happens once a generation, if then.

Whereas Hardy's first two published novels, though very different from one another, had each shown a uniformity of approach, *A Pair of Blue Eyes* is an experimental novel, in which, presumably deliberately, Hardy was trying out a variety of subjects and methods of treatment.[22] This is why it can be characterised by Michael Millgate as a 'rag-bag' of different elements,[23] and why it is possible to trace an intimate connection between two such apparently dissimilar novels as *A Pair of Blue Eyes* and *Far from the Madding Crowd*. For, in crude terms, Hardy selected from *A Pair of Blue Eyes* its most successful elements for further development in his next novel, and jettisoned those which had been less effective. His strategy may not be immediately obvious, simply because the approaches which most predominate in *A Pair of Blue Eyes*, particularly in its first half, are the ones which are later jettisoned, while the experimental narrative techniques of the second half of the novel are developed in *Far from the Madding Crowd*.

Looking first at the less effective aspects of the novel, the most fundamental characteristic of *A Pair of Blue Eyes*, which is also perhaps its most fundamental weakness, is described succinctly by Robert Langbaum: '*A Pair of Blue Eyes* is a powerful novel of manners in which the principal characters, except for the socially rising hero, are upper class. . . . [If the novel] does not count as major, it is probably because Hardy never does quite as well with novels of manners as with novels that emerge from pastoral.'[24] This is indeed a novel of manners, set very largely in a middle- or upper-class world. Of course, the tension between Stephen's professional position as an architect and his working-class origins is of significance, but the focus of the novel is on '[t]he quality, as the upper classes in rural districts are designated by the lower with so much true discrimination', to borrow Trollope's beautifully ironic words.[25] In terms of place this encompasses Endelstow Rectory, Endelstow House, Knight's chambers in Bede's Inn and Rotten Row; and in concerns: architecture, reviewing, novel-writing, the Church, dress (remember the extraordinary, detailed description of the 13 rings worn by Mrs Swancourt) and marriage as social and financial advancement. The narrative voice analyses the characters' feelings and thoughts at length, and adds intellectual weight to the narrative by numerous aphorisms and by allusions to a whole gallery of painters: the first description of Elfride alone defines her features in terms of the paintings of Raphael, Rubens and Correggio. There is occasional social satire: the Rotten Row scene is the most obvious and extended example, but there are many little touches, like Mr Swancourt's claim that he was always inclined to suspect Stephen 'because he didn't care about sauces of any kind. I always did doubt a man's being a gentleman if his palate had no acquired tastes' (Ch. 9). There is little action, but a high proportion of dialogue, particularly verbal fencing between the lovers, with much ponderous philosophising from Knight. It is unfortunate that both Elfride and the narrator appear to share admiration for the conversation of this 'musing mentor' (Ch. 27), though on one occasion Elfride does effectively (if perhaps unwittingly) puncture him: 'I see', she says, 'that is, I should if I quite understood what all those generalities mean' (Ch. 17). Various stock comic techniques are used. Characters are given humorous names, like William Worm and Robert Lickpan, and, with Hardyan irony, Felix (i.e. 'lucky') Jethway. They are characterised by the use of repeated phrases and mannerisms. Mr Swancourt, in a way reminiscent of Jane Austen's Sir Walter Elliot, talks frequently of the advantages of 'blue blood', and laughs to himself at stories too bad to tell, while Worm talks constantly of the sound of frying fish in his head.

The problem with all of this is that it never really seems to engage Hardy's interest sufficiently to raise the novel above the level of a pleasant read. The narrative tone is too heavy for the effect apparently intended, and there is a paucity of invention. In the more populated canvases of a Dickens, numbers of characters, particularised by physical characteristics and verbal mannerisms, interact with one another. In *A Pair of Blue Eyes* such a small number of characters, each with one or two characteristic actions or phrases, simply become irritating: we tire of hearing of Worm's fizzing head and Mr Swancourt's stories. It is the same with the humorous names. In *Barchester Towers* Trollope introduces Mrs Lookaloft (a social climber), Farmers Greenacre and Subsoil, the Quiverfuls, Bobbins (a draper) and Mr Vellem Deeds (a 'dashing attorney'), to name but a few. Worm and Lickpan seem rather isolated in comparison. Indeed, the first half of the novel has, perhaps surprisingly, much in common with Trollope, who was active in much the same literary world; the issue of the *Graphic* which carried its review of *A Pair of Blue Eyes* also included a note that 'Mr. Anthony Trollope's New Serial Story, PHINEAS REDUX . . . will be commenced in our issue of

Saturday next.'[26] Unfortunately, one has to concede that Trollope does this sort of thing much better.

Perhaps it is simply that Hardy had only observed the world of polite drawing-rooms as an outsider. Perhaps he cannot command the urbane tone and level narrative pace and stance appropriate for a comedy of manners, or is unaware of, or unconcerned by, the disruption caused to this type of fiction by abrupt changes of mood, pace and narrative stance. Whatever the reason, it is significant that the novel flares into life in the scenes in the Smiths' homely cottage, episodes which are outside the main narrative development and social focus of the book, but in which we see as real people the characters – the real natives, as distinct from the incomers – who have previously been viewed as caricatured comic relief. The scene in which Stephen returns to his parents' home after his sojourn in India (Ch. 23), with its anecdotes about pigs, lively talk about gardening and finely judged evocation of Stephen's slightly uneasy participation in the convivial scene, is as fine as the scenes in Warren's Malthouse in *Far from the Madding Crowd*. But in the later novel the social centre of the book has been moved, with tremendous effect, away from the drawing-room and back to the social milieu of *Under the Greenwood Tree* – to the workplace, farm and cottage – so that the scenes in Warren's Malthouse and the Buck's Head are not on the fringes of the novel but at its centre.

Another marked characteristic of *A Pair of Blue Eyes*, particularly in its early stages, is of course its remarkable reliance on recent autobiographical material, particularly though not exclusively relating to Cornwall. Even conceding Hardy's claim that the basic plot was drawn up before he set foot in Cornwall, the indebtedness to his recent experience there is indisputable. Hardy himself acknowledged that the character as well as the appearance of Elfride were based on Emma Gifford, and the basic situation in the early chapters – a young architect coming to restore a church in north Cornwall and falling in love with the young lady at the Rectory – is incontrovertibly based on Hardy's own experiences, and has been often commented upon. What is really surprising is the sheer quantity of detail which tallies: the rotting bench ends in the church which are drawn by the architect (Hardy/Stephen Smith); the time of year of the architect's first visit (Hardy 7 March/Stephen Smith 21 February); the Rector suffering from gout at the time of the architect's arrival, so that the latter is greeted by the young lady (Emma/Elfride); the length of time that the young lady had been in the parish (Emma two years/the Swancourts 18 months), a funeral taking place at the beginning of the architect's visit. And so on. The places visited by the young couple are largely the same: the Valency Valley, Trebarwith Strand and Pentargon Bay; also Beeny Cliff, with Emma/ Elfride on horseback. The real names undergo minimal alteration, for example Pentargon Bay becomes Targan Bay. Other place names, like Egloskerry and Trewen, are borrowed for the names of minor characters.[27]

The whole way of life in this isolated area is described with fidelity, so that you can move without any sense of incongruity from the world of the novel to the reality of north Cornwall at that date, as described, for instance, in the 1873 edition of Kelly's *Directory*.[28] When Mr Swancourt complains about the lack of society in this isolated area, the *Directory* illustrates why: of St Juliot's total population of 220 (at the 1871 census) only Caddell Holder himself merited listing in the Private Residents/Court section of the *Directory* – the section which would comprise his social circle. In adjoining villages, the numbers of Private Residents were similarly small: Lesnewth and Otterham had one each, Trevalga had two and neither Minster nor Davidstow had any. Boscastle, with a population of 360, including seven Private Residents, was a 'small seaport town' with a range of services, and boasted not just tradespeople and craftsmen (shopkeepers, butchers, carpenters, blacksmiths, masons and shoemakers) but also professional people (accountant, surgeon, land surveyor, solicitor). This is where in the novel Lord Luxellian goes to seek a surgeon when the church tower falls on Mrs Jethway, and where Mrs Jethway herself has been to post her letter in the post-office: 'Post & Money Order Office, Post Office Savings Bank & Telegraph Office'. St Juliot has no such facilities: 'Letters through Boscastle, which is the nearest money order & telegraph office'. Boscastle is the place from which the carriers leave for Launceston every Tuesday, Wednesday and Saturday, and there are '[r]egular trips between Bristol & this port by vessel belonging to Jabez Brown & Co.' This is the vessel which features in the novel as the *Puffin*, Stephen's 'favourite route' back to Castle Boterel.[29]

North Cornwall is of course the Lyonnesse whence Hardy returned '[w]ith magic in [his] eyes'. Yet there is less feeling and vitality in the entire first half of the book than in 'When I Set Out for Lyonnesse', or in one wonderful sentence of the 1895 Preface to the novel: 'The ghostly birds, the pall-like sea, the frothy wind, the eternal soliloquy of the waters, the bloom of dark purple cast that seems to exhale from the shoreward precipices . . .'. The creativity that could be sparked so many years later when writing the 'Poems of 1912–13' was not fired while writing *A Pair of Blue Eyes*, and there's nothing in the novel to match the intensity of feeling and the marvellous evocation of place in 'After a Journey' and 'Beeny Cliff'. Perhaps he was simply too close to his material, and, like Wordsworth, needed to recollect in tranquillity; perhaps it is that his strength is in evoking landscapes and a way of life which had become part of him through long association rather than places and people observed, however closely, as a visitor. The descriptions of Cornwall are like those of London: excellent purely as description, but lacking feeling and any involvement with the plot and characters: no more than background and local colour.

And crucially, in the gentle world of this romantic comedy of manners, with a background accurately but rather detachedly described from the real, *nothing happens*. That is, there is virtually no action outside the scope of ordinary everyday events. The courting of Elfride and Stephen is succeeded by the verbal fencing of Elfride and Knight, with more walks, talks and games of chess. Even the abortive elopement to London and Elfride's walk around the parapet of the church appear rather perfunctory and low-key. And then, Elfride and Knight climb the Cliff without a Name and, moments after lecturing Elfride on the theory of air-currents, Knight is clinging on to the cliff-edge for his very life. On one level Hardy is demonstrating his mastery of one of the basic conventions of serial-writing, for his ending of the February episode of the serialisation with Knight hanging on 'in the presence of a personalised loneliness' is an archetypal cliff-hanger.[30] No doubt it succeeded in encouraging people to buy the next number of *Tinsleys' Magazine*, to see what happened. But it is far more than that, as has been universally recognised right from the novel's first reviewers to the critics of today. But this is not an isolated piece of fine writing; it is rather as if something in this scene finally sparked Hardy's creativity into life, so that the whole of the rest of the novel is far more effective than the first section. Obscure classical and artistic allusions thin out, as do the rather ponderous aphorisms on manners, women and social matters. And while the writing has pace and narrative suspense, it at the same time manages to appear leisured, immersing us in an imagined world through some delightful episodes, like the first scene in the Luxellian vault, which clearly draws on deepest memories of Stinsford and Bockhampton life rather than on recent experience in Cornwall. Moreover, many of the qualities shown in the second half of the novel were further developed in *Far from the Madding Crowd*, making the scene on the Cliff without a Name a pivotal point not just in this one novel but in the development of Hardy's writing. I would like to concentrate on two key aspects of Hardy's narrative technique.

The first is almost too obvious, but is nonetheless highly significant. The scene on the Cliff without a Name in Chapters 21 and 22 is high drama, breaking with terrific force into the low-key comedy of manners. And it is very effective purely as dramatic action, for Hardy has a remarkable ability to catch the reader's attention and to create dramatic suspense; indeed, even in *Desperate Remedies* the densely plotted story succeeds as a mystery thriller. The effectiveness of Hardy's writing in such scenes comes partly from the quality of the imagined material, and partly from the care with which he brings the action before the reader. Here, there are the carefully selected visual details of the 'tooth of quartz', the 'tuft of sea-pink' and the 'white border to a black sea'; the sense of touch in the ascending rain-drops which stick into Knight's flesh 'like cold needles'; and the precise description of the making and testing of the rope which is Knight's salvation. This precision helps to avoid the over-writing characteristic of melodrama.

But the scene on the Cliff without a Name also signals Hardy's use of dramatic action in a much more complex way. This scene is not just plot, not just a means of catching the reader's attention, but is a method of exploring the novel's characters and themes with a vitality and a subtlety which could not be achieved in pages of narrative analysis. Hardy's imagination is fired by the dramatic and the extraordinary, and he uses dramatic events, and particularly life-threatening situations, to demonstrate extremes of feeling. The life-and-death scene on the Cliff without a Name is the first of these classic moments in Hardy. Elfride's dramatic rescue of Knight through the removal of her underclothes reveals not just 'woman's wit' but a depth of passion, and despite the conventions of Victorian family fiction, the two fly into each other's arms when the rescue is completed, even though Elfride is wearing 'absolutely nothing' but 'her diaphanous exterior robe or "costume"'. The rescue also reveals a strength in Elfride previously hidden by Knight's mastery in conversation and chess. The tragic overtones, and the nearness of destruction, also indicate the potentially catastrophic destructiveness in their relationship, and contrast forcibly with the gentle courtship of Elfride and Stephen and their theoretical discussion on which of them Stephen would save if both Elfride and Knight were drowning – an echo far more effective, because less overt, than the parallel chess games. The scene shows us the characters reacting to extreme circumstances with extremes of resourcefulness and feeling, and also acts as an image both of their relationship and of Stephen's displacement by Knight. Elfride has originally gone to the cliff to look out for the arrival of Stephen's boat, the *Puffin*, but as she and Knight celebrate the rescue by running into each other's arms, 'Elfride's eyes involuntarily flashed towards the *Puffin* steamboat. It had doubled the point, and was no longer to be seen.' The boat has disappeared, and Stephen has dropped out of her life. And this is not an exhaustive analysis of the possibilities of the scene as image, but merely an indication of the many levels of meaning it contains.

This scene is also the moment in Hardy's fiction when the landscape leaps from background to foreground: from well-described setting to an integral part of the novel's action and characterisation. Knight is pitted against natural forces much as Oak will be in the storm scene in *Far from the Madding Crowd*, and the later novel shows a consistent use of the natural world both as a force against which individuals define themselves, and as an objective correlative of their emotions and actions. The summer of Troy's courtship of Bathsheba is succeeded by an autumn in which Fanny dies and Troy deserts Bathsheba. This portrayal of an intimate connection between people and their environment is of course one of Hardy's main strengths, as he acknowledged by classifying all his greatest novels as 'Novels of Character and Environment'.[31] He also uses the scene to place the action of the novel in a still wider perspective, showing us Knight not just pitted against natural forces but against the span of geological time.[32] Inspired by this vision, Hardy's prose suddenly gains a wonderful resonance: 'He was to be with the small in his death.'

There is nothing in *A Pair of Blue Eyes* up to this point which remotely approaches the richness of the scene on the Cliff without a Name; the narrative mode has precluded this kind of intensity and drama. But this use of dramatic events to display and develop characters and relationships *is* a notable feature of the second half of the novel. Examples include the meeting of Knight, Elfride and Stephen in the vault of East Endelstow Church, the eventful sea-voyage from London to Plymouth, the falling of West Endelstow church tower, Elfride's distraught appearance in Knight's rooms in London after his rejection of her, and the final train journey of Knight and Stephen to Cornwall: it can't be said that nothing happens in this part of the novel. These scenes are not all of equal quality, but it is clear that Hardy is aware of their potential and is building on his earlier success. There is sometimes a tendency to overemphasise the symbolism: Elfride's reference to Knight as her 'strong tower', just moments before the church tower collapses, rather hammers home what would otherwise have been an effective image of Knight's imminent rejection of her. But the sea-voyage in Chapter 29 is well done, with the bustle and enjoyment of the first part of the voyage succeeded by effectively ominous foreshadowings of the collapse of the lovers' relationship in the 'floundering and rushing' of the sea and the suspected presence of Mrs Jethway.

And *Far from the Madding Crowd* develops further this use of dramatic events. Indeed, the *Westminster Review* commented rather tartly that in this novel 'sensationalism is all in all',[33] having evidently noted the number of dramatic episodes but failed to realise that they were not simply an end in themselves, as they had been in the sensation novels which were so popular in the 1860s. For the dramatic events which do indeed form a key component of the novel's structure are the means through which Hardy consistently shows us characters and relationships, and the place of people in the natural environment. The key word is of course 'shows', for it is when he is *showing* rather than *telling* that Hardy brings his characters fully alive, and particularly when the events shown are charged with drama. The enduring relationship of Oak and Bathsheba is defined through a series of such events: Bathsheba rescuing Oak from suffocation in his hut, Oak distinguishing himself in the fire, Oak treating the 'blasted' sheep, the pursuit of Bathsheba on the road to Bath, the saving of the ricks from the thunderstorm. In many of these extreme situations, sudden death is a real threat, and, as on the Cliff without a Name, the imminence of death shows us relationships unconstrained by social convention. Other dramatic events used in this way include Fanny's journey to Casterbridge Union, the opening of her coffin and the shooting of Troy. Hardy also uses events which, though less extreme than such life-and-death situations, similarly show characters and relationships through 'moments of vision': heightened events and images which leap out of the page with a stunning visual and quasi-symbolic force. The scene in 'The hollow amid the ferns' (Chapter 28) is a classic example, showing us the nature of the relationship of Bathsheba and Troy through brilliant detailed description and an inspired overall image; the sexual imagery is combined with that of a battle which is 'murderous and bloodthirsty'. What is most remarkable is that these wonderful 'moments of vision' and multi-layered dramatic events are not simply incidental fireworks in the text: they actually compose one of the key elements in the novel's structure, and it is a structural pattern which has its origins in the Cliff without a Name.[34]

The other key characteristic which I would like to explore is Hardy's use of precise visual angles and in particular his presentation of events through the perspectives of individual characters. As with the use of dramatic events to portray character and relationships, and often used in these scenes, Hardy is again drawing the reader into the imagined world by showing rather than telling. A fascination with visual angles is of course a marked characteristic of Hardy right from the very beginning of his first published novel. We remember Cytherea watching her father fall to his death through the window of the Town Hall, so that the scene appears like 'an illuminated miniature' (Ch. 1.3). The dramatic denouement of *Desperate Remedies*, in which Manston is followed by no fewer than three people as he re-buries his wife's body, achieves dramatic suspense by being described as seen by one of the participants, Anne Seaway (Ch. 19.5–6). But in these early instances, the narrator describes to us from the outside what the character is seeing, using such words as: 'she was now engaged in watching the scene', and '[t]he picture thus presented to a spectator' (Ch. 1.3). While we are shown the character's view, our standpoint remains that of a spectator watching the character watching the event. It is during the course of *A Pair of Blue Eyes*, as one might expect from the prominence of the word 'eyes' in the title, that Hardy starts to make that small, subtle but immensely significant shift to presenting events actually through the eyes of his characters.

The early chapters largely follow the method shown in *Desperate Remedies*. The narrator has an eye for pictorial effect, but although we see events and people with clarity, we remain outside the action, and uninvolved. Then in Chapter 22, we *are* suddenly involved in the scene: we share Knight's perspective as he sees 'the vertical face curving round on each side of him' and stares at the fossil trilobite, we enter his thought-processes as 'Time closed up like a fan.' Instead of simply watching Knight hanging to the cliff, we share his viewpoint, see the cliff as it appears to him, and see the images which pass before his 'inner eye'. Then suddenly 'something disturbed the outline of the bank above him. A spot appeared. It was the head of Elfride.' How effective to see the rescuer only through the eyes of the person being rescued. The narrative remains third-person, and modulates in and out of Knight's consciousness. But nevertheless there has been a crucial change in narrative perspective from the earlier examples; we can still see Knight from the outside, we can still analyse his thoughts; but at the same time we have undergone this traumatic experience with him, have seen it through his eyes. This apparently minor change of approach in fact transforms Hardy's writing. It increases dramatic suspense, it involves the reader in the very being of key characters, and the cinematic zooming in from the wider view to the individual and out again conveys a wonderfully rich vision in which we both feel the uniqueness of each individual life and see the individual in the wider context of the community, the natural world and infinity. The vision reaches its zenith in *Tess of the d'Urbervilles*, in which most readers feel an intense personal relationship to Tess, but in which we also see her from the outside: as a member of the community – family member, dairymaid, field-woman; as part of the natural world; and as 'a fly on a billiard-table of indefinite length' .[35]

Viewing events through a character's eyes inevitably increases one's sympathy with him or her. In the crucial chapter in which Knight rejects Elfride (Chapter 34), we again view events not through Elfride's eyes, but through Knight's, just as in the drama on the Cliff without a Name. Before Elfride comes downstairs, Knight glances up at her window and, in a prefiguring of the opening incident in *Far from the Madding Crowd*, sees Elfride looking at herself in the mirror. After their parting, we are again with Knight who 'could not forbear turning his head. He saw the stubble-field, and a slight girlish figure in the midst of it – up against the sky.' Similarly, when Stephen goes to West Endelstow Church in Chapter 24 to await the promised meeting with Elfride, we hear the sounds that he hears, and wait with him:

> The faint sounds heard only accentuated the silence. . . . Among the minutest where all were minute were the light settlement of gossamer fragments floating in the air, a toad humbly labouring along through the grass near the entrance, the crackle of a dead leaf which a worm was endeavouring to pull into the earth, a waft of air, getting nearer and nearer, and expiring at his feet under the burden of a winged seed.
>
> With all these soft sounds there came not the only soft sound he cared to hear – the footfall of Elfride.

This is brilliant, precise evocation, like the description of the sounds of Egdon Heath in *The Return of the Native*, but it also intensifies the feeling of suspense, of waiting – and we share it with Stephen.

The power of Hardy's technique in such instances is indisputable, but at this experimental stage, he has not yet worked it into a coherent pattern. When, at such key moments, we share the perspectives of Knight and of Stephen, we are of course distant from Elfride, and this alienation is increased by her disappearance from the novel after her brief visit to Knight's London chambers. We discover about Elfride's death only with Knight and Stephen on their arrival at Camelton station, and learn of her marriage only with them as, in an effective *coup de théâtre*, they read the coffin-plate as they shelter from the rain in the smithy (Ch. 40). Elfride's eyes feature in the title, and are much mentioned, but they are looked at rather than seen through: 'Her eyes seemed to look at you, and past you' (Ch. 17). In *Tess of the d'Urbervilles*, Hardy was to use the sharing of Tess's view of events to reinforce the reader's sympathy for her;[36] in the earlier novel the heroine is a much more distant figure, seen at crucial moments through the eyes of her disappointed lovers. Perhaps this explains in part the lack of any real tragic power in *A Pair of Blue Eyes*. At any rate, despite the narrative ambivalence towards Elfride, it seems more likely that Hardy had not yet achieved full control of his new technique than that he was deliberately using these limited perspectives to undercut our sympathy for his heroine.

But even if their localised success may not be part of a larger plan, the use of limited visual perspectives *is* a marked feature of the second section of the novel, and is the source of much of its vitality. This is Stephen, looking over the 'valley containing Elfride's residence' just after his return from India in Chapter 23, with the visual angle precisely described: 'A leaf on a bough at Stephen's elbow blotted out a whole hill in the contrasting district far away; a green bunch of nuts covered a complete upland there, and the great cliff itself was outvied by a pigmy crag in the bank hard by him.' And then we watch with him: 'And at the same time he noticed, coming over the hill from the cliffs, a white speck in motion. It seemed first to be a sea-gull flying low, but ultimately proved to be a human figure, running with great rapidity. . . . While he meditated upon the meaning of this phenomenon he was surprised to see swim into his ken from the same point of departure another moving speck, as different from the first as well could be, insomuch that it was perceptible only by its blackness.' Without knowing it, he is watching the light figure of Elfride, followed by the menacingly black figure of Knight, returning from their adventure on the Cliff without a Name. We have all the immediacy of Stephen's view, but because of our knowledge of the earlier events, realise that he is unwittingly watching the return of the couple from an incident which effectually removes him from the picture. It is beautifully done.

These varied perspectives are developed more systematically in *Far from the Madding Crowd* where the technique is used consistently to involve the reader in the novel and to manipulate our sympathies for the characters. In the very first chapter we view Bathsheba through Gabriel Oak's eyes, so being involved from the very beginning in the indelible impression she makes on him. Shortly afterwards we watch with Oak as Bathsheba feeds the sick cow, as she rides flat on the horse's back through the plantation and as she leaves the cattle-shed. Indeed, this is so marked a characteristic of the book that some critics believe that Oak (or even the narrator) is being presented as a voyeur. I would rather see it as part of a pattern by which Hardy seeks to involve us in the viewpoints of his key characters, for it involves more than one character and goes beyond merely seeing, to sharing the individual's experience.

When Bathsheba rescues Oak from the fire-fumes in his lambing-hut, we experience the whole incident with him as he returns to consciousness: 'His dog was howling, his head was aching fearfully – somebody was pulling him about, hands were loosening his neckerchief. . . . The young girl with the remarkably pleasant lips and white teeth was beside him. More than this – astonishingly more – his head was upon her lap, his face and neck were disagreeably wet, and her fingers were unbuttoning his collar' (Ch. 3). This is not voyeurism, nor even simply a visual angle, but a limited perspective involving sight, sound and touch, so that we gradually piece together with Oak from the evidences of his senses what has been happening. We gain both dramatic immediacy and a sense of shared experience, the limitation of the perspective to only what Oak can see, or feel, or hear bringing us right inside the character, the resulting closeness of reader and characters being one of Hardy's most notable attributes in his major fiction. And the technique is not restricted to Oak. There are many occasions when we experience events with Bathsheba. A memorable example is in her first meeting with Troy. She is on her evening rounds of the farm, and going through a dark plantation when she 'fancied she could hear footsteps entering the track at the opposite end. . . . The noise approached, came close, and a figure was apparently on the point of gliding past her when something tugged at her skirt and pinned it forcibly to the ground.' And then, when the lantern-door is opened and 'the rays burst out from their prison' she sees that 'The man to whom she was hooked was brilliant in brass and scarlet. He was a soldier' (Ch. 24). We share the immediate and striking impression which Troy makes on Bathsheba; moreover, because his name is not given until the end of the encounter we can share Bathsheba's reactions without being influenced by our prior knowledge of Troy's relationship with Fanny. In scenes like these, Hardy ensures that we experience many of the novel's crucial moments with Oak and with Bathsheba, his most sympathetic characters. It is significant that we do *not* share the perspectives of Troy and Boldwood to any extent.

This is the first novel in which Hardy shows a complete mastery of this gliding into and out of the consciousness and viewpoints of his characters, so that we gain all the benefits of a first-person narration without its limitations. As E. M. Forster said, 'this power to expand and contract perception (of which the shifting viewpoint is a symptom), this right to intermittent knowledge – I find it one of the great advantages of the novel-form'.[37] And, I would add, Hardy is, from *Far from the Madding Crowd* onwards, one of its foremost exponents.

Far from the Madding Crowd is indeed Hardy's first great achievement, and his first major novel. To some extent the reason does lie in his selection of theme and setting: while the novel is based on pastoral and shows an awareness of literary models,[38] in depicting the farming community of Weatherbury, Hardy was also dealing with a whole way of life familiar to him from his earliest recollections and from the stories told him by his grandmother and other elders. As in *Under the Greenwood Tree*, he could recreate both the community and the environment from his innermost knowledge, without resort to guide-book descriptions or careful observation of the manners of a social class in which he was not brought up. The author is clearly at home in all he describes, in a way that he is not in Endelstow Rectory. But the success of the novel is not just due to choice of subject. It is the deliberate structuring of the novel around a series of dramatic episodes revealing characters and their relationships, combined with a marvellous facility in using limited perspectives to help the reader to experience sights, sounds and emotions with the imagined characters, which raise the novel to new heights.

My key point is that these narrative strategies, which so contribute to the achievement of *Far from the Madding Crowd*, are there in great part in the second half of *A Pair of Blue Eyes*, where we can watch Hardy trying out these new ideas, honing his skills. To those people reading *A Pair of Blue Eyes* as it appeared month by month in *Tinsleys' Magazine* or in its first volume edition, all these techniques would have been a revelation, and they explain the sense of excitement palpable in those early reviews.

From our perspective today, we of course regard more highly the first novel in which they reached full development, but it is still possible to share the excitement of those first readers as we feel the novel soar into creative life as Henry Knight hangs on the Cliff without a Name. Indeed, this revelation of Hardy's full potential as a novelist remains one of the most exciting moments in Victorian fiction.

Notes

Quotations from Hardy's novels are taken from The World's Classics Edition (Oxford: Oxford University Press, 1985–93), except for those from *Desperate Remedies* which are taken from the Penguin Classics Edition, ed. Mary Rimmer (London, 1998). Chapter references for quotations are given in parentheses in the text.

1. Thomas Hardy, *The Life and Work of Thomas Hardy*, ed. Michael Millgate (London: Macmillan, 1984), p. 102.
2. Lascelles Abercrombie, *Thomas Hardy: a Critical Study* (London: Secker, 1912), pp. 68, 103, 63.
3. A rare exception is Michael Steig's 'The Problem of Literary Value in Two Early Hardy Novels', *Texas Studies in Literature and Language*, Vol. XII, no. 1 (1970), 55–62. Steig argues that *A Pair of Blue Eyes* 'is a superior work to *Far from the Madding Crowd* because it offers no reassurance to reconcile us to the claims of the super-ego, of society and convention'.
4. *Pall Mall Gazette*, 25 October 1873. My thanks to Lilian Swindall and the Dorset County Museum for making a copy of this review available to me.
5.. Michael Millgate puts this passage in the section 'Selected Post-Hardyan Revisions' in *Life and Work*, p. 507.
6. *Spectator*, 28 June 1873. For Hardy's correspondence with Tinsley on this matter see *Collected Letters*, I. 21–2.
7. *Graphic*, 12 July 1873. The title was criticised in a number of reviews, including those in the *Spectator* and *Pall Mall Gazette* which were in other respects so positive.
8. *Saturday Review*, 2 August 1873. Reprinted in *Thomas Hardy: the Critical Heritage*, ed. R. G. Cox (London: Routledge, 1970), pp. 15–18 (subsequently cited as *Critical Heritage*). The writer of this review was probably Horace Moule.
9. *The Times*, 9 September 1873; *Athenaeum*, 28 June 1873; *John Bull*, 6 September 1873.
10. This traditional view is again well established: 'With *Far from the Madding Crowd*, Hardy leapt at one bound into the front rank of living novelists', William R. Rutland, *Thomas Hardy* (London: Blackie, 1938), p. 65; 'It was his fourth published novel . . . which established him as a novelist with a growing reputation on both sides of the Atlantic', Norman Page, *Thomas Hardy* (London: Routledge, 1977), p. 10.
11. Many have been reprinted in *Critical Heritage* and in *Thomas Hardy and His Readers: a Selection of Contemporary Reviews*, eds Laurence Lerner and John Holmstrom (London: Bodley Head, 1968).

12. *Saturday Review*, 9 January 1875. Reprinted in *Critical Heritage*, pp. 39–45. See also *The Times* of 25 January 1875: 'Mr Hardy showed signs last year, in *A Pair of Blue Eyes*, of having raised for himself a higher standard of excellence than that with which ordinary novel-writers and ordinary novel-readers are well content. In his new book, *Far from the Madding Crowd* . . . there is still further evidence of his possessing a certain vein of original thought, and a delicate perceptive faculty . . .'. Three of the four reviews of *A Pair of Blue Eyes* which I have quoted at length compare Hardy with George Eliot, making more understandable the *Spectator*'s note on the first, anonymous, episode of *Far from the Madding Crowd* in the *Cornhill* that if it were not by George Eliot, 'then there is a new light among novelists' (3 January 1874). There was indeed, but he had arrived on the scene with his previous novel!
13. *Collected Letters*, Vol. II, p. 65.
14. *Academy*, 30 November 1878. Reprinted in *Critical Heritage*, pp. 48–50.
15. *Gleanings from Popular Authors, Grave and Gay*. Originally issued in 24 parts, forming two volumes: 1 (London: Cassell, 1882); 2 (London: Cassell, 1883).
16. Basil Champneys, *Memoirs and Correspondence of Coventry Patmore* (London: George Bell, 1900), Vol. II, pp. 261–2; Coventry Patmore, 'An English Classic: William Barnes', *Fortnightly Review*, November 1886, 669; *Life and Work*, p. 325.
17. *Life and Work*, p. 108.
18. Robert Louis Stevenson, *Memories & Portraits* (London: Chatto and Windus, 1887), pp. 292–3. Patmore and Stevenson shared both an admiration for early Hardy and a dislike of *Tess of the d'Urbervilles*.
19. Lionel Johnson, *The Art of Thomas Hardy* (London: Mathews & Lane, 1894), p. 39. The Preface is dated 1892, and the final proofs had been passed by that date.
20. William Tinsley, *Random Recollections of an Old Publisher* (London: Simpkin, Marshall, Hamilton, Kent, 1900), Vol. I, p. 128.
21. *Life and Work*, p. 116; *Collected Letters*, IV. 291; *Collected Letters*, V. 313–14.
22. The initial list of 'The Persons', as in a play, is another experimental idea tried out here and in this case not used elsewhere in Hardy's fiction.
23. Michael Millgate, *Thomas Hardy: His Career as a Novelist* (London: Bodley Head, 1971), p. 67.
24. Robert Langbaum, *Thomas Hardy in Our Time* (London: Macmillan, 1995), p. 69.
25. Anthony Trollope, *Barchester Towers*, Ch. 35: World's Classics edition, ed. James R. Kincaid (Oxford, 1980), Vol. II, p. 84.
26. *Graphic*, 12 July 1873.
27. Many of the transparent place-names were introduced in later editions, as Hardy undertook systematic 'Wessexisation' of his novels, and, following the death of the people involved, felt no need to continue the disguise of the St Juliot background. Targan Bay, however, went by this name even in the first edition. See Pamela Dalziel's 'A Note on the History of the Text' in the Penguin Classics edition of *A Pair of Blue Eyes* (London: Penguin, 1998), and Simon Gatrell, *Hardy the Creator: a Textual Biography* (Oxford: Clarendon Press, 1988), pp. 118–31.
28. *Post Office Directory of Devonshire and Cornwall* (London: Kelly, 1873).

29. The correlation of real and imagined worlds is so close that it is almost a surprise when a detail in the novel does *not* tie in with the actuality of north Cornwall in the 1870s, as with the placing of Endelstow House in the vicinity of Lesnewth, and the extension of the railway. In the course of the novel the railway is extended from St Launce's to Camelton, but in reality this extension did not take place until 1893, twenty years after the novel had been published. However, the requisite powers had been granted in 1864, and no doubt the long-anticipated coming of the railway would have been a natural topic of conversation when Hardy reached St Juliot Rectory at the end of his long journey.

30. This is the end of Chapter 21. Similarly, the November episode ended with Stephen and Elfride *en route* for London (end of Chapter 11), and the March one with Stephen entering the Luxellian vault: ' "Who is dead?" Stephen enquired, stepping down' (end of Chapter 5).

31. The position of *A Pair of Blue Eyes* on the borders of Hardy's major fiction is illustrated by Hardy's own uncertainty over where to classify it in the Wessex Edition. He did consider 'Novels of Character and Environment' before finally choosing 'Romances and Fantasies'. See *Collected Letters*, IV. 209.

32. See Phillip Mallett, 'Hardy and Time', in *Reading Thomas Hardy*, ed. Charles P. C. Pettit (London: Macmillan, 1998), pp. 156–71.

33. *Westminster Review*, January 1875. Reprinted in *Critical Heritage*, pp. 31–5.

34. Hardy may have been encouraged in the use of this technique by Leslie Stephen's injunction that 'though I do not want a murder in every number, it is necessary to catch the attention of readers by some distinct and well arranged plot', but what is significant is not the number of dramatic episodes, but how Hardy uses them. Stephen's letter is quoted in Richard Little Purdy, *Thomas Hardy: a Bibliographical Study*, revised edition (Oxford: Oxford University Press, 1968), p. 336.

35. *Tess of the d'Urbervilles*, eds Juliet Grindle and Simon Gatrell (Oxford, 1988), p. 110.

36. See my 'Hardy's Vision of the Individual in *Tess of the d'Urbervilles*', in *New Perspectives on Thomas Hardy*, ed. Charles P. C. Pettit (London: Macmillan, 1994), pp. 172–90.

37. E. M. Forster, 'The Art of Fiction' (transcript of BBC radio talk broadcast in 1944), printed as Appendix D in his *Aspects of the Novel* (Harmondsworth: Penguin, 1976), p. 186.

38. Hardy's earliest reference to *Far from the Madding Crowd* to Leslie Stephen describes it as 'a pastoral tale' (*Life and Work*, p. 97) and the word 'pastoral' is used on at least four occasions in the early, tone-setting chapters: George the dog is concerned at the 'serious turn pastoral affairs seemed to be taking' (Ch. 4); the title of Chapter 5 is 'Departure of Bathsheba: a pastoral tragedy'; Oak is referred to as a 'pastoral king' and thinks over his misfortunes 'amorous and pastoral' (Ch. 6).

2
Geology, Genealogy and Church Restoration in Hardy's Writing

Sophie Gilmartin

In 1879 Henry James wrote in his study of Nathaniel Hawthorne,

> History, as yet, has left the United States but so thin and impalpable a deposit that we can very soon touch the hard substratum of nature. ... A large juvenility is stamped upon the face of things. . . .[1]

James implies here that the soil or deposits are thin in America for narrative, as there has not yet been enough history in that young nation to prove fertile ground for stories. As he writes earlier in the same book: 'The moral is that the flower of art blooms only where the soil is deep, that it takes a great deal of history to produce a little literature.'[2] James is of course privileging history pertaining to 'Old World' populations, from the Europeans in America mainly, and ignoring the history of Native Americans. Controversial as his assertions about history and narrative may be, they accord with the ideas of his English contemporary, Thomas Hardy. While James eventually transplanted himself from that 'hard substratum of nature' in the United States to the presumably richer soil of Sussex, Hardy refused to travel in the other direction, to America. He expresses his reasons for this refusal in his poem, 'On an Invitation to the United States'.

In the first stanza Hardy refuses the invitation because, 'since Life has bared its bones' to him, he 'shrink[s] to seek a modern coast' where the inhabitants have no history, no tragedy, no 'centuried years' behind them. The 'new regions' of America 'claim them[selves] free' of the burden of centuries of memory, but it is precisely this burden, gathering weight and substance over the generations, which serves as a crucial catalyst for narrative in Hardy's writing. I give the second stanza in full:

For, wonning in these ancient lands,
Enchased and lettered as a tomb,
And scored with prints of perished hands,
And chronicled with dates of doom,
Though my own Being bear no bloom
I trace the lives such scenes enshrine,
Give past exemplars present room,
And their experience count as mine.

'Life has bared its bones' to Hardy, but his response in this second stanza is to give flesh to those bare bones through his particular type of story-telling. His writing takes bare bones – in tombs or in the skeletons of 'perished hands' – and gives them life. The 'ancient lands' are 'enchased and lettered as a tomb'; Hardy takes a date on a tomb or a quirk in a pedigree and enchases it – places it in a setting, surrounds it in detail – and thereby 'letters' it, giving it narrative force.

It is interesting that Henry James employs a geological metaphor to describe the state of history in the United States: the workings of geo-logical time upon landscape often serve as crucial metaphors in Hardy's writing as well. The marks left by ancient rivers, seas, glaciers and other traces of geological time are of course just as apparent in America as in Europe, but James views the American landscape of human history almost as a *tabula rasa*, covered only with a 'thin deposit'; for him as for Hardy, it is the Old World which has the 'deep soil' essential for history and narrative.

While Henry James writes metaphorically of soil and deposits, he was hardly likely to muddy his hands with the literal material in his writing. The rich loam around Marlott; the frozen earth of Flintcomb-Ash in *Tess*; the digging and tree-planting in *The Woodlanders*; the rock face to which Henry Knight clings for his life: for Hardy the case is quite dif-ferent, and the layers of soil and stone in his writing work on a literal and figurative level as the very substance of place and time. The various soils and rock mark out the land, designate region, which is so signifi-cant to Hardy, and they are also the materials which record the traces of different time-scales. The earth and stone are worked by human hands in a single life-span such as Tess's or Marty South's, by the hands of many generations of workers (genealogical time), and are in them-selves the products of sedimentary and igneous processes in geological time.

So in this essay I want to discuss the soil and earth in Thomas Hardy's writing, the earth's genealogical and geological layers, and also those 'bare bones' of 'perished hands' and the skeletons buried in the earth, the human deposits which Hardy gives flesh to in his narratives. I shall begin this exploration by turning to a consideration of the nostalgia, through much of the Victorian period, for the village or country churchyard. Hardy shared with his contemporaries a preoccupation with 'God's acre', but, more than this, his writings reveal his intensely idiosyncratic interest in the burial ground.

In *Tess of the d'Urbervilles*, the Lady-Day migrations of agricultural workers, and the loss of the leasehold on their family home, leads the destitute Durbeyfield family back to Kingsbere, to sleep (quite literally) among the tombs of their d'Urberville ancestors. This movement of return to the ancestral burial-place in *Tess of the d'Urbervilles* is an ironic reversal of the movement at this time away from the ancestral home. This movement was an aspect of the rapidly increasing agricultural migration of country-dwellers partly to escape the grinding poverty of rural areas in order to find work in the city. Those who did move away from their ancestral village tended to look back nostalgically to their family home, especially those later on in the century whose parents or grandparents had left the countryside; the distancing of one or two generations did much to remove the memory of the cruel hardships of agricultural life, and to idealise the rural community and the 'joys' of nature. In the poetry and literature of the nineteenth century a focus of this nostalgia often lay in the depiction of the country or village churchyard. The graveyard could be viewed as the last bastion of pedigree for those families who had left their village. They could return to the graveyard to read their genealogical record on the tombstones. Indeed, for the poor who had no written or emblazoned pedigree, the graves were frequently the sole written record of their ancestry. Without these records, there was only oral tradition to combat the possibility that the blood-lines, alliances and the stories associated with them would fade from memory.[3]

The village churchyard was hallowed in the poetry, painting and novels of the Victorian era as a place of peaceful community between the living and the dead. But this communal sensitivity is clearly felt much earlier as in, for instance, Gray's 'Elegy Written in a Country Churchyard' (1750), and in Wordsworth's 'Essay upon Epitaphs' (1810). Wordsworth writes:

> A village church-yard, lying as it does in the lap of nature, may indeed be most favourably contrasted with that of a town of crowded population. . . . The sensations of pious cheerfulness, which attend

the celebration of the sabbath-day in rural places, are profitably chastised by the sight of the graves of kindred and friends, gathered together in that general home towards which the thoughtful yet happy spectators themselves are journeying. Hence a parish church, in the stillness of the country, is a visible centre of a community of the living and the dead; a point to which are habitually referred the nearest concerns of both.[4]

Of the associations and connections between the family-names in the country churchyard, Wordsworth claims:

As in these registers the name is mostly associated with those of the same family, this is a prolonged companionship, however shadowy; even a Tomb like this is a shrine to which the fancies of a scattered family may repair in pilgrimage; the thoughts of the individuals, without any communication with each other, must oftentimes meet here. – Such a frail memorial then is not without its tendency to keep families together; it feeds also local attachment, which is the tap-root of the tree of Patriotism.[5]

In many of Hardy's novels and poems, a sense of 'local feeling' or attachment to region is mapped on to the rather more abstract or spiritual topographical space of 'God's Acre' – the burial ground. The names and family connections which appear on a family tomb or on the graves of generations of the same family in a country churchyard provide a family history of sorts.

But the movement of workers from the country to the city in the nineteenth century meant that these migrants were no longer buried in the family plot. The move to the city resulted not only in an overcrowding of the city of the living, but in the city of the dead as well. In the 1830s and 1840s there was public outrage over official reports on the state of city necropoli, and particularly those of London. In his book *Gatherings from Graveyards* (1839), G. A. Walker drew attention to an article in the *Quarterly Review* which stated that 'many tons of human bones every year are sent from London to the North, where they are crushed in mills constructed for the purpose, and used as manure.'[6] Walker, whose work is thought to have influenced the Parliamentary enquiry of 1843 into methods of interment, writes:

Decently to dispose of the dead, and vigilantly to secure their remains from violation, are among the first duties of society; our domestic endearments – our social attachments – our national prepossessions, respect and sanctify the resting place of our forefathers. . . .[7]

Commercial undertakers resold coffins or used them for firewood, and those visiting the grave of a loved one in a city cemetery could not be sure whether the bones of the beloved were lying under the gravestone or enriching the soil of some northern field. It is understandable then that a nostalgia for the peace and sanctity of the country churchyard grew as the nineteenth century advanced. Hardy's particular concern at the overcrowding in city cemeteries is mainly with the loss of family and communal associations, as is clear in the following passage from his short story, 'The Son's Veto' (1894). It is a story which opposes the ties of family and community in the country with the barrenness of a London suburb:

> Mr. Twycott had never rallied, and now lay in a well-packed cemetery to the south of the great city, where, if all the dead it contained had stood erect and alive, not one would have known him or recognised his name.[8]

Resurrected souls in a city churchyard would be strangers to each other, as Hardy claims here, whereas in a country or village churchyard the social and communal attachments, the bringing together of families through visits to the grave of a deceased relative or friend, would be still possible.

Henry Alexander Bowler's Pre-Raphaelite painting, *The Doubt; 'Can These Dry Bones Live?'* (1855), is one of a number of Victorian paintings which exhibits this nostalgia for the country churchyard. A young woman leans in contemplation over the gravestone of 'John Faithful', regarding his exhumed remains of skull and bone. The doubt over the possible resurrection and after-life of the bones is expressed in the woman's furrowed brow. This religious doubt is answered, according to Michael Wheeler, with

> a surplus of signs of hope of resurrection over signs of death: the message of the inscriptions on the two gravestones in the foreground ('I am the Resurrection and the Life' (John 11:25) and 'Resurgam') is reinforced by two symbols of new life and resurrection – the germinating chestnut on the flat stone, and the butterfly which sits on the skull.[9]

Figure 2.1 Henry Alexander Bowler, The Doubt: 'Can These Dry Bones Live?' (Courtesy of the Tate Gallery, London)

The still, peaceful moment in the country churchyard of the painting seems to agree with Wordsworth's edicts for the ideal burial-place:

> when death is in our thoughts, nothing can make amends for the soothing influences of nature, and for the absence of those types of renovation and decay, which the fields and woods offer to the notice of the serious and contemplative mind.[10]

In Bowler's painting the 'soothing influences of nature' are represented in sharp realistic detail: the effect of sun through leaves, the trailing ivy, individual blades of grass crisply set forth. The young woman also, with details such as the lace on her contemporary style of dress, and the lines in her face, is realistically presented. In the midst of all this realism, what is the viewer of the painting to make of the skull and bones lying on top of the gravestone? Wheeler comments on their role in the painting: 'the stark reality of the exhumed bones is not erased, or explained away, but rather held in tension with the hope of resurrection offered by John 11 on the gravestone'.[11]

Michael Wheeler provides a religious interpretation for the disturbing, jarring effect of the exhumed bones within this painting; the bones, even if starkly real, are yet symbolic. The representation of a human skeleton, or of a skull and bones, has been employed in paintings and funerary monuments for centuries to symbolise the nearness of death in life – the theme of *Et in Arcadia Ego* – or the close community of the living and the dead. This is certainly an important level of interpretation of Bowler's painting, and it is also the case that the Pre-Raphaelites did return to the symbolic motifs of earlier artistic traditions, particularly the medieval, in many of their works. Nevertheless this cannot entirely account for the strangeness of seeing the skull and bones placed within the intense realism of this Victorian painting. It is unusual, and was disturbing to some contemporary reviewers, to see this representation of death, which usually functions on a symbolic level, placed within a Victorian artistic tradition which does not seem entirely commensurate with the *Et in Arcadia Ego* motif; because although this painting is a well-known example of the Pre-Raphaelite style, it also has much in common with the popular 'Keepsake' paintings which often depicted attractive young women in sentimental, pretty situations (that is, not bending over a partly exhumed grave). Perhaps it was the disparity between the symbolic and realistic levels of the skull and bones (as well as sexism) which led a contemporary reviewer from the *Art Journal* to comment that a man would have been more appropriate at the centre of the painting; a clash of artistic traditions left a sense that something did not quite fit in Bowler's work. A consideration of *why* the bones in this painting are so jarring, why they seem so disturbingly out of place, may reveal that there are other tensions and resonances here aside from the admittedly prominent ones of religious doubt and the question of resurrection.

Bowler's painting was exhibited at the Royal Academy in 1855, at the height of public outrage over the exhumation and disposal of corpses in city churchyards. If for a moment we concentrate upon the skull and bones as actual, literal remains rather than just symbolic, then an interpretive trace which may have existed for Victorian viewers but which is now lost to us may perhaps be recovered; an alternative, more literal interpretation of this 'problem painting' may lie in the anxiety that the last bastion of eternal rest – the country churchyard – is showing signs of grave-disturbance. To those Victorian city-dwellers who had moved away from an ancestral village (or whose parents or grandparents had moved), this meddling with the buried could hamper alarmingly their nostalgic sense that their family history and a community of the living and the dead lay, still intact, in their ancestral churchyard. As G. A. Walker wrote, violation of the grave meant that 'the identity of relationship is destroyed' between the dead and the living.[12] Once the body has been disinterred, and consequently disconnected from the narrative of the gravestone, there can be no meaning or purpose in a visit to the grave. The signified is disassociated from signifier, the language of epitaph no longer has a referent, and the continuity of the family line between the living and the dead is arrested, rendered meaningless. The possibility of a return to the country churchyard to trace family origins and history is destroyed when the graves are disturbed. Blood-lines are cut, and with the passing of a few generations the city-dweller will come to the countryside as a tourist, with little or no memory of family or communal origin there.

Bowler's painting invites various interpretations because it stills a number of narrative alternatives within its frame; the gravestone tells a story which is framed by the narrative frame and then by the literal frame of the entire painting. Bowler extended this narrative *mise en abyme* by entitling the work with words based upon the opening to Ezekiel 37, and intending the painting as an illustration to Tennyson's *In Memoriam*.

Like Wordsworth, Gray and county historians, Thomas Hardy was very much aware of the narrative potential and power of gravestones. As in Bowler's painting, gravestones in his writing often serve as a narrative within the narrative. They tell stories within the frame of his novels and poems, stories which are crucially connected to the frame story. In his tales of the gravestone, the churchyard becomes the site, not of a harmonious community of the living and the dead, but of disconnection, either of lovers or of families.

The gravestone, as in that of Bowler's painting, partly reveals the tale of its occupant, but often leaves much of its familial or romantic history to conjecture. Hardy often writes the narrative inspired by the gravestone, the story which it could not tell. As in his poem 'In Death Divided', this is often a narrative of severance, of disruption. In the first stanza, he writes:

> I shall rot here, with those whom in their day
> You never knew,
> And alien ones who, ere they chilled to clay,
> Met not my view,
> Will in your distant grave-place ever neighbour you.

And, in stanza 4:

> The simply-cut memorial at my head
> Perhaps may take
> A rustic form, and that above your bed
> A stately make;
> No linking symbol show thereon for our tale's sake.

Hardy provides those 'linking symbols' for his 'tale's sake' in much of his writing which links lovers' histories and family lines. Often, however, he connects the linking symbols of graves with his tale, only to destroy the connections and to reveal the futility of hoping for any permanence to the stories behind the inscriptions on tombs. In *Far from the Madding Crowd*, for instance, Troy selects an expensive gravestone for Fanny; one which, according to the stone-cutter, is warranted 'to resist rain and frost for a hundred years without flying'.[13] But the grave is placed under a grotesque gargoyle on the church tower, and the waterfall from its spout after the night's rain destroys the flowers that Troy sentimentally planted on her grave. In future years the stone and its inscription will be worn away, and the only memorial of Fanny as beloved of Troy will be obliterated. Hardy's description of the violence of the water-spout upon her grave may even imply that one day her very remains will be disinterred by its force.

As in Bowler's painting, the peace of the country churchyard cannot guarantee a quiet resting place, and Wordsworth's belief in the 'soothing influences of nature' in the country churchyard pales in comparison with the violent and obliterative 'vengeance' of the gargoyle. Troy's determination to make Fanny's grave a place of lasting remembrance is futile. No monument to her name can compensate for the fact that Troy did not join his name with hers in marriage, or for the fact that the possibility of carrying on her memory through children is ended with their dead baby who lies in the grave illegitimate, nameless, and unnamed on the gravestone. In Hardy's early novel, *A Pair of Blue Eyes*, and his late novel *The Well-Beloved*, monuments, whether graves or statues, are created as memorials to stave off a forgetting of the dead one's life stories, and to stave off a sense of disconnection between the family and community of the living and the dead. As the son of a stonemason, and as an architect specialising in church restoration, Hardy's experiences gave him a peculiar perspective on these stone memorials. I want to consider this idiosyncratic perspective and how it influences the presentation of geology and genealogy in Hardy's writing, and particularly in *A Pair of Blue Eyes* and *The Well-Beloved*.

Thomas Hardy and church restoration

Hardy was a young architect with literary aspirations when in 1865 he took on an unusual and macabre assignment for his employer, Arthur Blomfield. In the *Life*, Hardy relates how this came about:

> Mr Blomfield (afterwards Sir Arthur) being the son of a late Bishop of London, was considered a right and proper man for supervising the removal of human bodies in cases where railways had obtained a faculty for making cuttings through the city churchyards, so that it should be done decently and in order. A case occurred in which this function on the Bishop's behalf was considered to be duly carried out. But afterwards Mr Blomfield came to Hardy and informed him with a look of concern that he had just returned from visiting the site on which all the removed bodies were said by the company to be reinterred; but there appeared to be nothing deposited, the surface of the ground lying quite level as before. Also that there were rumours of mysterious full bags of something that rattled, and cartage to bone mills. He much feared that he had not exercised a sufficiently sharp supervision, and that the railway company had got

over him somehow. 'I believe those people are all ground up!' said Blomfield grimly.[14]

Shortly after this, Blomfield was asked to supervise 'the carrying of a cutting by the Midland Railway through Old St Pancras Churchyard, which would necessitate the removal of many hundreds of coffins, and bones in huge quantities'.[15] This time Blomfield was determined that the bones, so unceremoniously moved from their eternal bedchambers, would find a decent resting place, and he asked Hardy to attend the railway works every evening in the autumn and winter, to keep an eye on the proceedings. Many years later, in 1890, Hardy wrote in *A Group of Noble Dames* of 'dear delightful Wessex, whose statuesque dynasties are even now only just beginning to feel the shaking of the new and strange spirit without, like that which entered the lonely valley of Ezekiel's vision and made the dry bones move'.[16] Certainly Hardy was not quite thinking of the 'shaking of the new and strange spirit' as a *train*, but the railway was, as he witnessed every evening of that autumn and winter, clearly making the 'dry bones move'.

As an architect in the 1860s, Hardy was active in two very different evocations of a 'new and strange spirit' of progress and change; one of commerce and industry in the form of the railway, and the other a religious force, a new zeal in the Church of England for church restoration. Each of these very different activities involved both a symbolic and literal disruption of that seemingly last bastion of changelessness – that is, a disturbance of the grave, that 'eternal' resting place from which people do not expect to be moved, at least until the Day of Judgement.

Church restoration was Hardy's principal work as an architect. The removal of walls and particularly the repaving of the old church floors with their ledger stones marking the graves underneath involved a disturbance and confusion of who was buried where. In the *Life* Hardy writes that through his restoration work he was 'passively instrumental in destroying or altering' much old architecture 'beyond identification – a matter for his deep regret in later years'.[17] At another point he remembers 'seeing the old font of —Church, Dorchester, in a garden, used as a flower-vase, the initials of ancient godparents and church-wardens still legible upon it. A comic business – church restoration.'[18] If this 'altering beyond identification' both of architecture and of graves caused him regret, it also became a fascination in his writings, both in the poetry and the novels. Mixed-up graves, lost family names on gravestones, inform his idiosyncratic delight in what he called 'satires of circumstance'. Sometimes the plight of the buried elicits a tragic tone, as in the poem 'I Found Her Out There', one of the 'Poems of 1912–13', in which he imagines his first wife Emma's body underground, buried in the wrong place, far away from her beloved Cornwall:

> Yet her shade, maybe,
> Will creep underground
> Till it catch the sound
> Of that western sea
> As it swells and sobs
> Where she once domiciled,
> And joy in its throbs
> With the heart of a child.

But, just as often, there is a satirical or tragi-comic tone as in this poem of 1882, 'The Levelled Churchyard', which deals directly with church restoration:

> 'O passenger, pray list and catch
>   Our sighs and piteous groans,
> Half stifled in this jumbled patch
>   Of wrenched memorial stones!
>
> 'We late-lamented, resting here,
>   Are mixed to human jam,
> And each to each exclaims in fear,
>   'I know not which I am!' . . .
>
> 'Where we are huddled none can trace,
>   And if our names remain,
> They pave some path or porch or place
>   Where we have never lain!'[19]

It seems as if Hardy cannot leave graves alone; like a zealous church restorer he is always disturbing the bones, shifting the gravestones, and all the time there is his sense of regret at the loss of the names of the buried, and the life-stories that went with their names.

Geology and genealogy

In his early, and most autobiographical novel, *A Pair of Blue Eyes* (1873), Hardy combines the elements of church restoration, disturbance of graves, pedigree and geology. A young architect, Stephen Smith, comes from London to a remote parish on the Cornish coast to restore the ancient crumbling church at Endelstow. There he falls in love with the vicar's daughter, Elfride Swancourt. Elfride has been loved before, unrequitedly, by a young farmer now dead, and his mother, the lonely Widow Jethway, blames Elfride for his death. The widow has commemorated the name of her only son in an expensive tomb of white marble. Differing from all the other gravestones which are hewn from the 'dark blue slabs from local quarries',[20] Jethway's tomb stands out in the moonlight in several crisis scenes of the novel. It provides a seat, for example, for Elfride and Stephen, as they plan their secret elopement. Stephen has been confessing to Elfride the fact of his humble ancestry, but when he discovers that he is sitting on the tomb of Elfride's former admirer, the discussion turns from preceding ancestors to preceding lovers. Elfride is able to resign herself to 'the overwhelming idea of her lover's antecedents' (78), but Stephen is disturbed momentarily that there was someone in Elfride's life before him. With the assurance of Elfride's love, however, this soon passes from his mind.

Jethway's tomb haunts the narrative, and is returned to again and again: as Elfride plays the organ in church and realises she is falling in love with Henry Knight, Stephen's 'successor' in love, she looks up from Knight to see 'the bleak barren countenance of the Widow Jethway' who has chosen her seat so that, 'From the gallery window the tomb of her son was plainly visible' (177); as Stephen waits for Elfride in the churchyard after his return from India he is almost literally haunted by the tomb:

> Turning the corner of the tower, a white form stared him in the face. He started back, and recovered himself. It was the tomb of young farmer Jethway, looking still as fresh and as new as when it was first erected (231).

While Stephen is away in India hoping to earn enough to marry Elfride, Henry Knight has come to Endelstow and gradually usurped Stephen's place in her heart. Another scene takes place near Jethway's tomb. Knight browbeats Elfride into a confession of her former 'lovers'. Unlike Stephen, Knight cannot reconcile himself to his romantic antecedents. He reprimands her: 'I hardly think I should have had the conscience to accept the favours of a new lover whilst sitting over the poor remains of the old one'; and 'in moody meditation, (he) continued looking towards the tomb, which stood staring them in the face like an avenging ghost' (310).

There are many other returns and repetitions involving Jethway's tomb in the novel, and, later in the novel, repetitions involving the tomb of the noble Luxellian family. Why is it that a tomb in a remote village churchyard punctuates this novel about a young woman's experience of love and her broken engagements? A clue to answering this question is given in Knight's sullen comments to Elfride about accepting the favours of a new lover while sitting above the 'poor remains' of the old one, the remains of Felix Jethway. What does it mean to become 'poor remains'? To Knight, Felix's bodily remains are 'poor' because they are to be pitied; they are all that is left of one who has been replaced, superseded by another man. This fear of being forgotten is a central anxiety of the novel. Tombs do not merely signify death here, but also, what is perhaps much worse, they signify the forgetting rather than the remembrance of the deceased, and in that forgetting, a death of love.

What is at stake here for Knight is a fear that he will not be the first and only of Elfride's lovers, but that instead he will be added to an unsung 'pedigree' or line of lovers, becoming one day forgotten like the 'poor remains' of Felix Jethway. Knight's fear of being forgotten, of becoming an empty shell of love, can be seen on a geological scale in the well-known cliff-hanging episode, midway through the novel. Knight faces death as he hangs from a cliff, waiting to be rescued by Elfride. The moments that he hangs suspended give him an opportunity to contemplate the shelf of slaty rock against which his face is pressed. It is layered with the impressions of trilobites, molluscs and other shells of former life:

> opposite Knight's eyes was an imbedded fossil, standing forth in low relief from the rock. It was a creature with eyes. The eyes, dead and turned to stone, were even now regarding him. It was one of the early crustaceans called Trilobites. Separated by millions of years in their lives, Knight and this underling seemed to have met in their place of death. . . . Zoophytes, mollusca, shell-fish, were the highest developments of those ancient dates. The immense lapses of time each formation represented had known nothing of the dignity of man. They were grand times, but they were mean times too, and mean were their relics. He was to be with the small in his death (209).

The impersonality of the trilobite's dead eyes impresses upon Knight his own smallness in geological time and perhaps also in the layers of memory of those he knows and loves. His own body will become 'poor remains', a shell of extinct life and love, to be forgotten in layers of time among a multiplicity of other lovers.

In contrast to the unpedigreed single grave of Felix Jethway is the Luxellian family tomb in the neighbouring churchyard. Chapters 26 and 27 of the novel take place mainly inside this tomb which is being set in order for a new inmate, the recently deceased Lady Luxellian. Stephen's father, John Smith, relates the story of Elfride's grandmother, also named 'Elfride', who was a Luxellian and who is buried in the tomb. She had run away with the singing-master and died giving birth to the heroine's mother. Smith comments upon the female Luxellian line: 'That trick of running away seems to be handed down in families, like craziness or gout. And they two women be alike as peas' (246), meaning Lady Elfride Luxellian and her granddaughter, Elfride Swancourt.[21] Of course, neither Smith nor his fellow villagers can know the extent to which these Elfrides will actually repeat one another; they do not know of Elfride's cancelled elopement with Stephen, or that in the future the present Elfride will become another 'Lady Elfride Luxellian', and die as she did, giving birth to a first child.

John Smith introduces the story of Elfride's grandmother by addressing his fellow workman and villager: 'Simeon, I suppose you can mind poor Lady Elfride, and how she ran away with the singer? . . . I think it fell upon the time my father was sexton here' (246). Smith's 'do you mind?' and his reference to his father's time reinforce the sense of a strong communal memory here (and Smith is also relating the story to his son 'who had frequently heard portions of the story', carrying the narrative through at least three generations in this instance). But even for Stephen's father it is difficult to distinguish between these various incarnations of an 'Elfride'. The two women begin to merge into one another in the layers of his memory, which is of a wider scope than that of the young Stephen, Knight or Lord Luxellian. Knight's fear when confronted with the trilobite's dead and impersonal eyes, that he 'would be with the small in his death' is connected to his fear that he will be forgotten in the time of one generation – in Elfride's life – by becoming a forgotten layer in her memory, one of a row of lovers. John Smith's conflation of the two Elfrides emphasises this forgetting; even in one generation the similar stories of lovers begin to merge and become lost in one another.

In *A Pair of Blue Eyes* the mark of the human is slowly but decisively erased. Some graves are left untended and forgotten, some graves cannot yield up the stories of their buried, and always in the background there are those graves which are destroyed by church restoration. Even in the human time of the local villagers, the Luxellian tomb begins to conflate the stories of the two Elfrides buried there, erasing their individuality.

Geological time is frightening and alienating in its vastness, but even within genealogical time, the human trace is at risk of being misread or forgotten. A silting process is beginning in the Luxellian tomb which will place Elfride, if not quite yet among the geological layers, then as a tiny layer among the many layers of the Luxellian succession. She is, after all, by the novel's close, the second wife of the lord, and the reason that she, Stephen and Knight met in the Luxellian tomb to begin with was because it was being prepared for the *first* Lady Luxellian. Future visitors to the tomb will see two Lady Elfride Luxellians there, both having died in childbirth, and with the passage of time no one will be able to distinguish between them or their separate stories.

Another generational repetition across the female line, similar to that of *A Pair of Blue Eyes*, is found in Hardy's late novel, *The Well-Beloved* (1897),[22] which tells the story of three generations of women, all named Avice Caro,[23] and how they merge into one woman in the eyes of the sculptor Jocelyn Pierston, who loves all three. In Pierston's case, statues of his own creation become involved with both the geological and genealogical layers of his native island. These time-spans dwarf his own life-span, and his statues – his only offspring – make a mockery of his attempts at marital union and sexual consummation.

The vacant sadness Jocelyn experiences when confronted with the successive empty shells of each former 'well-beloved' is related to Knight's fear in *A Pair of Blue Eyes* when confronted with the empty shells of molluscs in the slaty rock of the Cliff without a Name. The anxiety over being forgotten, of joining an arbitrary universe in a forgotten layer of memory pervades Hardy's work. It is the impulse behind elegy, the inscriptions on tombs, and the creation of monuments, or, as in the case of Pierston, of statues. For Pierston, the departure of the well-beloved leaves behind nothing but a lifeless shell, without colour, voice or substance to call him to her. This is the case, at least, until the well-beloved takes up abode successively in the three generations of Avice Caro.

Jocelyn attempts to control this fear of the arbitrariness of love and the forgetting that accompanies the passing of love, by sculpting in stone images of his 'well-beloved'. His artistic medium is taken from the 'stratified walls of oolite' from the quarries of his native isle. The geological layers of this Portland stone serve his art, and also, by calling to his mind his father's quarry on his native isle, serve to connect him with the genealogical layers of intermarrying families of his birthplace.

The mutability of his well-beloved during the 20 years between the first and second parts of the novel is such that he struggles to fix the spirit in a 'durable shape', sculpted in stone. But the stone that he sculpts is the limestone of his native isle, and this fact undermines Jocelyn's attempts to 'fix' the 'well-beloved' in sculpture: this oolite is made up of millions of fossilised shells – like the dead shells of all the women in whom he has fleetingly seen the well-beloved. Hardy describes the stone in the opening of Chapter 1, as 'the melancholy ruins of cancelled cycles'; the geological stratifications of the island rock undermine the art with which he tries to give life to the dead shapes of his artistic fiction. This line from Shelley's 'Prometheus Unbound' was a favourite of Hardy's – he uses it in *Tess* also – and these 'cancelled cycles' so often manifest themselves as geological and genealogical layers or traces left in the earth in his writing. The dead eyes of the trilobite in *A Pair of Blue Eyes*; Elfride's burial with her firstborn, probably marking the end of the Luxellian line; Jocelyn Pierston's failure to marry and produce children with any of the three generations of Avice Caro: all these failures of continuity point to Hardy's fascination with 'cancelled cycles'.

Edward Said has written of the role of genealogy and narrative in *Jude*:

> Hardy's case in *Jude the Obscure* is, I believe, the recognition by a great artist that the dynastic principles of traditional narrative now seemed somehow inappropriate. . . . Both Little Father Time's name and his presence yield up further observations which, we may feel . . . do great damage to the sacrament of ongoing human life. For the boy is neither really a son nor, of course, a father. He is an alteration in the course of life, a disruption of the archaeology that links generations one to the other.[24]

Similarly, in *The Well-Beloved*, Jocelyn Pierston is a 'disruption of the archaeology that links generations': as Hardy writes of him, his 'inability to ossify with the rest of his generation threw him out of proportion with the time' (144).[25] Pierston is a genealogical 'disruption' because he could have been either the father of the second Avice or the grandfather of the third; instead, he bears no familial relationship as husband, father or grandfather to any of the three generations of island women, a particularly isolated genealogical condition on an 'island' where most people are related through generations of intermarriage. With Jocelyn's failure to unite himself with any of these women, 'the dynastic principles of traditional narrative' are not only 'inappropriate', as Said argues, but positively end-stopped. While Hardy's writing is concerned intensively, almost obsessively, with variously juxtaposed time-scales and cycles, those 'deposits' of history, generations and geology which provide him with a thick and fertile soil for narrative, he is less interested or inspired by continuity and ongoing generations than he is by sterile repetition or a failure to continue the genealogical line. Enamoured as he is with 'the melancholy ruins of cancelled cycles', Hardy seems finally, with *Jude the Obscure* and *The Well-Beloved*, to have taken the decision to cancel his own narratives which rely so crucially upon cycles of generation.

Notes

1. Henry James, *Hawthorne*, ed. Tony Tanner (1879; London, 1967), p. 31.
2. Henry James, *Hawthorne*, p. 23.
3. In a letter to Rider Haggard in March 1902, Hardy responded to Haggard's enquiries relating to his 'opinion on the past of the agricultural labourers' in Dorset. Hardy wrote that 'down to 1850 or 1855 their condition was in general one of great hardship', but that 'things are of course widely different now. . . . Their present life is almost without exception one of comfort, if the most ordinary thrift be observed.' Hardy attributes the migration of agricultural workers from the country to the city largely to 'insecurity of tenure' – the loss of leasehold which he describes, for instance, in *Tess* and *The Woodlanders* – and certainly not from choice in most cases: 'That these people have removed to the towns of sheer choice during the last forty years it would be absurd to argue, except as to that percentage of young, adventurous, and ambitious spirits among them which is found in all societies.' In this letter, Hardy expresses his regret over the loss of village traditions and communal memory resulting from migration, and points to the churchyard as one of the places where continuity with the past is being severed: 'there being no continuity of environment in their lives, there is no continuity of information, the names, stories, and relics of one place being speedily forgotten under the incoming facts of the next. . . . For example, if you ask one of the workfolk . . . the character and circumstances of people buried in particular graves; at what spots parish personages lie interred . . . they [*sic*] can give no answer: yet I can recollect the time when the places of burial even of the poor and tombless were all remembered, and the history of the parish and squire's family for 150 years back known' (*Life and Work*, pp. 335–7). See Keith Snell's *Annals of the Labouring Poor: Social Change and Agrarian England 1660–1900* (Cambridge, 1985) for a more sceptical account of the condition of the agricultural labourer in Dorset during the period of composition of Hardy's novels.
4. William Wordsworth, 'Essay upon Epitaphs, I', in *The Prose Works of William Wordsworth*, eds W. J. B. Owen and Jane Worthington Smyser, Vol. II (Oxford, 1974), p. 55.

5. Wordsworth, 'Essay upon Epitaphs, III', edn cit., p. 93.
6. G. A. Walker, *Gatherings from Graveyards; Particularly Those of London* (London, 1839), p. 380.
7. *Gatherings from Graveyards*, p. 380.
8. Thomas Hardy, 'The Son's Veto', *Life's Little Ironies*, ed. F. B. Pinion (London, 1977), p. 38.
9. Michael Wheeler, *Death and the Future Life in Victorian Literature and Theology* (Cambridge, 1990), p. 59.
10. Wordsworth, 'Essay upon Epitaphs, I', edn cit., p. 54.
11. Wheeler, *Death and the Future Life*, p. 61.
12. Walker, *Gatherings from Graveyards*, p. 188.
13. Thomas Hardy, *Far from the Madding Crowd*, ed. Suzanne Falck-Yi (Oxford and New York, 1993), p. 322.
14. *Life and Work*, p. 46.
15. *Life and Work*, p. 46.
16. Thomas Hardy, *Wessex Tales and A Group of Noble Dames*, ed. F. B. Pinion (London, 1977), p. 246.
17. Hardy, *Life and Work*, p. 35.
18. Hardy, *Life and Work*, p. 129.
19. Hardy, 'The Levelled Churchyard', stanzas 1, 2 and 4.
20. Thomas Hardy, *A Pair of Blue Eyes*, ed. Alan Manford (Oxford and New York, 1985), p. 231. Further quotations from the novel will be indicated by page number within the text.
21. The page layout in the Wessex edition suggests that this speech should be assigned to John Smith; in the World's Classics edition, it is given to Simeon.
22. Thomas Hardy, *The Well-Beloved*, ed. Tom Hetherington (Oxford and New York, 1986). Quotations from the novel will be indicated by page number in the text.
23. In fact the 'second' Avice is named 'Ann Avice Caro', but upon first meeting her, Jocelyn insists that, 'Well, Ann or otherwise, you are Avice to me' (p. 80). This second woman in the generational sequence is subsequently referred to as Avice. She is 'Ann Avice Caro', but to Jocelyn, 'an Avice Caro', or simply another of the first.
24. Edward Said, *Beginnings* (New York, 1978), p. 138.
25. Said's reference to the layering through time implicit in his term 'archaeology' is worked out as geological and genealogical layers in *A Pair of Blue Eyes* and *The Well-Beloved*.

3
'Gifted, even in November': the Meanings of *The Well-Beloved*

Michael Irwin

The opening of *The Well-Beloved* will strike seasoned Hardy-readers as familiar. Place, time and season are specified. The location is the Isle of Slingers – very obviously Portland Bill. It is 'about two o'clock, in the middle of the summer season'. Along a steep, dusty road walks a solitary pedestrian, revisiting his native place after an absence of several years. But the landscape appears strange to him:

> What had seemed usual in the isle when he lived there always looked quaint and odd after his later impressions. . . . The towering rock, the houses above houses, one man's doorstep rising behind his neighbour's chimney, the gardens hung up by one edge to the sky, the vegetables growing on apparently almost vertical planes, the unity of the whole island as a solid and single block of limestone four miles long, were no longer familiar and commonplace ideas. All now stood dazzlingly unique and white against the tinted sea, and the sun flashed on infinitely stratified walls of oolite. . . .[1]

Usually Hardy's pedestrians traverse open country of a kind to be mentally visualised in terms of, say, a Constable landscape. Here Jocelyn confronts the strange geometry of an obstructive, populated rock, visually flattened and stylised after the manner of Cézanne. The strong verticals are offset by the implied horizontality of the 'single block of limestone'. Hardy is signalling to the reader that this particular novel will be atypically distanced from the conventions of realism. As the narrative unfolds, the hint is developed: the Isle of Slingers is to be predominantly a figurative locale, characterised by 'eternal saws . . . going to and fro upon eternal blocks of stone' (12).

This is and is not Hardy country. On such inhospitable ground there can be no crops, no sheep, no cows, therefore no 'chorus' of rural labourers. Quarrying seems to offer the only land-based employment. The grounds of Sylvania Castle contain the sole plantation of trees which the island can boast. The diverse murmurings and singings of wind among leaves, a recurrent soundtrack in so many of the Wessex novels, will be absent here. So, too, will be bird and insect life. This is arid terrain indeed, potentially as inhospitable as Flintcomb-Ash. Hardy makes it plain within a few pages that he has set aside vital dimensions of his art, contextual, visual and aural. He is to show patterned lives against a patterned background. It might seem that he is condemned to create little more than a diagrammatic fable, prioritising ideas at the expense of dramatised life and emotion.

Diagrammatic *The Well-Beloved* certainly is; lifeless it proves not to be. Already in the opening chapter we are shown why. When Pierston stops walking and sits down in the sun

> He stretched out his hand upon the rock beside him. It felt warm. That was the island's personal temperature when in its afternoon sleep as now. He listened, and heard sounds: whirr-whirr, saw-saw-saw. Those were the island's snores – the noises of the quarrymen and stone-sawyers. (10)

So far from being inert geological matter the Isle is personified as a warm sleeping animal. It has life and is a source of life. Certainly it fulfils a variety of utilitarian functions: from where Pierston is sitting he sees a cottage which is 'like the island . . . all of stone, not only in walls but in window-frames, roof, chimneys, fence, stile, pigsty and stable, almost door' (10). The islanders live off the island as Hardy's Woodlanders live off the woods they inhabit, feeding on its very substance. Yet the stone which provides fences and pigsties has also been fashioned into pagan temples and Christian churches – even into St Paul's Cathedral. Pierston himself shapes it into sculptures: Aphrodites, Freyjas, Nymphs and Fauns, Eves, Avices. . . . The stuff of the island is made to minister to a full range of human needs. One way of reading the novel is to see the stone as representing, metaphorically, the raw appetites and impulses which can be alternatively the activating force behind day-to-day work and living or the source of religious, romantic or artistic aspiration.

Just as the dead rock can sponsor rich life, so can a routine narrative flower into powerful episodes. It is not incongruous, therefore, though it can appear so on a first reading, that this narrative features lavish fluctuations of circumstantiality and intensity. Pierston's whole artistic career is essentially accounted for in a paragraph of seven words:

He prospered without effort. He was A.R.A. (50)

The paragraph which relates the transference of his affections to Marcia Bencomb is similarly meagre:

In the course of ten minutes he adored her. (31)

This transference might itself seem to be functional in origin. When he walks through the storm with his arm round Marcia, Pierston becomes conscious

of a sensation which, in its incipient and unrecognised form, had lurked within him from some unnoticed moment when he was sitting close to his new friend under the lerret. Though a young man, he was too old a hand not to know what this was, and felt alarmed – even dismayed. It meant a possible migration of the Well-Beloved. (29)

The inference that Hardy is referring to a physical reflex a good deal commoner in life than in Victorian fiction is confirmed within a couple of pages, when Pierston is drying Marcia's wet clothes and the rising steam sends him into a reverie:

He again became conscious of the change which had been initiated during the walk. The Well-Beloved was moving house – had gone over to the wearer of this attire. (31)

Hardy would appear to be smuggling past Mrs Grundy a fact of life she chose not to acknowledge, but to draw attention to his stratagem is to risk producing a misleading emphasis. His very point is that the awkward fact is in itself of limited interest. Just as the stone which makes a pig-sty can make a temple, so, to use Pope's formulation in *An Essay on Man*:

> Lust, thro' some certain strainers well refin'd,
> Is gentle love, and charms all womankind . . .
> (II, 189–90)[2]

Hardy's acknowledgement of the force of physical desire is merely a background to his exploration of idealised love. The former he can sketch diagrammatically or (as here) refer to in passing; the latter he will want to bring to full sensual and poetic life.

Hence the calculated unevenness of *The Well-Beloved*. A couple of pages of perfunctory narrative, perhaps spanning several years and several relationships, may be followed by a detailed account of a single episode in Hardy's most luxuriant descriptive vein – an assignation, a funeral, a birth, a sea-trip without oars. In overall effect the novel is like a scrawny, wiry vine, which bears here and there a large and luscious fruit.

This peculiar characteristic no doubt alienates a number of Hardy's usual admirers. Of the other novels probably *A Pair of Blue Eyes* comes closest – similarly a schematic, yet deliberately melodramatic, anatomisation of love, similarly based upon a sequence of four love-affairs. But the earlier novel is twice as long, though spanning three years rather than 40, and is brought far more consistently to full fictional life. There, too, Hardy is sometimes offhand in his modes of stylisation, but not, as often in *The Well-Beloved*, to the extent of reducing passages of connecting narrative to the scantiest of enabling matter. Elfride and her lovers are substantially developed: an essay on characterisation in *The Well-Beloved* would have nothing to feed upon. The obvious inference is that Hardy didn't take his last novel too seriously. The fact that he chose to rewrite it pretty drastically before putting it between hard covers could well be taken as evidence that he felt dissatisfied with it.

But that inference might be too hasty. His topic is one which had intrigued Hardy all his life, and had in one way or another informed most of his fiction. Already in *Far from the Madding Crowd* Oak and Boldwood are specifically victims of the 'idealisation in love' which many years later is to bedevil Clare and Pierston.[3] And while these passions are embodied in richly-developed characters and situations Hardy recurrently steps back to offer detached, diagnostic comment on the pathology of the emotions concerned – for example, this on Boldwood:

> The insulation of his heart by reserve during these many years, without a channel of any kind for disposable emotion, had worked its effect. It has been observed more than once that the causes of love are chiefly subjective, and Boldwood was a living testimony to the truth of the proposition. No mother existed to absorb his devotion, no sister for his tenderness, no idle ties for sense. He became

surcharged with the compound, which was genuine lover's love. (127)

Here is Hardy's home-brewed brand of naturalism. Love may be uplifting, irradiating, a source of drama and poetry, but it is also a species of psychological by-product or secretion, all but open to material analysis. Comments of this kind were to become familiar in his fiction. Fitzpiers remarks: 'people living insulated, as I do by the solitude of this place, get charged with emotive fluid like a Leyden jar with electric, for want of some conductor at hand to disperse it'.[4] Pierston himself comes to think that one of his amorous attachments 'had been solely owing to the highly charged electrical condition in which he had arrived by reason of his recent isolation' (58). These observations, and many others like them, show Hardy's deep interest in love as a *condition* – something not unlike an illness. It is hardly surprising, therefore, that he should have wanted to devise, at least as an occasional resort, a mode of fiction which could investigate it on just such terms. *The Well-Beloved* can be seen as complementary to the more orthodox *Tess*, or *Far from the Madding Crowd*. Whereas in those novels the dramatisation of love is intermittently diversified by analytic comment, in *The Well-Beloved* an analytical account of a series of affairs is only occasionally amplified by a romantic scene in Hardy's best manner, with the wind blowing, the rain flying, the sea pounding. . . . What he gains from this approach is a comparative element – one such affair in the series can be cross-related to another – and the chance to work systematically, rather than incidentally, in the diagnostic mode.

The Well-Beloved thus has the kind of special interest often to be derived from the minor, or 'failed' works of a major writer, such as Fielding's *Amelia*, or Eliot's *Romola*. Where it 'goes wrong' – if it does – is through pursuing wholeheartedly, and arguably to an awkward conclusion, an interest of the author's which elsewhere has constituted no more than an animating sub-taste of anomaly. Such a work can be enlightening precisely through being unsatisfactory. The reader may be granted a back-stage view of a preoccupation.

Unfortunately that relatively smooth introductory account leads abruptly into rougher terrain. There is a further complicating factor in relation to *The Well-Beloved* which makes the novel difficult to come to terms with. That factor in turn interacts with more superficial complications – that there are two versions of the novel, each open to more than one interpretation and featuring more than one potential ending. Meanings and permutations of meaning proliferate. To work through the whole sequence of possible readings is a tiresomely pedantic task but a necessary one.

The starting-point is that Hardy's recurrent interest in idealising love is here compounded with a second theme. Pierston differs from the likes of Oak, Eustacia or Clare in two apparently related ways. He is not merely a subjective lover, but a *serial* subjective lover. Moreover he is an artist. Hardy himself seemed uncertain as to how much stress to put on this latter point. He wrote to Swinburne that *The Well-Beloved* was 'a fanciful exhibition of the artistic nature', but the novel is sub-titled merely *A Sketch of a Temperament*.[5] In his Preface Hardy refers to Pierston giving 'objective continuity and a name to a delicate dream which in a vaguer form is more or less common to all men'. When the sculptor describes his problem to Somers his friend comments:

> 'You are like other men, only rather worse. Essentially, all men are fickle, like you; but not with such perceptiveness.' (40)

If Somers is right then the story we are being told is simply a local version of the Don Juan legend. But Pierston makes two points in his defence. One is that he strives to be faithful to the abstract 'elusive creature' itself. The claim seems a feeble one, since by his own account inner compulsion gives him no choice in the matter. His second comment – that the recurring migration of the Beloved has been a 'racking spectacle' to him – carries more weight. Don Juan is not noted for such regrets. But whether the defence is sufficient to mark him out as a special case, *qua* artist, is open to doubt.

The revised ending of the novel bears very directly upon these issues. In the serial version Pearston's[6] suicide attempt induces a near-fatal illness and inflicts a wound serious enough to threaten his sight. He wakens to find himself being tended by Marcia, with whom he had passed a short spell of uneasy married life 40 years previously. When he is at last permitted light enough to see his nurse, the appearance of this former sweetheart, so long a stranger, appals him:

> the face of Marcia forty years ago, vanished utterly. In its place was a wrinkled crone, with a pointed chin, her figure bowed, her hair as white as snow. To this the once handsome face had been brought by

the raspings, chisellings, stewings, bakings and freezings of forty years. The Juno of that day was the Witch of Endor of this. (255)

This decayed visage is brought into direct juxtaposition with an enlarged photograph of Avice:

The contrast of the ancient Marcia's aspect, both with this portrait and with her own fine former self, brought into his brain a sudden sense of the grotesqueness of things. His wife was – not Avice but that parchment-covered skull moving about his room. An irresistible fit of laughter, so violent as to be an agony, seized upon him, and started in him with such momentum that he could not stop it. He laughed and laughed, till he was almost too weak to draw breath . . .
    'O – no, no! I – I – it is too, too droll – this ending to my would-be romantic history!' Ho-ho-ho! (256)

It is a black, sardonic ending – effectively a reversal of the fairy-story conclusion (as in 'The Wife of Bath's Tale', for example) where the old witch turns into a beautiful maiden. A chapter in *The Well-Beloved* is called 'Juxtapositions'. Here Hardy has invoked that favourite technique of his to dramatise an unpalatable truth – that however passionately, or idealistically, you court a young woman (or man), the best you can hope is that you will wind up married to an old one. The concluding 'Ho-ho-ho!', outside the inverted commas, would seem to represent the author's own last grim laugh at a fate which he himself was experiencing all too painfully at the time of writing.
    The revised ending is appreciably less harsh. Marcia's altered face is described in pretty much the same terms – though Hardy adds 'the thinkings of more than half a lifetime' to the ageing factors, and omits the reference to the Witch of Endor – but these changes only become apparent to Pierston once he has persuaded her to discard her make-up. Previously he has thought of her as 'remarkably good-looking, considering the lapse of years': 'You are fair and five-and-thirty – not a day more.' (199) The revelation does not prompt hysterical mirth – indeed he is moved by the fortitude with which she accepts and reveals her transformed state: 'Marcia, you are a brave woman . . . I admire you from my soul.' (200) In this version of the story he is *not* already married to her, but he eventually proposes (his fifth proposal of the novel) in a spirit of friendship and they go through a valetudinarian wedding ceremony. Admittedly they have been under social pressure:

'It is extraordinary what an interest our neighbours take in our affairs,' he observed. 'They say "Those old folk ought to marry; better late than never." That's how people are – wanting to round off other people's histories in the best machine-made conventional manner.' (203)

Despite the hint that he is compromising with public opinion in marrying off his 'old folk', Hardy has modified mood and tone as well as events, to produce an effect altogether gentler than that of the serial version.

Less obviously he has altered the very significance of the conclusion. In the serial version the realisation that his wife is 'that parchment-covered skull' all but drives Pearston to drastic action: 'He put up his hand to tear open his wound, and bring eternal night upon this lurid awakening.' (256) The 'eternal night' referred to is not death but blindness, his doctor having warned him that 'the wound is such that you may lose your sight if you are allowed to strain it prematurely' (255). The inference is that it is sight, the ability to perceive beauty, which has been the root of his problems. In his earlier farewell note to Somers, however, the emphasis was different again: 'My youth, so faithful to me, so enduring, so long regarded as my curse, has incontinently departed within the last few weeks.' (250) In neither case are his artistic ideals invoked.

Seen in this light Pearston's problems would appear to be pretty much those of Everyman – or of an immature Everyman. He is responsive to physical beauty in women and plagued with an untiring susceptibility to it. One of Hardy's remarks about himself seems relevant here: 'I was a child till I was 16; a youth till I was 25; a young man till I was 40 or 50.'[7] Like Pearston he has had a 'faithful' and 'enduring' youth. The fact of him writing *The Well-Beloved* would seem to imply that, equally with his fictional creation, he found it a curse, and looked to age or death for a cure. But again the affliction doesn't necessarily seem to relate to 'art'.

In the hardcover version the case is presented differently. Pierston survives his illness, but physical and emotional stress have combined to precipitate a late-life crisis. Its full ramifications emerge in stages. He goes to his studio, and is repelled by his own works: 'They are an ugliness to me!' (201) But it is not that he has become more self-critical. A visit to the National Gallery elicits a similar reaction: 'He saw no more to move him, he declared, in the time-defying presentations of Perugino, Titian, Sebastiano, and other statuesque creators than in the work of the pavement artist they had passed on their way' (201). In sum, he finds 'his sense of beauty in art and nature absolutely extinct' (202). The change is a source of relief to him: 'Thank Heaven I am old at last. The curse is removed' (202). But this 'curse' is not the one bewailed by his serial *alter ego*. It is implicitly clear that, having lost his sexual desires, Pierston has lost with them his aesthetic sense. He regrets neither loss, believing that these attributes in tandem have caused his wretchedness.

To spell out more clearly the distinction between the two versions: it would seem that Pearston's romantic problems might derive merely from a susceptible 'temperament'. He might have suffered equally had he been a carpenter or a plumber. With hindsight Somers's charge of mere fickleness looks persuasive: in fact, if Pearston makes a good recovery from his illness, the Well-Beloved may conceivably ride again. With his successor the case is different. The artistic impulse is central, and when that dies the Well-Beloved is gone for good. But the fable can still be read in two ways. Pierston's art may be seen as merely a by-product of sexual disappointment. He could be a frustrated Everyman with a compensatory talent for statue-making. As he himself says, the 'idiosyncrasy, or whatever it is, which would be sheer waste of time for other men, creates sober business for me' (52). His amorous dreams, 'translated into plaster', make him money and build him a name. On this reading it is still clear – as was not the case with Pearston – that his art is intrinsic to his erotic life, but this is merely at the level of sublimation.

The alternative view is that he could *never* find romantic satisfaction because he is indeed a special case. His is the 'artistic temperament' which truly does oblige him to pursue an ideal female beauty – to which any individual woman can only roughly approximate – as opposed to settling for a compromise relationship with some reasonably satisfactory particular specimen. This interpretation would see the artist as doomed to unhappiness as long as he stays true to his highest aspirations. Pierston is relatively unusual among Hardy protagonists in that he is still alive (albeit with little in hand) when the fiction in which he figures comes to an end. He is even relatively contented, sufficiently prosperous and newly married to a wife whom he at any rate likes and esteems. But this is precisely because he is dead as an artist: 'the curse is removed'. His aesthetic sensibility has been a kind of illness, which he is glad to have shaken off.

It is a further complication that Hardy hedges his bets on a crucial aspect of this reading – the quality of the art concerned. Pierston may talk about 'sober business' and is indeed described at one stage as enjoying popular success; but his friend Somers tells him he is the country's 'only inspired sculptor': 'You are our Praxiteles' (74–5). Then again the older Pierston comes to feel that he 'had not for years done anything to speak of – certainly not to add to his reputation as an artist' (172). On that showing it might seem that his eventual decline into artistic impotence is no great loss. But that possibility is itself left open to question by one of those equivocal final sentences so characteristic of Hardy's novels:

> At present he is sometimes mentioned as 'the late Mr. Pierston' by gourd-like young art-critics and journalists; and his productions are alluded to as those of a man not without genius, whose powers were insufficiently recognised in his lifetime. (206)

It may well have been the case that the modest and reticent Hardy did not care to present as an incontrovertible genius a character who might be taken for an oblique self-portrait. There is, however, good reason to think that he did not want Pierston to be regarded simply as a hack sculptor with a venereal itch. That reason lies in the novel's structure. It was suggested earlier that the changed ending in the second version represents a marked shift of emphasis. Neither ending, however, resolves all the issues raised by the preceding narrative. Indeed, neither is given final authority even within the version in which it appears. Hillis Miller points out that there are two further possible endings implied within the texts themselves: Jocelyn's suicide attempt might have succeeded, or he might have pursued his plan of emigrating to America.[8] There are yet further possibilities beyond these. Pierston tells Somers of an earlier suicide project, induced by the departure of one Elsie Targe (38). On that occasion he was deterred by fear of crabs. More radical is a sixth alternative which Hardy explores at some length. Apart from Marcia and the three Avices it is the young widow, Mrs Pine-Avon, 'from every worldly point of view . . . an excellent match for him' (111), who most nearly engages Jocelyn's affections. However, their developing relationship is marred by a misunderstanding, and by the time this has been put right the second Avice has come upon the scene. Mrs Pine-Avon follows Pierston to the Island, but she arrives too late:

> He knew what a fool he was, as he had said. But he was powerless in the grasp of the idealising passion. He cared more for Avice's finger-tips than for Mrs. Pine-Avon's whole personality. (112)

Within a page or so his friend Somers, who has happened to pass her on the road, inquires who she is. When Pierston has briefly explained her presence, Somers remarks 'abruptly': 'I'll marry her myself, if she'll have me. I like the look of her' (113). And he proceeds to do exactly that. Here Hardy provides his allegory with a 'control'. Somers is an artist himself, but his philosophy of love is at opposite poles from that of his friend:

'When you have decided to marry, take the first nice woman you meet. They are all alike.' (114)

He marries Mrs Pine-Avon on Pierston's behalf, so to speak. His future will be what Pierston's would have been had the original relationship not been accidentally disrupted. When he reappears as a married man the change is marked: 'Alfred Somers, once the youthful, picturesque as his own paintings, was now a middle-aged family man with spectacles . . . and a row of daughters tailing off to infancy' (161). His wife herself has now 'retrograded to the petty and timid mental position of her mother and grandmother' and is indeed said to represent a retrogressive trend among contemporary women of her kind, 'their advance as girls being lost in their recession as matrons' (161). In trying to make money to keep his family Somers has lost his idiosyncrasy as a painter, instead addressing himself – successfully – 'to the furnishing householder through the middling critic' (161). Presumably Pierston's eventual fate, whatever ironies may be involved, is not to be seen merely as a reduplication of his friend's. There must be *some* sense in which he, unlike Somers, is a 'possessed' artist.

How, if at all, are these contrarieties and complexities to be resolved? Normally one would expect a diagrammatic, quasi-allegorical work to be successful roughly in proportion to the crispness of the resolution it achieves. To list these variant readings and sub-readings of *The Well-Beloved* is therefore to put a question-mark against it. But they can also serve to suggest that Hardy's novella does not work as at first it might seem to. The plurality, or incompleteness, of the allegory is intrinsic to its meaning.

If Pierston is accepted as being a man of genius for the purposes of the novel, *The Well-Beloved* is a direct precursor of Robert Graves's *The White Goddess*. Though Graves is writing of 'the poet' it would seem reasonable to apply many of his comments to 'artists' in general. In any case it would be 'the poet' who would be foremost in Hardy's own thoughts. Graves is characteristically forthright:

> The test of a poet's vision, one might say, is the accuracy of his portrayal of the White Goddess and of the island over which she rules. The reason why the hairs stand on end, the eyes water, the throat is constricted, the skin crawls and a shiver runs down the spine when one writes or reads a true poem is that a true poem is necessarily an invocation of the White Goddess, or Muse, the Mother of All Living, the ancient power of fright and lust.[9]

To most readers the system of ideas of which this claim is the core will probably seem no more than engagingly dotty, at least at first glance. It looks significantly less so if one takes fuller account on the one hand of the very concept of the Muse, which can boast a formidable pedigree, or on the other of the numerous individual artists, including Yeats, Janacek, Picasso and Graves himself, whose later work, especially, seemed to be fuelled by renewed sexual energies and/or some particular lover/muse. Each of them might have seemed to be seeking a third Avice. Many aspects of Hardy's novel could be comfortably assimilated to Graves's views. We are told that 'The Goddess, an abstraction to the general, was a fairly real personage to Pierston' (148). When the sculptor is forced to part from the second Avice he feels that 'Aphrodite, Ashtaroth, Freyja, or whoever the love-queen of his isle might have been, was punishing him sharply, as she knew but too well how to punish her votaries when they reverted from the ephemeral to the stable mood.' (131) Graves addresses himself to just this possibility:

> A poet writes, as a rule, while he is young, and has the spell of the White Goddess on him. . . . In the result, he either loses the girl altogether, as he rightly feared; or else he marries her and loses her in part. Well, why not? If she makes him a good wife, why should he cherish the poetic obsession to his own ruin? (455–6)

It was suggested above that since Somers enacts this latter alternative Pierston's case is to be differentiated from his. In a later passage Graves comes remarkably close to discussing the sculptor's dilemma in his own terms:

> A Muse-poet falls in love, absolutely, and his true love is for him the embodiment of the Muse. As a rule, the power of absolutely falling

in love soon vanishes; and, as a rule, because the woman feels embarrassed by the spell she exercises over her poet-lover and repudiates it; he, in disillusion, turns to Apollo who, at least, can provide him with a livelihood and intelligent entertainment, and reneges before his middle 'twenties. But the real, perpetually obsessed Muse-poet distinguishes between the Goddess . . . and the individual woman whom the Goddess may make her instrument for a month, a year, seven years, or even more. The Goddess abides; and perhaps he will again have knowledge of her through his experience of another woman. (490–1)

Pierston 'turns to Apollo' for a livelihood at times, but not – as does the married Somers – in perpetuity. He is at any rate an *intermittently* obsessed Muse-poet, or Muse-artist, and presides over the second version of the novel in that capacity.

Hardy's sketch of the 'artistic temperament' is altogether uncannily close to Graves's account. Yet the latter would seem readily and tidily amenable to translation into allegory. Why, then, should *The Well-Beloved* be so relatively ragged a work? The question is lent added force by the fact that Hardy himself seems to have found a suitable allegory ready to hand. Pierston, he suggests, is 'the Wandering Jew of the love-world' (65); the sculptor is 'urged on and on like the Jew Ahasuerus' (148). Having found the parallel, however, he chooses not to develop it – or not to develop it in remotely predictable terms. It is in the change he makes that he parts company with Graves.

The vital emendation is that Pierston-Ahasuerus finds himself not on an endless pilgrimage through an open world of women, but on a treadmill, condemned to love generation after generation of Avices. There are several possible explanations for this stratagem. The simplest is that Hardy felt a need to impose some sort of shape on potentially miscellaneous material. Any re-telling of the Ahasuerus or Don Juan legend potentially goes on *ad infinitum*. Hardy's generational device subsumes repetitiousness into series and thereby creates a form for his work. Beyond that, perhaps, is an implicit suggestion that the tastes of a Don Juan may not, after all, be indiscriminate. Perhaps each of us has hidden patterns of preference. A simple version of such patterning is implied in casual conversation when someone remarks (for example) that X has married a woman resembling his mother, or has deserted his wife for a woman who looks just like her. In *The Well-Beloved* the continuities may be similar in kind, but they go deeper than physical resemblance. The first Avice is described as 'local to the bone'. When Pierston, at a London party, hears of her death, he immediately begins to visualise 'the old,

old scenes on Isle Vindilia which were inseparable from her personality' (70). Various local sights, repeatedly mentioned in the novel, come to life before his mind's eye: the quarries, the Castle, the ocean, the lighthouses. In contrast Nichola Pine-Avon shrivels in his regard: 'she became a woman of his acquaintance with no distinctive traits' (70). That night he pictures Avice in her winding sheet, 'irradiated' by the moonlight, reached only by the island sounds: 'the tink-tink of the chisels in the quarries, the surging of the tides in the Bay, and the muffled grumbling of the currents in the never-pacified Race' (73). He returns to the Island and actually witnesses her funeral – but only from a distance of a quarter of a mile. His eyes take in a surrealistically diverse scene, the coffin of his former lover moving, on human legs, among or against a church, a cemetery, a lighthouse, the sea, a fishing-boat, a school of mackerel. . . . Dramatised in this wonderful description are a host of the sights and sounds which Pierston links with his lost love. In re-experiencing them he resumes contact with her. That evening he lingers in the churchyard by moonlight, 'disinclined to leave a spot sublimed both by early association and present regret' (77) – and thinks for a dizzy moment that he sees Avice herself. It is, of course, her daughter that he has seen, and he comes to find in her, too, this charm of 'early association'. Despite the gap in years he longs to marry 'one in whom seemed to linger as an aroma all the charm of his youth and his early home' (105).

In effect the diagnosis concerning Art is subsumed in a larger diagnosis concerning Love. To use Graves's terminology, Hardy is at least as interested in the Island as in the Goddess. His suggestion is that every man – or every man of the sketched 'temperament' – has this instinctive tendency to assimilate abstract longings of one kind or another into romantic love for a woman whose physical appearance triggers the relevant associations. Pierston is ultimately (and recurrently) drawn to a physical type which he associates with the Island, very much as Eustacia is attracted by a man whom she links with Paris, or Angel Clare by a milkmaid whose face and demeanour seem to epitomise the traditional rural life to which he has committed himself. The inference is that although Everyman's Well-Beloved may assume a diversity of forms, the most powerful, the most insistent, will be those that bear directly on a hidden predilection. Pierston is not pursuing merely an abstract ideal.

Thus the potential patterns of the fable subside into reflexivity. At her own funeral Avice the first is aggrandised as she metaphorically dissolves once more into the great seascape which for Pierston she personifies. A few chapters later the process is shown in reverse, as her daughter, in his eyes, entirely eclipses the natural background:

> How incomparably the immaterial dream dwarfed the grandest of substantial things, when here, between those three sublimities – the sky, the rock, and the ocean – the minute personality of this washer-girl filled his consciousness to its extremest boundary, and the stupendous inanimate scene shrank to a corner therein. (102)

True love for Pierston (as presumably for Hardy) is organic and holistic. It suffuses; it synthesises. Its antithesis is the fragmented life of fashionable London, which has him contemplating 'shoulderblades, back hair, glittering headgear, neck-napes, moles, hairpins, pearl-powder, pimples, minerals cut into facets of many-coloured rays, necklace-clasps, fans, stays, the seven styles of elbow and arm, the thirteen varieties of ear . . .' (61–2) An Avice is not such an assemblage of spare parts, but a hieroglyph, a personified environment.

Outside Hardy's diagnosis of art, then, lies a diagnosis of love. But even that diagnosis is subsumed in a larger one. The 40-year time-span of *The Well-Beloved* helps to emphasise the brevity of human life. Two of the Avices die; Pierston is reduced to feebleness. But flesh is not unique in its frailty. If Marcia's face has been chiselled and eroded, so has the very rock of her native island. Hardy reminds us that our sense of geological stability is a delusion, derived from the relative brevity of human apprehension. His 'peninsula, carved by Time out of a single stone' (Preface) has been further worn by the waves and plundered by quarrymen. On the same slow time-scale, however, comes a possibility of replenishment. Deep in the Island 'a forest of conifers lay as petri-factions' (87). Such inexact renewal is everywhere visible: two castles lie in ruins, but another has been built; a church has gone down in a cliff-fall, but it has been replaced; the Avices are recycled like the trees: one produces another, who produces a third. The people, the plants, the buildings, the very rocks which we see as 'products' are expressions of an interminable *process*. This is the point Hardy makes when describing how the 'periodic' moaning of the second Avice in child-birth is accompanied by a similarly rhythmical moaning from the sea nearby, 'so that the articulate heave of the water and articulate heave of life seemed but differing utterances of the selfsame troubled terrestrial Being – which in one sense they were' (133).

Yet it is hard to decide just where Hardy sits in relation to his own perception. When Pierston is beginning to woo the second Avice, whom he employs to do his washing, he engages her in a conversation about the appropriate methods to use:

> All this time [he] was thinking of the girl – or as the scientific might say, Nature was working her plans for the next generation under the cloak of a dialogue on linen. He could not read her individual char-acter, owing to the confusing effect of her likeness to a woman whom he had valued too late. He could not help seeing in her all that he knew of another, and veiling in her all that did not harmonise with his sense of metempsychosis. (90)

Pierston talks severely of mangling and starching, but he is falling in love – although his heart is with a woman 20 years dead and his mind is clouded with this 'sense of metempsychosis'. All three impulses can be seen as mere by-products of a breeding urge, a life-force. That, however, would be the 'scientific' view, which Hardy doesn't neces-sarily endorse. His reworking of the novel, and the plurality of possible 'endings' in either version, represent a refusal to endorse *any* simple view. He has raised a series of questions which push outwards from immediate and personal feeling towards abstraction. Is romantic love no more than a rationalisation of animal desire? Is art the product of unappeasable idealisation or of sexual dissatisfaction? Is the capacity to go on falling in love a symptom of immaturity, or of vitality, or of renewed aesthetic aspiration? In ostensibly loving another human being are we really responding to a projection of our private appetites and associations? Are not all these impulses, whatever their intrinsic emphases, alternative manifestations of an indifferent life-force? Hardy's refusal to offer a final answer to such questions is not timorousness or hesitancy. His task is not to solve the problems but to induce his readers to ponder them. Implicitly his novel asserts that in these matters any 'answer' must be delusive or provisional. The ultimate untidiness of his allegory is an acknowledgement that the argument is inescapably open-ended.

   The open-endedness carries the corollary that abstract reasoning is in any case likely to be an inadequate guide to conduct. Most of his readers will find it reassuring that Hardy's subsequent career did not reflect the pessimism or defeatism of Jocelyn Pierston. More than 20 years after the serialisation of *The Well-Beloved* he married for a second time. And however well or ill that decision sat with his personal experience of the Well-Beloved it is certain that he went on composing great poetry until his death.

Notes

1. *The Well-Beloved*, ed. Tom Hetherington (Oxford: Oxford University Press, 1986), p. 9. Subsequent references to this edition are given in parenthesis.
2. *The Poems of Alexander Pope*, ed. John Butt (London: Methuen, 1963), p. 522.
3. *Far from the Madding Crowd*, ed. Suzanne B. Falck-Yi (Oxford: Oxford University Press, 1993), p. 100. Subsequent references to this edition are given in parenthesis.
4. *The Woodlanders*, ed. Dale Kramer (Oxford: Oxford University Press, 1985), p. 89.
5. *The Life and Work of Thomas Hardy*, ed. Michael Millgate (London: Macmillan, 1984), p. 305. Subsequent references are given in parenthesis.
6. The sculptor is named Pearston in the serial version, *The Pursuit of the Well-Beloved*, but Pierston in the revised hardcover edition.
7. See *Life and Work*, p. 408.
8. See the Introduction to *The Well-Beloved*, ed. J. Hillis Miller (New Wessex Edition: London, 1975), p. 17.
9. Robert Graves, *The White Goddess* (London: Faber and Faber, 1961), p. 24. Subsequent references are given in parenthesis.

4
A Feast of Language: Hardy's Allusions

Mary Rimmer

I begin with an allusion of my own, from Shakespeare's *Love's Labour's Lost*. 'A feast of language' is adapted from the cutting aside the page Moth makes about three pedants (his master Don Armado, Sir Nathaniel, and Holofernes) as they flourish learned greetings at each other: 'They have been at a great feast of languages, and stol'n the scraps' (V.i). Moth refers in part to the pedants' habit of sprinkling their talk with ostentatious Latin words, and to their obsessive quibbling over the meanings, proper uses and even pronunciation of words, but his comment, especially as I have paraphrased it for my title, can also refer more generally to the ridiculous figure pedants cut by making a display of their learning. They attempt to lay claim to the rich feast of linguistic or literary tradition, but manage only to steal a few scraps.

For many of his critics, the Thomas Hardy who makes quotations and allusions, whether to literary texts or to odd bits of esoteric knowledge, risks becoming just such a pedantic scavenger and gatecrasher at the feast of learned language. Unlike the three in *Love's Labour's Lost*, however, he seems not a figure of fun, but rather a victim of his spotty formal education, embarrassingly keen to demonstrate the range of his knowledge and unconscious that his efforts to do so reveal rather than obliterate his background. Accordingly, he has been slated for awkward quotation, for 'showy rather than functional' allusions,[1] and for dropping the names of authors and painters in an effort to prove his cultural credentials.

The disapproval is sometimes vociferous and sometimes muted, but there is still an overall sense that Hardy's best, as Raymond Chapman puts it, 'is found when he turns from the richness of allusion to the simplicity which the language offers equally with its complexity'.[2] There are some exceptions: Marlene Springer's *Hardy's Use of Allusion*, for instance, and Rosemarie Morgan's *Cancelled Words*, which comments perceptively on allusion in *Far from the Madding Crowd*.[3] But even Springer finds it necessary to distinguish between Hardy's 'successful' allusions on the one hand, and on the other, those which show him as 'a prime example of the self-educated man attempting to prove himself to the English Establishment'.[4] Likewise, to Jean Jacques Lecercle, Hardy's style is marked by contradictions between 'the speaker of dialect' and 'the reader of penny cyclopaedias, desirous to share his knowledge'. Lecercle sees these contradictions as central to Hardy's use of language, and credits Raymond Williams with destroying the 'myth' of Hardy as autodidactic pedant, yet his own reference to penny encyclopaedia reading has a condescending edge none the less.[5]

The discomfort caused by Hardy the allusionist is closely related to the well-worn view of him as a 'dogged, leisurely, old-fashioned story-teller',[6] who by rights should have stayed not only with 'simple' language but also with rural subjects and material taken 'from life' rather than from books. And despite his impatient remark in the *Life* about contemporary readers of *Far from the Madding Crowd* who seemed to expect him to write 'for ever about sheepfarming',[7] Hardy himself provided some support to this view of his work when he divided it under sub-headings for the 1912 collected edition, and in his General Preface to that edition referred to the first category, the 'Novels of Character and Environment', as containing the books 'which approach most nearly to uninfluenced works'.[8] Over the last few years that portion of the Preface and its ramifications for Hardy criticism have been ably analysed by a number of critics, notably Peter Widdowson and Charles Lock;[9] I will therefore not repeat the specifics of those analyses, but simply note that to call something an 'uninfluenced work' begs several questions, and that the Preface echoes and responds to contemporary reviews to such an extent that it cannot be taken as an unproblematic statement of value, especially given Hardy's characteristic vagueness about what he means by 'influence'. None the less, critics have persistently quoted the classification and his comments on it, and have used them to define the nature of his fiction, and the negative consequences for his work of literary and cultural 'influences', whether general ones such as the constraints of serial publication and the form of the nineteenth-century novel, or particular ones such as Wilkie Collins, or Hardy's childhood favourites Harrison Ainsworth and G. P. R. James. Hence the 'real' or 'good' Hardy becomes the unbookish one, 'influenced' only by his experience of rural life and oral culture.

Yet Hardy himself seems to have seen no absolute divide between the lived and the learned, the rural and the urban, the oral and the written. Indeed, 'rural life' itself is a more complex phenomenon than many commentators seem to assume. Even when Hardy was growing up, in the 1840s and 1850s, Dorchester and Higher Bockhampton were separate worlds, but also ones which communicated with each other fairly frequently. In the *Life* Hardy notes the radical difference between the county-town 'which had advanced to railways and telegraphs and daily London papers' and the 'hamlet three miles off, where modern improvements were still regarded as wonders',[10] but he does so in the context of commenting on his own daily movement between hamlet and town, movement which formed part of his life for over ten years as schoolboy and architect's pupil. Dorchester was after all a place you could go to from Bockhampton without much difficulty – to buy books, to get a better education, and to begin a professional life which would eventually take you into the metropolitan world of London.

As Hardy navigated his passages between these separate but connected worlds, he made increasing use of notebooks for collecting and storing quotations and observations, and of printed anthologies. On both counts he was very much of his age. As Michael Wheeler points out in *The Art of Allusion in Victorian Fiction*, the Victorian predilection for anthologies, whether bought or self-constructed, reflected

> the widely held belief that change in the century following the Industrial Revolution was too rapid and disruptive. An indication of this uneasiness in an age of rapid change was the apparently universal habit of hoarding and sharing inherited and contemporary wisdom from which a sense of moral and psychological security could be gained. The garnering of old saws and new apothegms was evident wherever one turned.[11]

Hardy's own extensive study and use of anthologies such as *The Golden Treasury*, and the charmingly titled *Beautiful Thoughts from Latin Authors*, reflect that hoarding and sharing habit, as do his notebooks, though as I shall argue I think his uses of the material read and collected in this way tend if anything to undermine 'moral and psychological security'. But certainly his anthology-reading and notebook-keeping suggest his close connections with contemporary culture at least as much as they suggest the audodidact's lack of cultural ease.

To be fair, though, critical objection to the allusions stems from their actual effects as well as from assumptions about Hardy. To an extent they simply share with all quotations and allusions the power to disrupt reading, if only by reminding us that the 'world' we are immersed in is a literary one. Moreover, since it enters the host text as fragments, any material quoted or alluded to is easily manipulated and distorted; the allusion may therefore end up challenging our assumptions about the source text as well as our reading of the host text. As A. S. Byatt puts it in *Babel Tower*, quotation 'gives a kind of papery vitality and independence to . . . cultural clichés cut free from the web of language that gives them precise meaning'.[12] Frederica, the protagonist of *Babel Tower*, uses quotation and other forms of what she calls 'cut-up' to try to master the various clichés and documents (legal, personal, and literary) that threaten to control her life. For Byatt the disruption built into quotation and allusion can be harnessed for creative and personal purposes; even clichés, once 'cut free' from their context, take on a 'papery vitality'. Quotation may appear to invoke the cultural authority of a source text (Homer, for instance, or Shakespeare), but it also erodes cultural authority, for it asserts the quoter's right to manipulate any text, including highly prestigious or even sacred ones. We may think here of Sue Bridehead's Bible in *Jude the Obscure*, cut up and rearranged in order to turn it into a historical document like any other, and subject it to her editorial control. Or we may think of the extended allusion Hardy makes to Virgil's *Aeneid* in *Desperate Remedies*, one which links that most virtuous of Roman heroes, Aeneas, to the villain Aeneas Manston and (through a quotation from the *Aeneid*) the chaste virgin warrior Camilla to the prostitute Anne Seaway.[13] Are we supposed to see their classical *alter egos* as elevating Manston and Anne? Or do we rather see Hardy as having a sly dig at Virgil's concepts of heroism and chastity?[14]

Equally problematic, though in a different way, are allusions to the obscure and unexpected – in *Far from the Madding Crowd*, for example, where Fanny Robin is compared to 'the clever Jacquet Droz, the designer of automatic substitutes for human limbs',[15] or in *Desperate Remedies*, where the narrator informs us that readers 'who remember Greuze's 'Head of a Girl' in one of the public picture-galleries, have an idea of Cytherea's look askance'.[16] Since most of us will not know Droz or recall the Greuze painting, both allusions are likely to bring our reading to a halt, and tease us away from Fanny and Cytherea as 'real' characters involved in suspenseful struggles for shelter and livelihood. Ultimately, then, both serve primarily to remind us that the novels are constructs, like Droz's artificial limbs, Fanny's improvised crutches, Greuze's painting and Cytherea's backward glance (a movement the narrator even describes as 'one of her masterpieces').

Conventionally, allusions are deployed as subtly as possible, in order to minimise such disruption. Hardy, however, seems actively to court the anti-realist energies of quotation and allusion, in line with his characteristic tendency to push realism to and beyond its limits. From the very beginning of his novel-writing career in 1868, when he submitted a manuscript to Macmillan entitled 'The Poor Man and the Lady: a Story with no Plot', Hardy was working against the grain of nineteenth-century realism even while he produced it. 'Plot' is central to realism; the realist impression thrives on the crowding of event upon event, story-line upon story-line. Interestingly, when he referred to 'The Poor Man' in his old age in the *Life*, Hardy wrote of it not as a realist novel, but as a cultural and philosophical grab-bag: 'a sweeping dramatic satire of the squirearchy and nobility, London society, the vulgarity of the middle class, modern Christianity, church restoration, and political and domestic morals in general, the author's views, in fact, being obviously those of a young man with "a passion for reforming the world"'. A little later on Hardy notes that the style had 'the affected simplicity of Defoe's', but he makes it plain that 'this naïve realism' amounted almost to a hoax: in later years he was surprised to think 'that his inexperienced imagination should have created figments that could win credence from such experienced heads' as Alexander Macmillan's and John Morley's, his first two readers.[17]

Never very far from the surface in Hardy, the consciousness that a novel consists of 'figments' works through in various ways, even in his language. In *Hardy's Literary Language and Victorian Philology*, Dennis Taylor notes that 'there is throughout Hardy a persistent questioning of the idioms of language, as though he will not allow us to fall into idiomatic drowse, but keeps us awake with slight jars of the language, not great enough to be solecistic'.[18] Hardy's allusions appear to work in a similar way: they refuse to fold smoothly into the surface of his works, and interrupt our desire to drowse in a complete fictional world. Interestingly, immediately before the sentence just quoted, Taylor identifies a need for a more thorough study of allusion, and comments that Hardy seems to set his face against 'the urbanity of allusiveness which confirms a high culture'.[19] Later, he suggests that allusion in Hardy, especially in his poetry, resists

> the history of allusive phrasing, which Eliot was probably most thinking about when he celebrated the poet 'getting as much as possible of the whole weight of the history of the language behind his word' . . . Hardy evokes a different history, more anomalous, more

rooted in the impersonality of the historical dictionary, less literary and learned, less the fitting accompaniment of a well-educated person.[20]

It is just that anomalous, stubbornly un-urbane spirit that informs Hardy's allusions, and in a sense does reflect his self-education, not because he is anxiously showing off, but because his heterodox attitude towards his acquired culture questions not only the conventions of realism, but also those of 'high culture' as defined by the later nine-teenth century. Hardy did possess his culture, perhaps more securely than many who had not had to fight so hard for it, but he was enough of an outsider to resist many of its assumptions. Adept at the art of working sly subversions into his text, he will take a phrase from a dic-tionary or an encyclopaedia as readily as from a literary work. In his very miscellaneousness, as well as in his unexpected applications of 'good literature', he calls cultural categories into question.

Hardy's resistant ownership of culture comes through most clearly in allusions within dialogue. The novels contain numerous awkward moments in which characters' degree of cultural knowledge comes to define their social place, often quite painfully. Stephen Smith in *A Pair of Blue Eyes*, for instance, leaps to complete a Latin quotation that Mr Swancourt has been muttering to himself, in part because, like Mr Swan-court, he finds the quotation relevant to his fortunes in love. But Mr Swancourt's response ('I am delighted with you, Mr. Smith, for it is so seldom in this desert that I meet with a man who is gentleman and scholar enough to continue a quotation, however trite it may be') underlines the issues involved here.[21] Stephen is in a precarious social position: a guest from London, a professional man, and a tacitly accepted suitor for Elfride Swancourt, he is also the son of John Smith, the local stonemason, a fact which, if known, would disqualify him from visiting the Swancourts at all. Uneasily poised as he is between two worlds, his ability to recognise and complete a Latin quotation is a crucial assurance that he is 'gentleman and scholar enough' for the role he is trying to play. At the same time, Mr Swancourt's comment on the triteness of the quotation suggests that both of them may be making a misleading display of learning here by remembering the quotation as a tag or anthology piece rather than directly from Horace. Mr Swancourt may, however, be a little in advance of his naïve guest in recognising that to remember a 'trite' quotation is slim grounds for boasting, and once he discovers who Stephen is, he calls the episode up as evidence of the young man's failure to make the mark: 'the Latin line he gave to my quotation; it was very cut and dried, very; or I, who haven't looked into a classical author for the last eighteen years, shouldn't have remembered it'.[22]

Allusive contests in Hardy can be more open, as in *The Woodlanders*, where the bitter memory of one fuels George Melbury's desire to have Grace well-educated, and in a sense drives the entire plot. This is of course his memory of being asked by the parson's son and his friends, 'Who dragged Whom round the walls of What', and hearing them shout with laughter when instead of making the 'correct' response about Achilles, Hector and Troy, the young George responds 'Sam Barret, who dragged his wife in a wheeled chair round the tower when she went to be churched'.[23] Melbury's tale of crying over the shame of the moment that night until his pillow was wet, and his vow to starve before anyone laughs at any child of his for similar ignorance, demonstrate the potential costs of not knowing one's way around the allusive minefield. Yet like Stephen's Latin, the knowledge Grace gains as the result of her father's vow makes her no less vulnerable, though superficially she is able to gain the upper hand, as she does when she muses about her supposed new role as Mrs Charmond's companion and amanuensis, and indulges in literary name-dropping in front of Giles. Her cultivation, though it does stop Fitzpiers from simply seducing her, provides no defence against the more comprehensive social snare of marriage, which is both the 'right' end for someone of her education, and a dead-end for her, tied as she is to a man whose scientific exploits seem no more promising than his performance as a husband.

Stephen and Grace both believe to a greater or lesser extent in what Melbury calls the 'freemasonry of education'[24] and its power to level social distinctions based on birth, but they find that in fact education and reading distance them from their original class while offering little advance towards social improvement, especially for Grace, whose status will be determined primarily by whom she marries. Ethelberta Petherwin takes a more cynical view of the value of cultural background. One of Hardy's most sophisticated manipulators of words and texts, she borrows from the Gothic novel and Defoe, chooses ironically appropriate passages from *Paradise Lost* to read over Milton's grave, and uses Defoe's *The Shortest Way with the Dissenters* to make a covert joke about employers' attitudes towards their servants. Nevertheless, she remains shrewdly aware that reverence for literary and other received texts can block as easily as foster social advance. She warns her sister not to believe in inherited wisdom, here represented by the old saw about honesty as the best policy: 'don't you go believing in sayings, Picotee:

they are all made by men, for their own advantages. Women who use public proverbs as a guide through events are those who have not ingenuity enough to make private ones as each event occurs.'[25] Though Ethelberta focuses on women here, *The Hand of Ethelberta* as a whole suggests that to gain the 'advantage' in class as well as gender terms takes ingenuity rather than honesty, and skilful manipulation of texts rather than simply cultured knowledge of them.[26] When she moves into public storytelling, for instance, she uses Defoe's style to invent a new genre, or at least to reinvent an old one, and keep the public guessing about her background or origins, much as the young Hardy used the 'affected simplicity' of Defoe to fool 'experienced heads'. Ethelberta knows not only that education without birth and material goods to back it up does not go very far, but also that in order to make it go farther one has to use it rather than trust to it as a social passport.

Although Hardy's narrators' allusions naturally work a little differently from those characters use, similar ironies circulate around them, as for instance in the cluster of references and quotations which surround Eustacia Vye in *The Return of the Native*, arguably the most allusively described character in Hardy. Indeed, the barrage of references the *Return of the Native* narrator applies to her, especially in the 'Queen of Night' chapter, has seemed excessive to many, even a little silly attached to a young woman pining away on Egdon Heath because she has been banished from watering-place life in Budmouth. How clear an idea can we form of a Eustacia who resembles everything from goddesses to roses? The sense that the portrait is fluid, perhaps even chaotic, is reinforced when we consider Hardy's several changes to the allusions he uses for her: in Chapter VI, for instance, the manuscript and the *Belgravia* serialisation have the narrator refer to her features as suggesting those of Marie Antoinette and Byron, though resembling neither. Hardy changed this to the features of Marie Antoinette and Mrs Siddons for the first edition, and then to Sappho and Mrs Siddons in the 1895 edition.[27] The changes do reflect a shift in Eustacia's characterisation in later editions, but they also suggest a certain arbitrariness in the parade of references: since none of the comparisons does define her, one can be substituted for another, and Sappho take the place of Marie Antoinette, without much altering the description.

Rather than make all these references add up to a coherent characterisation, Hardy seems to have designed them to dramatise Eustacia's troubled relationship to the various texts and cultural icons which surround her in the narration. To begin with, he places the early accounts of Eustacia after another description, that of the Heath itself. True, the narrator applies far fewer allusions to the Heath than to Eustacia, but the terms applied to her do echo the North/South imagery central to the description of Egdon. Its 'mournful sublimity' is at several points seen as explicitly Northern, contrasted to 'the vineyards and myrtle-gardens of South Europe',[28] and associated with the Celts who built Rainbarrow, the Druids and followers of Thor and Woden whose rites are the ancestors of the heath-dwellers' Guy Fawkes bonfires. As the antithesis of Southern sympathies and Southern/classical concepts of beauty, the Heath in November preserves intact 'that sinister condition which made Caesar anxious each year to get clear of its glooms before the autumnal equinox, a kind of landscape and weather which leads travellers from the south to continually describe our island as Homer's Cimmerian land'.[29] Thus, when Eustacia's lips are described as suggesting buried fragments of forgotten marbles, because their line forms 'the curve so well-known in the arts of design as the cima-recta, or ogee',[30] the very awkwardness of the technical terms makes sense: Eustacia becomes a curve, a fragment of a statue, subsumed into the North/South contrast that characterises Egdon Heath. The description, which at first appears to elevate her, turns her into a mere textbook example that brings the Heath's Northern character into sharper relief.

The Southern associations, along with other elements of her description, obscure rather than clarify Eustacia. An anomalous 'apparition' on Egdon, she is defined in curiously negative terms: 'It was felt at once that that mouth did not come over from Sleswig with a band of Saxon pirates whose lips met like the two halves of a muffin.'[31] Like the earlier description of her face as being 'without ruddiness, as without pallor', this historical reference tells us primarily what Eustacia is not.[32] Similarly, we hear of the things she does not wear (coloured ribbon and metallic ornaments) and in the manuscript and serial versions we also hear of her refusal to use perfume. Even in the 1895 and subsequent texts, where Hardy substantiates her Southern characteristics by giving her a father from Corfu, the mention of his nationality comes halfway through the chapter, too late to turn the negative edge of her description. (In the *Belgravia* serialisation she is briefly half-Belgian, again suggesting that generalised foreignness is more important to our reading of her than any specific nationality or origin.)

The ironic references to goddesses which open the 'Queen of Night' chapter and crop up again at intervals as it goes on reinforce the sense that absences define Eustacia, for they underscore her lack of power. The narrator comments that if it were possible 'for the earth and mankind to be entirely in her grasp for a while' she would be as capricious and unjust as fate or the gods usually are[33] – but of course Eustacia has no Olympian sphere of action, and would have none even if she escaped to Budmouth or Paris as she so longs to do. Indeed, as the narrator remarks, her quasi-divine dignity depends on her having nothing; whereas 'A narrow life in Budmouth might have completely demeaned her', her negative position, 'without realms or hearts to queen it over', paradoxically makes her queenly, because she can 'look as though [she has] lost them'.[34]

Perhaps the most telling use of allusion to erode Eustacia occurs in the paragraph which catalogues the things her presence, moods, motions and voice call to mind. In the first place, the catalogue, like much of the chapter, is a little too inclusive to be taken quite seriously:

> Her presence brought memories of such things as Bourbon roses, rubies, tropical midnights and eclipses of the sun; her moods recalled lotus-eaters, the march in *Athalie*, her motions, the ebb and flow of the sea; her voice, the viola. In a dim light, and with a slight rearrangement of her hair, her general figure might have stood for that of either of the higher female deities. The new moon behind her head, an old helmet upon it, a diadem of accidental dewdrops round her brow, would have been adjuncts sufficient to strike the note of Artemis, Athena, or Hera respectively, with as close an approximation to the antique as that which passes muster on many respected canvases.[35]

The very miscellaneousness of the lists makes their limitations as a character summary clear; instead of emerging as the sort of 'rounded' character we expect in a realist novel, Eustacia appears as a series of others' memories and associations, a figure for the romantic desires of her observers. The paragraph ends by considering her suitability, not for becoming a goddess this time, but for representing one: with a few props and in a dim light, she could 'strike the note' of Artemis, Athena or Hera and achieve 'as close an approximation to the antique as that which passes muster on many respected canvases'. Moreover, even these limited possibilities for fame and a wider life are denied on Egdon, hardly the place to be discovered as an artist's model, or to construct tableaux of classical goddesses; the closest Eustacia will get to such a thing is the Mummers' play, the 'fossilised survival' in which she plays the Turkish Knight.[36] As the narrator slightingly notes, her 'celestial imperiousness, love, wrath, and fervour' are 'somewhat thrown away on netherward Egdon'.[37] Further, as a woman, she inhabits a world where, even beyond Egdon, 'doing means marrying'; her schemes have 'the comprehensive strategy of a general', but her life offers her little scope for their exercise.[38]

Eustacia's own attempts to find herself an allusive niche have no greater success. Her 'high gods' William the Conqueror, Strafford, and Napoleon come to her third-hand, through 'the Lady's History' she has read at school, and the Bible seems to be her only direct source for heroic narrative. Her preference for Saul, Sisera, the Philistines and Pontius Pilate over more orthodox choices such as Jacob and David marks her 'forwardness of mind', and yet there is also something a little pitiful in this schoolgirl idea of heroism which, as the narrator comments, is only original by virtue of Eustacia's isolated situation 'among the very rereward of thinkers'.[39] And, of course, on Egdon she finds nothing closer to her ideals than Wildeve, whose inadequacies are plain to her even at the most intense moments of their love affair, and Clym, whose delusions are as complete as her own. Her field of reference is limited, true, but even the narrator, with a much wider range of texts to choose from, can find only ironic allusions for her.

The references pile up around Eustacia only to convince us that we cannot read them in conventional terms at all. They seem there to reveal their own failure to describe her, and to suggest the trap that she and others fall into by expecting a romantic and mythical world instead of the intransigently unromantic circumstances which constrain them. Like the 'sayings' Ethelberta warns Picotee about, created and handed down by others and making an indifferent fit with the shifting exigencies of a particular life, stories of gods, goddesses, heroes and kings turn out to be as insubstantial as 'memories' of music or roses. The allusions lead us off in a variety of different and frustrating directions as we try to call up the image of a 'southern marble' or remember who Strafford was.[40] We end up with an often inharmonious chorus of names and ideas rather than an imaginary, almost-real woman we could recognise as 'Eustacia'. Paradoxically, she becomes present to us as a puzzle, a figure we must try to piece together from the fragmentary allusions which swirl around her.

Like the allusive descriptions of Eustacia, Hardy's texts often engage us through the very things that are supposed to be wrong with them. Just as his own relationship to literature and culture was more complex than that implied by the notion of 'Hardy the autodidact' or 'Hardy the rural teller of tales', so his texts deploy allusions to that learning or culture neither in the urbane, high-culture tradition, nor with the gaucherie of the newly learned or half-learned show-off. His not-quite-conventional perspective on culture allows him to question the urbane tradition, and its illusory but seductive offer of a word made comprehensible by literature and inherited wisdom. As Hardy uses allusion it turns back on itself, and begins to interrogate the structure of knowledge it derives from: it becomes a weapon, a tool of advancement likely to cut the hand of those who try to use it, or an echoing chorus of reference that can define only hopeless desire for unattainable things. 'Writing', John Goode argues, 'is at the very root of Hardy's self-consciousness', not as something which codifies and makes sense of the world, but as a 'dead metaphor' which both dislocates experience and allows outsiders 'a mode of access to the culture'.[41] Hardy's 'stol'n scraps' and 'cut-up' disrupt the 'feast of language' that is inherited print culture, but they also assert his right to be at the feast, not as respectful visitor or scavenger, but as a full participant, whose right of access includes the right to manipulate the inheritance as he chooses.

Notes

1. S. F. Johnson, 'Hardy and Burke's "Sublime"', in Harold C. Martin, ed., *Style in Prose Fiction*, English Institute Essays, 1958 (New York: Columbia University Press, 1959), p. 79.
2. Raymond Chapman, *The Language of Thomas Hardy* (London: Macmillan, 1990), p. 57.
3. Rosemarie Morgan, *Cancelled Words: Rediscovering Thomas Hardy* (London: Routledge, 1992). See for instance pp. 25–8, and references to allusion in the notes (pp. 173, 175–7 and 179–80).
4. Marlene Springer, *Hardy's Use of Allusion* (London: Macmillan, 1983), pp. 4–5.
5. Jean-Jacques Lecercle, 'The Violence of Style in *Tess of the d'Urbervilles*', in *Alternative Hardy*, ed. Lance St John Butler (New York: St. Martin's Press, 1989), p. 22.
6. Albert J. Guerard, *Thomas Hardy* (1949; rpt. Norfolk, CT: New Directions, 1964), p. ix.
7. *The Life and Work of Thomas Hardy*, ed. Michael Millgate (London: Macmillan, 1984), p. 105.
8. 'General Preface to the Novels and Poems' (1912), rpt. in *Thomas Hardy's Personal Writings*, ed. Harold Orel (Lawrence: University of Kansas Press, 1966), p. 44.
9. Peter Widdowson, *Hardy in History: a Study in Literary Sociology* (London: Routledge, 1989), pp. 48–55, and Charles Lock, *Criticism in Focus: Thomas Hardy* (London: Bristol Classical Press, 1992), pp. 51–4.
10. *Life and Work*, p. 36.

11. Michael Wheeler, *The Art of Allusion in Victorian Fiction* (New York: Barnes and Noble, 1979), p. 14.

12. A. S. Byatt, *Babel Tower* (London: Vintage, 1997), p. 385.

13. *Desperate Remedies*, ed. Mary Rimmer (London: Penguin, 1998), p. 356.

14. Interestingly, Virgil's praise for Camilla works against his own cultural tradition, in which the female warrior was by no means a figure of chastity. Hardy in a sense undoes Virgil's careful balancing act by connecting Camilla to Anne Seaway.

15. *Far from the Madding Crowd*, ed. Suzanne B. Falck-Yi (Oxford: Oxford University Press, 1993), p. 274. Pierre Jacquet Droz (1721–90) was a designer of mechanical figures. Springer cites the Droz reference as an example among others in *Far from the Madding Crowd* of 'what seems to be a compulsion to impress his audience by dropping obscure allusions which add little to the story save distraction' (p. 57). Later she suggests that the 'over-intellectual' allusions in this episode reflect Hardy's 'possible discomfort with the overt pathos of the scene' (p. 68).

16. *Desperate Remedies*, p. 58.

17. *Life and Work*, p. 63.

18. Dennis Taylor, *Hardy's Literary Language and Victorian Philology* (Oxford: Clarendon Press, 1993), p. 293. My work on allusion has benefited greatly from the erudition and insight of Taylor's work on Hardy's language.

19. The 'high culture' referred to here is that defined in the first instance by Matthew Arnold in *Culture and Anarchy* (1867), as 'the study of perfection'; to Arnold 'The great men of culture are those who have a passion for diffusing . . . the best knowledge of their time.' *Culture and Anarchy and Other Writings*, ed. Stefan Collini (Cambridge: Cambridge University Press, 1993), pp. 59, 79. T. S. Eliot, a later advocate of Arnoldian high culture, also figures in Taylor's discussion.

20. Taylor, p. 295. The quotation is from T. S. Eliot's essay 'The Three Provincialities' (1922), rpt. in *Essays in Criticism* I.

21. *A Pair of Blue Eyes*, ed. Alan Manford (Oxford, 1985), p. 51.

22. *A Pair of Blue Eyes*, p. 85.

23. *The Woodlanders*, ed. Dale Kramer (Oxford: Oxford University Press), p. 23.

24. *The Woodlanders*, p. 44.

25. *The Hand of Ethelberta*, ed. Tim Dolin (London: Penguin, 1996), p. 145.

26. Even Ethelberta's brother Sol, apparently the blunt, straightforward opposite to his devious sister, suggests that it is important to make a wise choice of texts: 'I don't care for history. Prophecy is the only thing can do poor men any good' (*The Hand of Ethelberta*, p. 377).

27. The manuscript is in the library of University College, Dublin, and available in facsimile, edited by Simon Gatrell (New York: Garland Press, 1986). The novel ran as a serial in *Belgravia* in 1878, and the first edition was published in three volumes by Smith, Elder (1878). The 1895 edition is part of the collected edition of Hardy's novels published by Osgoode, McIlvaine (1895–96).

28. *The Return of the Native*, ed. Simon Gatrell (Oxford: Oxford University Press, 1990), p. 4.

29. *The Return of the Native*, p. 50.

30. *The Return of the Native*, p. 64.

31. *The Return of the Native*, p. 64.
32. *The Return of the Native*, p. 63.
33. *The Return of the Native*, p. 63.
34. *The Return of the Native*, p. 66.
35. *The Return of the Native*, p. 64.
36. *The Return of the Native*, p. 122.
37. *The Return of the Native*, p. 64.
38. *The Return of the Native*, p. 68.
39. *The Return of the Native*, p. 67.
40. Sir Thomas Wentworth, 1st earl of Strafford (1593–1641), served under Charles I in various capacities. He managed to please neither king nor Parliament most of the time, and eventually was caught between them, impeached and executed: he was known for ruthlessness. In the *Literary Notes* Hardy records two references to Strafford, both negative. See *The Literary Notebooks of Thomas Hardy*, vol. I, ed. Lennart A. Björk (London: Macmillan, 1985), pp. 16, 19. He later adapted the Clarendon passage, which describes the impeachment as a 'triumph of justice, but a mockery of law', to comment on the guerrilla tactics Diggory Venn deploys to keep Wildeve home at night (*The Return of the Native*, p. 273).
41. John Goode, *Thomas Hardy: the Offensive Truth* (Oxford: Blackwell, 1988), pp. 2–3.

5

'As near to poetry . . . as the conditions would allow': the Presence of the Poet in Hardy's Novels

William Morgan

In the years after 1898, Thomas Hardy spent a good deal of his intellectual and emotional energy making the case that he had been a poet all along – even during the years when he was writing novels. Sometimes he tried to make this case by denigrating his fiction and doing all he could to turn his readers' attention away from his novels and towards his poetry, but in his most extended commentary on the relationship between his prose and verse – the paragraphs on that topic near the beginning of Chapter 24 of *The Life and Work of Thomas Hardy* – he takes a different approach and argues instead for the similarities between his work in the two genres. The chapter is called 'Collecting Old Poems and Making New', and one of its main objects is to account for the career change from popular novelist to poet in a way that celebrates Hardy the poet without denigrating Hardy the novelist. Here is the key passage:

> The change, after all, was not so great as it seemed. It was not as if he had been a writer of novels proper, and as more specifically understood, that is, stories of modern artificial life and manners showing a certain smartness of treatment.[1]

In this construction, the novels are not the mere journeywork he sometimes called them but are instead serious literary efforts that are distinguished from most writing in a similar form ('novels proper') by the ways in which they resemble poetry. In the reckoning at work here – and we should remember that this is the view of Hardy the veteran poet preparing his autobiography in his mid-70s – the novelist and the poet are akin because their writer held his novels accountable to an older, higher, and more durable literary standard: the standard of poetry. 'He had mostly aimed', says the narrator of the *Life and Work*, 'to keep his narratives close to natural life, and as near to poetry in their subject as the conditions would allow, and had often regretted that those conditions would not let him keep them nearer still.' This account of the relationship between Hardy's novelist self and his poet self is premised upon an idea of the separation of genres and of the higher standing of poetry: his novels are better than most novels 'proper', he argues, in that they resemble and are modelled upon poetry, which is a higher form of writing, devoted to the depiction of the 'natural' instead of the 'artificial'. In the older Hardy's view, his literary vision of things or orientation towards the world exists in its pure form in the realm of poetry, from whence it descended for a time to elevate his fiction by its presence.[2]

I don't believe with Hardy that poetry is by definition a 'higher' genre than fiction; that idea of his seems rather quaint and old-fashioned to me. And I'm not sure that his reputation as a writer would fare very well if his work were reorganised hierarchically with all the poetry being elevated above all the fiction. There are plenty of Hardy poems – even volumes of poems – that have, to my mind, a considerably lower literary standing than *Tess of the d'Urbervilles*, and there are several novels that I would gladly sacrifice rather than give up, say, 'Wessex Heights', 'The Oxen', or the 'Poems of 1912–13' – or, if we want to compare books to books, then there are several novels I'd part with before I'd give up *Moments of Vision* or *Satires of Circumstance*. But Hardy worked consistently enough from his own premises that if one is looking as I am for the presence of the poet in the novels, it is virtually impossible *not* to address the topic on his terms – that is, by looking for the ways in which he brought the classic features of what he thought of as a more elevated form of discourse to the work of novel-writing. In the older Hardy's reductive terms, all that is native to the practice of prose fiction is narrative structure and social observation, while all that is best and most rewarding about the local texture – and, indeed, much of the overall narrative pattern – of his novels and stories is attributable to the influence of poetry. Let me be clear that while I think Hardy's stance about the hierarchy of genres is dated and defensive, I don't see that it did him any harm in either his fiction or his poetry: it seems a fairly benign form of snobbish prejudice. In fact, it's clear to me that, whatever their limitations as intellectual arguments in some absolute world, Hardy's beliefs about the relative status of poetry and fiction caused him to introduce into his novels a number of features that we are all glad to have there. I for one wouldn't have him change his beliefs if so doing would change the luxurious and resonant texture of much of his fiction.

The main body of this chapter will be given over to trying to name and analyse – and to a certain degree to celebrating – the effects of those quirky beliefs on Hardy's novels, and I hope to accomplish my ends by asking, as I suppose Hardy must have asked: what resources are available to one who sets about writing novels if he wants to bring his fiction nearer to the higher standard of poetry?

It will be apparent to anyone familiar with Hardy's work that such a question branches and shifts and spreads itself out into innumerable sub-questions. My answers can be at best only suggestive, bringing us closer to understanding Hardy on some fronts and merely raising additional questions on others.

In the broadest terms, Hardy's answer to that question seems to have been that he could make the language of his fiction resemble the language of poetry in as many ways as possible – as many ways as 'conditions' would allow. All of Hardy's readers and many of his critics are aware of poetic effects such as rhythmic language, highly-charged patterns of allegory and imagery, and so on, in his fiction (and I will return to some of those effects further on), but I wonder how many of us have noticed the degree to which Hardy actually introduces verse – his own occasionally but mostly that of others – into his novels and calls attention to it as such. Surely the most direct and uncomplicated means by which a writer may bring fiction closer to the conditions of poetry is to introduce lines of verse into the texture of the fiction. By my count, there are 243 separate appearances of verse in Hardy's fiction.[3] These verse passages range from a half-line to 32 lines in length, though most of them are somewhere around two-to-four lines. My inexact calculation tells me that when all is said and done there are something in the neighbourhood of 1000 lines – or 5000 to 6000 words of verse – in Hardy's novels and stories. To give you some perspective on those numbers, I'll point out that 1000 lines of verse is about the equivalent of a full book of *Paradise Lost* – or, to put the matter in more directly relevant terms, it's about half the number of lines to be found in *Wessex Poems*, Hardy's first published volume of verse. Even after working on this topic for some time, I am still somewhat staggered when I think of just how much verse a reader of Hardy's fiction will have taken in, in the course of reading through his novels and stories – surely more than is to be found in the work of any other novelist.

Here are a few more statistics: many of the instances of verse in Hardy's fiction are presented in the voices and sometimes the silent thoughts of characters; there are just over 100 such passages. As might be expected, the rural and less formally educated characters give voice mainly to folk songs and rhymes, psalms and hymns – in other words, to the various kinds of poetry that are the common property of the rural community. In the opening chapter of *Under the Greenwood Tree*, for example, Dick Dewey sings 'in a rural cadence' as he walks along,

> With the rose and the lily
> And the daffodowndilly,
> The lads and lasses a-sheep-shearing go.[4]

And of course in the same book the choir sings in verse on several occasions, most memorably, perhaps, in Chapter IV when they perform – and the novel prints – all four stanzas of 'Remember Adam's fall' outside Fancy Day's dark window. This event in *Under the Greenwood Tree* offers perhaps a good occasion for me to introduce one of my analytical points about the presence of lines of verse in Hardy's fiction: almost invariably, the verse passages slow down the reading experience. Even the fairly solemn prose that introduces the choir's performance is faster-paced than the hymn itself. Here's what the novel says:

> Then passed forth into the quiet night an ancient and time-worn hymn, embodying a quaint Christianity in words orally transmitted from father to son through several generations down to the present characters, who sang them out right earnestly:

> > 'Remember Adam's fall,
> > O thou man:
> > Remember Adam's fall
> > From heaven to Hell.
> > Remember Adam's fall;
> > How he hath condemn'd all
> > In Hell perpetual
> > There for to dwell. . . .'[5]

And so forth for three more stanzas. A reader who takes the pace of those 32 lines of verse and who reads them slowly and meditatively as they ask to be read, will have cut the speed of his or her reading approximately in half and will probably return to the surrounding prose with a different pace and a different attitude – at least for a short while.

Most Hardy readers will be able to think on their own of other occasions when Hardy's rustic characters speak or sing in religious or folk verse – Jan Coggan, Joseph Poorgrass and Bathsheba performing ballads after the Harvest Supper; Joan Durbeyfield singing as she rocks the cradle; Manston and the drunken postman marching along to the tune of 'When Joan's ale was new'; Grandfer Cantle intoning – 'in the voice of a bee up a flue', Hardy says – 'The kíng call'd dówn his nób-les áll, / By óne, by twó, by thrée'; Henchard ordering the choir to perform 'His seed shall orphans be, his wife / A widow plunged in grief' as a curse upon Farfrae; the marvellous scene in *Two on a Tower*, when Mr Torkingham tries to teach the choir more respectable diction so that he can hear the words of Psalm 53 presented with appropriate dignity – and several more. In Hardy's fiction at large, I find about 25 occasions of characters singing or quoting folk tunes or ballads and about ten instances of their doing the same with hymns and Psalms.

For the most part, the rural and less formally educated characters not only limit their verse utterances to the communal poetry, but they also speak their verse out loud in the presence of others; speaking in verse is usually (but not quite always – witness, for example, Dick's singing to himself) a social act among Hardy's rustics. The opposite is true for his better-educated characters: they tend first of all to quote the classic poets instead of ballads, folk-rhymes or the Psalms; and they often *think* the words of the poets – or perhaps murmur them to themselves – instead of saying them out loud. Consider, for example, Dr. Fitzpiers' half-audible quotation from Shelley's 'Epipsychidion' as he leaves Grace for a rendezvous with Mrs. Charmond:

> 'Don't wait up for me.' With these words he mounted his horse, turned into a branch road by the turnpike, and ambled down the incline to the valley. . . . Could she have heard Fitzpiers's voice at that moment she would have found it murmuring
>
> > ' – Towards the load-star of my one desire
> > I flitted, like a dizzy moth, whose flight
> > Is as a dead leaf's in the owlet light.'
>
> But he was a silent spectacle to her.[6]

Something similar happens between Knight and Elfride in Chapter 31 of *A Pair of Blue Eyes*, when Knight discovers that Elfride had kissed another man before he met her.

> Knight could not keep from his mind the words of Adam's reproach to Eve in *Paradise Lost*, and at last whispered them to himself –

'"Fooled and beguiled: by him thou, I by thee!"'

'What did you say?' Elfride inquired timorously.
'It was only a quotation.'[7]

But sometimes Hardy's better-educated characters insert a relevant quotation from a poet to make a particular kind of point in a conversation – even a conversation that may include a tense, emotional confession – as in Cytherea's use of some lines from Robert Browning's 'The Statue and the Bust' to explain to Edward in *Desperate Remedies* why she has married Manston:

> 'I am to blame, Edward, I am,' she said mournfully; 'I was taught to dread pauperism; my nights were made sleepless; there was continually reiterated in my ears till I believed it –
>
> > "The world and its ways have a certain worth,
> > And to press a point where these oppose
> > Were a simple policy."
>
> Edward, I married to escape dependence for my bread upon the whim of Miss Aldclyffe, or others like her.'[8]

These lines from Browning must have impressed Hardy, since he uses them again in 'The Waiting Supper', where Christine, who attributes them to 'a sensible, new-risen poet' whom she has been reading that very morning, speaks them to Nicholas to justify – oddly enough – her *opposite* conclusion: that she can *not* marry him until he betters himself; hence she adds the last half-line that Cytherea had left off: 'Better wait.'

There are something over 60 occasions on which Hardy's characters either think or speak in the words of Shelley (six times), Robert Browning (also six times), Shakespeare (four times), Milton and Horace (three times each), Byron, Burns, Dante Gabriel Rossetti, Swinburne, Keats and Newman (twice each), and Thomas Moore, Edgar Allan Poe and Thomas Campbell (once each). The extraordinary range and number of these references gives me the occasion to make another kind of point about the appearance of verse in Hardy's fiction: that the first readers – and indeed most of the readers of Hardy's work until the last 25 years or so – encountered all of these passages of verse quotation without the helpful notes that we are accustomed to finding at the back of the New

Wessex and World's Classics and Penguin Classics and other annotated editions such as I have of course used in preparing this chapter. When the narrator of *Jude* calls a particular Swinburne poem 'familiar', we modern readers may check the back of the book if we don't recognise the lines in question and thus learn – almost instantly – who wrote them and what work they come from: by so doing we can make the lines at least somewhat 'familiar' with rather little effort. Not so with Hardy's earlier readers: they either knew the lines straightaway or had to make do without knowing. The reader who knows the source of a given quotation is allowed not only to see the appropriateness of the sentiment expressed in the verse passage but also to join with character and narrator for a brief episode of shared understanding and perhaps self-congratulation; but the reader who doesn't 'get it' probably has to stifle a little feeling of inadequacy.

And how many of us would recognise a quotation from T. Watson (*Desperate Remedies*), or John Hoskins (*Ethelberta*), or William Henry Drummond (*A Laodicean*)? There are at least 11 verse passages in Hardy's fiction that have eluded the most assiduous efforts of his modern editors and are still unidentified – six of them spoken by narrators and five by characters. The verse occasions which Hardy's characters and narrators present to his readers, in other words, are not only highly allusive but a little slippery and elusive as well, and their overall effect might be seen as unsettling to a reader's confidence. Certainly the sheer range of the quotations has been unsettling to my mathematics in preparing this chapter. I can hardly say with certainty just how many verse passages come from, for instance, folk poetry or the work of Thomas Campbell or that of Bishop Ken if some quotations are so obscure that Hardy's most erudite modern editors haven't been able to track them down.

Well, how about the narrators? There are about 70 moments in Hardy's fiction in which they speak in verse – sometimes in the words of obscure writers such as the ones I've just been talking about, other times in the words of the very famous or moderately famous poets. Here's my tally: Hardy's narrators quote Shakespeare (eight times), Shelley and Tennyson (five times each), Swinburne, Robert Browning and Milton (four times each), Barnes and Vergil – the latter in Dryden's translation – (three times each), Whitman, Heinrich Heine and Drayton (twice each), and Chatterton, Gosse, Wordsworth, Dante Gabriel Rossetti, Keble, Ken, Homer (in Chapman's translation), Sheridan, Terence, Crashaw, Horace, Byron, Scott, Dryden, Butler and Keats (once each).

The poetic reading list of Hardy's narrators has a great deal of overlap with that of his better-educated characters: they have many of the same favourites, for instance – Shelley, Robert Browning, Shakespeare, Milton – though for some reason Hardy's narrators are more given to quoting Tennyson (five times) than are his characters (only once). And the narrators and educated characters quote from the poets with almost the same frequency: the characters some 60 times and the narrators some 70. There are a few shadings of difference, however: the narrators quote more frequently from the obscurer poets, whereas the characters reach no further outside the mainstream than Thomas Campbell and John Henry Newman. And the narrators quote from a higher number of different poets: 31 different poets for the narrators and only 14 for the characters. Broadly speaking, then, Hardy's narrators seem to be familiar with all the poets known to his characters but also with additional poets and with a broader range of poets.

So much for characters and narrators, but there is yet one more place where verse shows up in Hardy's fiction, and it tends to reinforce the pattern of difference I am trying to sketch between the characters' and narrators' use of poetic quotation: I am talking about the presence of verse in what might be called the *printed voice* of the book itself – that is, in epigraphs, mottoes, and the like – bits of text which cannot be attributed either to the voice of the characters or to that of the narrator but which are obviously a part of the book's self-presentation and which are meant to influence our reading of the rest of the text. For example, who 'says' or 'speaks' the epigraph from *Two Gentlemen of Verona*, 'Poor wounded name! My bosom as a bed / Shall lodge thee', which appears on the title page of *Tess*? Likewise, who 'speaks' or takes responsibility for the title page of *The Woodlanders*, which features this quatrain:

> 'Not boskiest bow'r,
> When hearts are ill affin'd,
> Hath tree of pow'r
> To shelter from the wind!'

This little poem was in fact supplied by Hardy himself, for the Osgood, McIlvaine edition of the novel in 1896. There are about 70 such verse epigraphs and mottoes at the heads of Hardy's chapters (or sometimes, as in the case of *The Woodlanders* or *Tess*, whole books), and they, like the narrators' quotations from the poets, tend to range more widely over the corpus of poetry than do the characters' quotations: the epigraphs include quotations from 22 different poets, some of them nearly universally known, and others somewhat obscure. Over half of these epigraphs, by the way, are to be found in two fictional texts: *An Indiscretion in the Life of an Heiress* and *A Pair of Blue Eyes*, since these two works have an epigraph for each chapter. Considered at large, the epigraphs come from Shakespeare (eight times), Scott and Tennyson (seven times each), Shelley, Burns and Robert Browning (four times each), Milton, Crashaw, Gray, Byron, Wyatt and Hardy himself (twice each), and Swinburne, Sappho, Keats, Marlowe, Gay, Wordsworth, Dryden, Waller, Vergil, and that great poet, Anon. (all once each).[9] The epigraphs, as might be expected, make reference to the same broad zone of poetry as do the quotations used by the narrators, and when one combines the two categories, it becomes clear that there is a kind of literary educational divide that separates the two authorial or nearly authorial voices of Hardy's fiction (the voices of the narrators and the 'voices' – if we may call them that – of the epigraphs, etc.) from even the better-educated characters: Hardy's closest representatives seem to have read and remembered more poetry and a broader range of poetry than even Jude or Sue or Clym or Fitzpiers.

So far as I am aware, the only strand of critical commentary on Hardy's abundant use of verse quotation in his fiction is the negative one that began with his earliest reviews and that is perhaps typified by the late Robert Gittings in his two-volume biography of Hardy published in 1975 and 1978. Gittings, like some of Hardy's first reviewers, saw Hardy's quotations and learned allusions as mostly pretentious and unfortunate. In his view, Hardy was parading his learning and defensively trying to claim equality with those who had more formal education than he did. Several subsequent critics have taken up Gittings's argument, and in some quarters it has become a fairly established interpretation: in this view, Hardy is a self-conscious autodidact who tries to compensate for a sense of social inferiority by demonstrating at every opportunity his abundant if somewhat eccentric learning. As you will have guessed, I wish to propose a different, and, I think, more interesting interpretation.

It will already be clear from what I've said that the kind of verse quotation practised by Hardy's rustic characters does not sort well with Gittings's arguments about Hardy's social defensiveness. The rustics ground their poetic vocabulary in the hymns and psalms and the folk rhymes and songs of the community and tend to speak or sing their poems *to* each other in a distinctly social context. Hardy presents the communal poetry, in other words, as part of the social 'glue' that holds the rural community together; it's a medium for the exchange and reinforcement of ideas and opinions already shared by the participants. Clearly this kind of verse quotation cannot be evidence of social snobbery or educational defensiveness on Hardy's part, since in these passages he is celebrating the language and customs of the rural working class and of his own birth culture – the mastery of which would not bring him any particular social credit: perhaps, in fact, the opposite. Further, the verse quotation that he allots to his rustics strikes me as having nothing in the nature of pretension about it; it is affectionate observation about the way a certain kind of poetry works in the rural community, and if anything, Hardy seems to look upon the rustics with nostalgic envy – not feeling superior to them and not setting them up as superior to himself or his readers: just presenting a clear and affectionate portrait of a kind of literary life – and make no mistake about it; his rustics do have a lively literary life – that neither he nor his readers is likely to have comfortable access to.

But Gittings's complaint is about what he sees as the pretentious quotation from and allusion to the classic poetic tradition, not the folk and religious tradition. Even here, however, I think he's mistaken – or at least ungenerous. In my view, Hardy is not quoting from Tennyson because Tennyson is the Poet Laureate or from Crashaw because he wants his readers to be impressed that he knows Crashaw; he's quoting to call attention not to who wrote the verse passages, but to the shape and substance of the quoted matter itself – its aptness for the occasion, its beauty, and so on. And the citations from the classic poets cooperate very well with other features of the texts and do some of the most important work of fiction-writing. They frequently serve, for example, to deepen character. If the rustics' use of verse offers a glimpse into their *communal* life, the verse citations of the better-educated characters most often offer us a look into their *individual* psychic lives. Of the many possible examples, I can perhaps cite just one to make the point – Sue's speaking the words of Thomas Campbell's poem called 'Song' as she and Jude walk away from the Parish clerk's house, having decided not to post their banns after all; the novel tells us she 'murmurs':

> 'Can you keep the bee from ranging,
> Or the ring-dove's neck from changing?
> No. Nor fetter'd love . . .' [10]

And she trails off into silence or ellipsis dots. In the manuscript, Hardy allows her to complete the line-and-a-half that follow: 'No. Nor fettered love from dying/In the knot there's no untying.' With or without that additional bit of text, the passage is telling: it shows us that Sue's feelings about the dangers of marriage are not exclusively centred on its alleged backwardness as a social institution: she is also concerned about its possible effect on the quality of their love. And given that she has just been talking with Arabella about *her* troubles, marital and otherwise, she might also be expressing her resolve not to taint herself with Arabella's proprietary attitudes about marriage. Hardy's more literate characters frequently speak verse this way: they come to life in association with and speak in the vocabulary of a poetic tradition that gives them words in which to couch their most powerful personal feelings – words that make them comprehensible to themselves, and sometimes to one another and to the readers as no other words could do. And the verse quotations employed by the narrators and appearing in the epigraphs and mottoes in their turn enrich the narrative consciousness at work in Hardy's fiction, the consciousness that offers the reader guidance about how to think critically concerning the characters and the action. The voices of the narrators, epigraphs and mottoes, in other words, represent a kind of consciousness that knows everything that the characters know – and *more* – and in the verse quotations they use, those voices register both kinship with the classically educated characters and at the same time their *greater* knowledge. In effect, Hardy's use of verse offers his readers the opportunity to experience three different mental frames, and each frame serves its own separate function in establishing the texture of the reading experience. While Hardy carefully distinguishes among the three – the consciousness of the rustic culture, the consciousness of the classically educated characters, and the arbitrating consciousness represented by the narrators, epigraphs and mottoes – he does not, to my mind, make any invidious distinctions or set up any hierarchies of value among them: all three of the modes by which verse gives voice to consciousness in Hardy's fiction receive full respect and the space in which to do their work.

In addition to serving some of the most traditional ends of fiction – character-building and moral/intellectual appraisal – Hardy's verse quotations may also be seen as a bold and innovative technique in that they function in the manner of a kind of meta-fiction fabricated into the very texture of the work and serving as a body of instruction about – to recycle one of Hardy's own titles – The Profitable Reading of Fiction. The verse passages, I suggest, may serve to teach us how to read Hardy's fiction. I mean this claim literally: the verse in the novels and stories often serves the function of instructing Hardy's readers in the art of reading the surrounding prose in the most appropriate and profitable way – that is, the way we read poetry. Just as Henry Fielding in the 1740s, perhaps intuiting that his audience would need some help in understanding and making sense of this new form, so appropriately named the *novel*, included incidental essays on character, plot, and probability in *Joseph Andrews* and *Tom Jones*, and just as John Barth and other postmodern writers, intuiting that they are writing in a difficult later mode that requires skills many readers may not have, have included passages of meta-commentary in their work so as to establish a relationship between the readers' existing skills and expectations and the demands of their texts, so Hardy, it seems to me, has included passages of verse as a kind of course of instruction – worked into the very fabric of his fiction – in reading fiction such as his, fiction that is derived from and modelled upon poetry and that is therefore not to be read as one reads most fiction. In *Joseph Andrews*, Fielding addresses what he takes to be his readers' lack of preparedness by lacing the novel with commentary on the moral usefulness of fiction, on the best way to read it, and so on: hence such chapter titles as 'Of writing lives in general, and particularly of *Pamela*; with a word by the bye of Colley Cibber and others' and 'Of Divisions in Authors' (by which he means chapter and book divisions) and 'Matter prefatory in praise of biography'. In his chapter on 'divisions in authors', Fielding takes the readers into his confidence thus:

> There are certain mysteries or secrets in all trades, from the highest to the lowest, from that of prime-ministering to this of authoring, which are seldom discovered, unless to members of the same calling. Among those used by us gentlemen of the latter occupation, I take this of dividing our works into books and chapters to be none of the least considerable. Now, for want of being truly acquainted with this secret, common readers imagine that by this art of dividing we mean only to swell our works to a much larger bulk than they would otherwise be extended to. . . .
>
> But in reality the case is otherwise, and in this, as well as all other instances, we consult the advantage of our reader, not our own; and indeed, many notable uses arise to him from this method: for, . . . those little spaces between our chapters may be looked upon as an inn or resting-place, where he may stop and take a glass, or any other refreshment, as it pleases him. . . . A volume without any such places of rest resembles the opening of wilds or seas, which tires the eye and fatigues the spirit when entered upon.[11]

The tone here – slightly flippant but playful and ingratiating – is fairly typical of the meta-fictional passages in Fielding's work. John Barth's tone is quite different; perhaps it is best described as desperate. In the title story of his collection called *Lost in the Funhouse*, for example, the main character's family is driving to Ocean City, Maryland, to spend the afternoon and evening having fun, but the story is stiff and won't go where it's supposed to, and Barth's narrator keeps getting distracted by a kind of hyper self-consciousness, and writes about matters of fictional technique instead of just telling his story:

> Thrice a year – on Memorial, Independence, and Labor Days – the family visits Ocean City for the afternoon and evening. When Ambrose and Peter's father was their age, the excursion was made by train, as mentioned in the novel *The 42nd Parallel* by John Dos Passos. . . .
>
> Description of physical appearance and mannerisms is one of several standard methods of characterisation used by writers of fiction. It is also important to 'keep the senses operating'; when a detail from one of the five senses, say visual, is 'crossed' with a detail from another, say, auditory, the reader's imagination is oriented to the scene, perhaps unconsciously. . . . The brown hair on Ambrose's mother's forearms gleamed in the sun like. Though right-handed, she took her left arm from the seat-back to press the dash-board cigar lighter for Uncle Karl. . . . The fragrance of the ocean came strong to the picnic ground where they always stopped for lunch. . . . The Irish author James Joyce, in his unusual novel entitled *Ulysses*, now available in this country, uses the adjectives *snot-green* and *scrotum-tightening* to describe the sea. Visual, auditory, tactile, olfactory, gustatory. . . . We should be much further along than we are; something has gone wrong; not much of this preliminary rambling seems relevant.[12]

These are fairly extreme cases of writerly self-consciousness from very early in the history of the English-language novel and from fairly late (Barth's story dates from the late 1960s), but as far apart as they are, they are alike in urging their readers to read not just the story but also *the means of its telling*; they make matters of technique a part of the subject of the novel and deny readers the opportunity to relax into the work as if the writer's language were a transparent medium by which we could gain uncomplicated access to the book's 'reality'. In short, they insist on a particular way of reading as the best or most profitable way.

Hardy, historically situated between the two, has nothing of this order of meta-commentary in his fiction. But I want to suggest that his verse quotations often do some of the same work – albeit much more subtly – that is being done by Fielding's or Barth's self-referentiality. Although Hardy does not use verse to direct his readers' attention to questions of writerly technique, he does use it, I believe, to try to influence our reading practices.

All of the instances of verse in Hardy's fiction have some of the effects I'm trying to examine here, but the quotations appearing in the voices of the narrators are the most direct means of delivering Hardy's 'reading lesson', and I think I can make my case with just a few examples drawn mainly from them. Broadly speaking, the narrators use verse to teach us three reading habits:

– that we should listen to the sound and rhythm of the language in Hardy's prose, and enjoy those features as a part of the aesthetic experience of reading;
– that we should allow his imagery and the comparisons it embodies to take us quickly and economically to unexpected new zones of insight and understanding;
– and that we should collaborate with the text in producing the imaginative texture of scene and the relationship between scene and meaning.

Consider the sounds and rhythms of the following passage from *The Woodlanders*, and ask if you could tell, without having the text before you, when Hardy's prose leaves off and the verse quotation (from Thomas Chatterton) begins:

beyond the yard were to be seen gardens and orchards, now bossed, nay encrusted, with scarlet and gold fruit, stretching to infinite distance under a luminous lavender mist. The time was early autumn,

> When the fair apples, red as evening sky,
> Do bend the tree unto the fruitful ground,
> When juicy pears, and berries of black dye
> Do dance in air, and call the eyes around.

The landscape confronting the window might indeed have been part of the identical stretch of country which the 'marvellous boy' had in his mind when he penned those lines.[13]

Hardy's prose approaches the quoted matter in a character very like that of the poem itself – even down to the alliteration of 'luminous lavender mist' and the embedded line of iambic trimeter in 'the time was early autumn' – and in so doing it virtually effaces the borderline between the two kinds of writing. This is what I mean by Hardy fabricating the verse quotations into the very texture of his prose. And he seems to take the rhythm of the verse passage, even if it's not Chatterton's loose iambics but instead Walt Whitman's galloping free verse, as in this passage from *Tess*, describing Angel's intentions in coming to Talbothays dairy:

> [H]e had come as to a place from which as from a screened alcove he could calmly view the absorbing world without, and, apostrophising it with Walt Whitman –
>
> Crowds of men and women attired in the usual costumes,
> How curious you are to me! –
>
> resolve upon a plan for plunging into that world anew.[14]

And here's another example, from the last chapter of *Far from the Madding Crowd*, in which Hardy's prose is barely distinguishable from the playful rhythms of the passage he quotes from the humorous 'Patty Morgan the Milkmaid's Story' by R. H. Barham:

> It was a damp, disagreeable morning. Nevertheless, at twenty minutes to ten o'clock, Oak came out of his house and
>
> Went up the hill side
> With that sort of stride
> A man puts out when walking in search of a bride,
>
> and knocked at Bathsheba's door.[15]

If you are looking at the passage on the page, you see that there is an inset quotation in lines, but Hardy's surrounding prose has allied itself so nearly with the sounds and syntax of the verse that we are encouraged to bring the same expectations and reading strategies to the two kinds of writing.[16]

Just as he surrounds verse passages with prose sharing similar features of sound and rhythm, so he also seems to heighten the texture of imagery in his prose in the passages that frame verse quotations. Consider this selection from *A Laodicean*, in which Somerset considers trusting his approach to the De Stancy castle to the guidance of the telegraph wire instead of the regular road:

> For a few moments Somerset doubted and stood still: the cut over the down had no mark of a path or drive, but on the other hand it might be a shorter though steeper way to the same place. The wire sang on overhead with dying falls and melodious rises that invited him to follow; while above the wire rode the stars in their courses, the low nocturn of the former seeming to be the voices of those stars,
>
> > Still quiring to the young-eyed cherubim.
>
> Recalling himself from these reflections Somerset decided to follow the lead of the wire. It was not the first time . . . that he had found his way at night by the help of these musical threads which the post-office authorities had erected all over the country for quite another purpose than to guide belated travellers.[17]

Lorenzo's fifth-act speech in *The Merchant of Venice* likens the music of the spheres to the singing of angels and assures his listeners that

> > There's not the smallest orb which thou behold'st
> > But in his motion like an angel sings,
> > Still quiring to the young-eyed cherubins

If celestial spheres can sing in Shakespeare, in Hardy electrical *wires* can *sing a nocturn*, the stars can *ride* in their courses, and singing telegraph *wires* can be *threads* of music. Perhaps it's heresy, but I prefer Hardy's fresher, more complex imagery here to Shakespeare's bald conventionality.

Here's another example of imagery in a prose passage doing the work of poetry – this one from *The Mayor of Casterbridge* – the scene in which Henchard asks Elizabeth-Jane to write out a contract for him:

> 'Now then – "An agreement entered into this sixteenth day of October" – write that first.'
>
> She started the pen in an elephantine march across the sheet. It was a splendid round bold hand of her own conception. . . . But . . . Henchard's creed was that proper young girls wrote ladies'-hand –

nay, he believed that bristling characters were as innate and insepa-rable a part of refined womanhood as sex itself. Hence, when, instead of scribbling, like the Princess Ida,

> In such a hand as when a field of corn
> Bows all its ears before the roaring East,

Elizabeth-Jane produced a line of chain-shot and sand-bags, he red-dened in angry shame for her, and peremptorily saying 'Never mind – I'll finish it', dismissed her there and then.[18]

The embedded quotation from Tennyson's *The Princess* likens the grace-ful slant of proper handwriting to the wind-bent symmetry of field crops moved by a breeze, and, as if he were bringing his prose to meet the imagery of the quotation, Hardy surrounds that image of handwriting with two of his own: first, that handwriting on the page is like the walk of an animal (a striking conception in itself), and Elizabeth-Jane's resem-bles an elephant; and secondly, that handwriting in its effects is like weaponry, and Elizabeth-Jane's is large and unsubtle – like 'chain-shot and sand-bags'. In Hardy's prose, as in the best poetry, imagery is not mere ornament but instead is an integral means of conveying knowl-edge; Hardy's imagery provokes a linguistic and intellectual activity that brings the reader quickly and strikingly to new understandings, whether of the intersection of technology and the cosmos or the meaning and function of handwriting.

And if poetry requires responsiveness to sound, rhythm and imagery, it also requires that a reader collaborate with its gestures meant to make palpable the scene of its happening and the links between that scene and the meanings of the poem. Numbers of passages in Hardy's fiction work the same way, in that they speak only a portion of what they require of their readers, and it becomes our job to complete the scene. Many such scenes, I have learned in the course of preparing this chapter, include verse quotations. Consider the following passage from *Tess*:

> Thus Tess walks on; a figure which is part of the landscape; a field-woman pure and simple, in winter guise: a grey serge cape, a red woollen cravat, a stuff skirt covered by a whitey-brown rough wrapper, and buff leather gloves. Every thread of that old attire has become faded and thin under the stroke of rain-drops, the burn of sunbeams, and the stress of winds. There is no sign of young passion in her now:

> The maiden's mouth is cold
> . . .
> Fold over simple fold
> Binding her head.

Inside this exterior, over which the eye might have roved as over a thing scarcely percipient, almost inorganic, there was the record of a pulsing life which had learnt too well, for its years, of the dust and ashes of things, of the cruelty of lust and the fragility of love.[19]

By describing her clothes – and only her clothes – Hardy manages in this passage to convey a sense of her physical shape against the backdrop of the land, of the season of the year, of the natural elements within which she has her being, of her emotional state, and of the personal history that has led to it. Although he attends almost exclusively to the clothing, we are moved to supply all the other materials making up the scene and to assign it the kind of meaning he would direct us towards. And the quotation from Swinburne's 'Fragoletta' – 'The maiden's mouth is cold. . . ./Fold over simple fold/Binding her head' – tucked into the middle of the passage is so fully integrated that the ear nearly passes over it. This is prose doing the work of poetry.

Hardy embodies these kinds of lessons in reading – urging us to attend to the sound and rhythm and imagery of his prose and putting us in the position of having to complete the scenery of his texts – for good reason: he is writing a kind of prose that both requires and rewards the kind of attention we might ordinarily reserve for poetry. And this is the case not only when he is embedding verse quotations and writing prose that matches the qualities of the verse, but over and over again. We will all have our favourite passages of Hardy's highly charged, poetic prose, but I've selected two particularly self-contained ones to help me make my point, because I'm persuaded that if the popular genre now called the prose poem had been invented when Hardy was writing, he would have adopted it and would have become one of its acknowledged masters. Here are two fairly famous paragraphs from Hardy's novels – one from the *Mayor* and the other from *Tess* – and I invite you to read them with the kind of attention Hardy has invited us to bring to his prose. From Chapter XXIV of the *Mayor*:

> Lucetta was very kind towards Elizabeth that day. Together they saw the market thicken, and in course of time thin away with the slow decline of the sun towards the upper end of the town, its rays taking

the street endways and enfilading the long thoroughfare from top to bottom. The gigs and vans disappeared one by one till there was not a vehicle in the street. The time of the riding world was over; the pedestrian world held sway. Field labourers and their wives and children trooped in from the villages for their weekly shopping, and instead of a rattle of wheels and a tramp of horses ruling the sounds as earlier, there was nothing but the shuffle of many feet. All the implements were gone; all the farmers; all the moneyed class. The character of the town's trading had changed from bulk to multiplicity, and pence were handled now as pounds had been handled earlier in the day.

Lucetta and Elizabeth looked out upon this, for though it was night, and the street lamps were lighted, they had kept their shutters unclosed. In the faint blink of the fire they spoke more freely.[20]

In addition to the striking images and the effects of sound and rhythm, the passage has a marvellous discipline and self-sufficiency derived from its series of balanced pairs: the market *thickens* and *thins*; the setting sun invades the town from its *upper end* to its *bottom*; the *riding world* yields to the *pedestrian world*; the *tramp of horses* is replaced by the *shuffle of feet*; *bulk* gives way to *multiplicity*; and *pence* succeed to *pounds*. Hence, succession – rather than loss – describes the character of change, and, through its overall rhetorical strategies, the passage makes an important argument about the nature of time and change – an argument that is particularly relevant and appropriate for this novel, since it is saturated with instances of succession: poverty succeeds prosperity for Henchard, Farfrae succeeds Henchard in virtually every way, a new Elizabeth-Jane succeeds the old one, and so forth. This passage is written in carefully nuanced, disciplined prose that deploys the devices of poetry to bring great richness and insight to the experience of reading – either *The Mayor of Casterbridge* or the texture of life itself.

And here's my second example of something like a self-contained prose poem from one of Hardy's novels – this one from Chapter XLIII of *Tess*:

After this season of congealed dampness came a spell of dry frost, when strange birds from behind the north pole began to arrive silently on the upland of Flintcomb-Ash; gaunt spectral creatures with tragical eyes – eyes which had witnessed scenes of cataclysmal horror in inaccessible polar regions, of a magnitude such as no human being had ever conceived, in curdling temperatures that no man could endure; which had beheld the crash of icebergs and the slide of snow-hills by the shooting light of the Aurora; been half blinded by the whirl of colossal storms and terraqueous distortions; and retained the expression of feature that such scenes had engendered. These nameless birds came quite near to Tess and Marian; but of all they had seen which humanity would never see, they brought no account. The traveller's ambition to tell was not theirs; and with dumb impassivity they dismissed experiences which they did not value for the immediate incidents of this homely upland – the trivial movements of the two girls in disturbing the clods with their hackers so as to uncover something or other that these visitants relished as food.[21]

This passage insists that the birds are something apart from the human sphere, but oddly, it calls them into service to represent something about the human sphere at the same time. They have known natural phenomena beyond human experience or endurance – events inaccessible even to the human imagination, much less to human experience: they are of another order of nature, and their experience is likewise of another order. But like Tess and Marian enduring the winter at Flintcomb-Ash, and implicitly, like all of us humans, the birds 'retained the expression of feature that such scenes had engendered' even though they thought little of the grandeur of their experiences, being reduced to 'dumb impassivity' by the need for food. Even as the passage pushes the birds away from the human to emphasise their status as other, it draws them back to stand as allegorical figures making a point about the consequences to the human psyche when life is reduced to mere survival – a condition in which the grandest of experiences is of little consequence alongside the need to sustain the merely physical life of the organism. Again in this passage, we have the language of prose doing the work of poetry, this time by effectively doubling the power and significance of a tiny bit of plot and giving it a symbolic resonance that connects Tess's suffering with something vaster than itself.

In at least three ways, then, Hardy works to give to the language of his fiction some of the qualities he associates with poetry: (1) he introduces verse itself into his fiction and uses it to slow down and complicate the reading experience; (2) he surrounds his poetic quotations with sound effects, rhythms, and imagery that make the movement into and out of verse almost seamless; and (3) he creates and sustains a prose style that has both a consistently poetic texture and some brilliant, self-contained passages of poetic prose resembling late-twentieth-century prose poems. Besides being a remarkable aesthetic gift to his readers, the embedded verse quotations and other poetic features of his prose are intellectually stimulating because of the way in which they provide a running commentary on themselves as well as what I've called a body of instruction for his readers about how to read poetic prose. Thus they deepen and extend the possibilities offered to readers of Hardy's fiction in that they serve equally well the reader who wishes to 'surrender' to the experience of a lavish text and the one who wishes to give his or her primary attention to the pleasures of self-conscious analysis.

Beyond the ones I've described here, I can think of at least two more ways in which Hardy the poet might be said to be present in the fiction, and I will name them briefly, although this is not the occasion for discussing them fully. The first is in what might be called recycled content that appears first in a novel and later shows up in a poem – or vice versa. I'm thinking here of such repetitions as Dairyman Crick's story about William Dewey playing the Nativity Hymn to deceive the bull which is chasing him – and that story's relationship to 'The Oxen' some 25 years later on; does the fact that a given bit of content appears – sometimes in a very different form – later on in a poem give it some kind of retroactive poetic standing in the novel in which it first appeared?[22] For any but a first-time reader, it seems to me that it must. And what about those early poems that Hardy tells us he 'dissolved into prose' and used in *Desperate Remedies*? Are there useful points to be made about the presence of the poet in such fictional moments? The second way that occurs to me for talking about the poet in the fiction is more directly biographical: what lessons from his five or six-year period of writing poetry in the 1860s did Hardy take directly over into his fiction? Can we learn anything from looking at his earliest poems and then looking for similar themes and techniques in the novels?[23]

I began by pointing out that the Hardy of *Life and Work* is writing as a poet when he attempts to account for his career change. As a gesture of last-minute candour, perhaps I should mention that since I last spoke before the Hardy Society Conference, I have myself become a poet in something like an official sense of the word. Had he known of it, Hardy would at least have smiled at the irony that one William Morgan, a mere critic, in his 58th year, and after something like 30 years of scholarly prose, has just published his first book of poems and has now presented himself to write about the poetry in Hardy's fiction – here in the centenary year of Hardy's first book of poems, likewise published in *his* 58th year, etc. I mention these parallels because of their gratuitous ironies and because the last four or five years (during which I have been concentrating my own writing mainly on poetry and at the same time have been re-reading much of Hardy's fiction) have given me a new appreciation for just how accomplished a writer he is. Like the Hardy of the *Life and Work*, I have written about Hardy's fiction in this chapter not from a position of lofty objectivity but from a particular place in my own writing life. And just as I think it must have changed Hardy's reading practices to think of himself as a poet, so I am sure that being now a poet myself has changed my way of reading Hardy's prose. I like to think that at last I have begun to read him as he took pains to try to teach me to – slowly, with attention to rhythm and image, as a participant in the creation of scene and meaning, and with a pleasant double awareness – of not only the wondrous places his writing can take me, but also of the remarkable skill and integrity of the disciplined language that takes me there.

Notes

1. Thomas Hardy, *The Life and Work of Thomas Hardy*, ed. Michael Millgate (London, 1984), p. 309.
2. In my thinking about this topic, I am indebted to the work of William Hickey, a member of a postgraduate seminar that I taught in 1996 at Illinois State University. Bill Hickey is a poet; hence, even though the seminar was about Hardy's fiction, he made it his business to show the rest of us the poet at work in Hardy's prose, and although my own argument takes a different direction from his, I learned a good deal from his papers.
3. I use 'about', 'approximately', and so forth in this context, since (1) some verse quotations in Hardy's fiction have not been identified and therefore cannot be attributed, and since (2) the distinction between an allusion and a quotation is not always easy to draw. Reasonable people, even those with high-order mathematical skills, could disagree about some of the totals.
4. *Under the Greenwood Tree*, ed. Simon Gatrell (Oxford, 1985), p. 11.
5. *Under the Greenwood Tree*, p. 32.
6. *The Woodlanders*, ed. Dale Kramer (Oxford, 1985), p. 155.
7. *A Pair of Blue Eyes*, ed. Alan Manford (Oxford, 1985), p. 304.
8. *Desperate Remedies*, ed. Mary Rimmer (London, 1998), p. 256 (Chapter 8 of Vol. II).

9. Sappho is, I think, the only female poet whom Hardy quotes in his fiction. It would be interesting to explore what this might mean.

10. *Jude the Obscure*, ed. Patricia Ingham (Oxford, 1985), p. 286.

11. Henry Fielding, *Joseph Andrews*, ed. Martin C. Battestin (Boston, 1961), pp. 73–4.

12. John Barth, *Lost in the Funhouse* (New York, 1969), pp. 70–1, 75.

13. *The Woodlanders*, p. 132. The 'marvellous boy' is of course the poet, Chatterton.

14. *Tess of the d'Urbervilles*, eds Juliet Grindle and Simon Gatrell (Oxford, 1988), p. 157.

15. *Far From the Madding Crowd*, ed. Suzanne B. Falck-Yi (Oxford, 1993), p. 413.

16. Another line of inquiry would involve examining Hardy holographs to try to determine when, in these passages of quoted verse, he was working from a printed text and when from memory. Some evidence might be gained by trying to sort out at what point in the evolution of the printed texts (ms, proofs, etc.) the quotations became block quotes. Rosemarie Morgan has indicated that at least some of the verse passages in the manuscript of *Far from the Madding Crowd* are not quoted in lines but are written continuously with the surrounding prose; see her *Cancelled Words: Rediscovering Thomas Hardy* (London, 1992). I interpret this to mean that in such circumstances Hardy is quoting from memory.

17. *A Laodicean*, ed. Jane Gatewood (Oxford, 1991), p. 21.

18. *The Mayor of Casterbridge*, ed. Dale Kramer (Oxford, 1987), p. 131.

19. *Tess of the d'Urbervilles*, p. 273.

20. *The Mayor of Casterbridge*, p. 170.

21. *Tess of the d'Urbervilles*, pp. 279–80.

22. Other examples would include 'Tess's Lament' and 'Beyond the Last Lamp', which is closely related to a scene in *Tess*; and 'Midnight on the Great Western', which recapitulates a scene in *Jude*.

23. Members of the seminar which followed the lecture on which this chapter is based made several impressive points about this last matter. One very striking observation was that in some of these early poems Hardy may be observed teaching himself to speak in a female voice (see, for example, 'She, to Him I–IV', 'Dream of the City Shopwoman', 'From Her in the Country', and 'Her Reproach').

6
Hardy's Architecture: a General Perspective and a Personal View

Timothy Hands

This chapter falls into two parts. The first is a brief introduction to Victorian architecture in relation to Hardy's experience of it. The second is a totally personal suggestion of how Hardy's career as an architect influenced his work as an author.

Whereas eighteenth-century architecture had been essentially classical in style, Victorian architecture was predominantly Gothic. An ideology of Gothic was developed by A. W. N. Pugin (1812–52), most famously in his *Contrasts* (1836); and by John Ruskin (1819–1900), whose chapter 'The Nature of Gothic' in *The Stones of Venice* (1851–53) imaginatively analyses the characteristics of the style. For Pugin, what he termed the Wonderful Superiority of Buildings of the Middle Ages must be readily apparent to every observer. For Ruskin, Gothic could be defined by savageness, changefulness, naturalism, grotesqueness, rigidity and redundance. Students of Hardy keen to understand the background of ideas against which the writer grew up will discover much of interest in these two highly individual texts.

In the early 1860s, a reaction against High Gothic began to set in. 'Gothic is barbaric art, after all', declares Sue Bridehead. 'Pugin was wrong, and Wren was right.'[1] The 'Modern Gothic' or 'Rogue Gothic' school centred on William Butterfield (1840–1900), E. B. Lamb (1806–69), S. S. Teulon (1812–73), F. T. Pilkington (1832–98), E. Bassett Keeling (1837–86) and W. W. White (1825–1900). These architects attempted to combine medievalism and modernity, traditional forms and new materials: their style was highly idiosyncratic and self-expressive, with particular emphasis on ornament, and they delighted in the use of new materials. Hardy studied with particular care Bassett Keeling's much-criticised Strand Music Hall, and visited one of White's early designs, All Saints Notting Hill. More radically, other architects, especially Norman Shaw (1831–1912) and W. E. Nesfield (1835–88), advocated a wider range of historical styles, such as Queen Anne: Hardy was to choose books by both these architects when in 1863 he won an Architectural Association prize.

As the century progressed, attitudes towards the issue of Gothic restoration also altered. The mid-Victorian architect, such as Sir George Gilbert Scott, with whom Hardy had tangential contact, might expect to spend at least as much of his time restoring old buildings as designing new ones, such restoration then being understood to include projects as considerable as rebuilding, redesigning, or even total destruction. The formation of the Society for the Protection of Ancient Buildings by William Morris in 1877 marked a change of mind and heart; the Ancient Monuments Protection Act (1882, amended 1900) provided supporting legislation.

Hardy's sound technical education and family knowledge of building eminently qualified him for an architectural training: there is no reason to suppose that, had he wished to, he could not have pursued an architectural career leading to prosperity and perhaps even distinction. He was proposed as a member of the Architectural Association by Arthur Blomfield in 1862. The next year he won first prize in the Association's competition for the design of a country mansion, a well as a silver medal awarded by the Institute of British Architects for his prize essay 'On the Application of Colored (sic) Bricks and Terra Cotta to Modern Architecture'. Hardy's principal employment was with three architects: John Hicks, Arthur Blomfield and G. R. Crickmay. In 1870 he worked intermittently for Raphael Brandon, a distinguished architectural writer and practitioner, with whose writings Hardy was well acquainted, and on whose chambers those of Knight in *A Pair of Blue Eyes* are based. In 1872 he worked for T. Roger Smith, a professor at the RIBA, for whom he prepared designs for a competition for London Board Schools. He found Smith able and amiable and the success of one design led to the offer of further employment from him: Hardy declined Smith's offer, though giving his surname to the hero of the novel he was currently writing, *A Pair of Blue Eyes*, and sending that hero on an architectural assignment to Bombay, where Smith himself had undertaken commissions in the 1860s.

This decision marked the formal conclusion of Hardy's architectural career, and Hardy's limited returns to architecture in later life were generally motivated by personal or sentimental reasons: the restoration of Stinsford church, for example, or the design of Max Gate. He did, however, become an early and regular correspondent for the Society for the Protection of Ancient Buildings, which he joined in 1881. His involvement with the Society between 1882 and 1926 on a total of 16 projects, mostly ecclesiastical and mostly in Dorset, is fully documented in Claudius Beatty's *Thomas Hardy: Conservation Architect* (Dorchester, 1995), where Hardy's address to the Society's AGM in June 1906, entitled 'Memories of Church Restoration', is also reproduced.

My personal view is that Hardy's career as an architect considerably influenced his writing. This is evident in both content and style. An obituary entitled 'The Master Craftsman' in the architectural journal *The Builder* implied that Hardy wrote throughout his career with an architect's eye and pen. 'Those who have entered a church in Mr Hardy's company', Edmund Blunden recalled, 'may remember the immediate sense of his mastery of all its various material detail. . . . The training he had undergone meant an additional quickness and rightness in his observation as a general habit, which was so valuable a resource in his novels and other writings.'[2]

Though only one novel (*A Laodicean*) is dominated by architectural discussion, three others (*The Poor Man and the Lady*, *Desperate Remedies*, *A Pair of Blue Eyes*) also have architects as their hero. Architectural conceptions and terms recur: Eustacia's lips and Lucetta's back are alike in their correspondence to 'the cima-recta'; and the prospect of Wintoncester in the final chapter of *Tess of the d'Urbervilles* has 'its more prominent buildings showing as in an isometric drawing', just as the lines in the buildings in Chief Street, Christminster in *Jude the Obscure* are 'as distinct in the morning air as in an architectural drawing'.[3]

The literature of the architectural Gothic had raised consciousness of the architectural merits of the parish church: the two copiously illustrated volumes of the Brandon brothers' *Parish Churches*, which Hardy had studied, prescribed personal inspection of the old churches of England as the only means by which the genius of medieval architects could be properly appreciated; *A Laodicean*, in perhaps over-carefully considered detail, opens with Somerset reverently practising the art. Hardy the writer often returns for his settings to the habits and interests of Hardy the architectural pupil. In the novels, scenes set in churches or churchyards are not only prominent but also frequently portentous (for example, in *A Pair of Blue Eyes*, *Far from the Madding Crowd* and *Jude*). In the poems, the Brandons' advice is turned almost into a recurrent genre piece (see, for example, 'Drawing Details in an Old Church', 'Copying Architecture in an Old Minster' and 'While Drawing in a Churchyard'): in the first edition of *Wessex Poems* 'The Impercipient' is illustrated with a detailed pencil sketch of the interior of Salisbury Cathedral. Many poems have ecclesiastical settings: 'At the Wicket Gate', 'A Church Romance', 'A Cathedral Facade at Midnight', 'The Clock-Winder', 'A Poor Man and a Lady', 'Her Dilemma', 'In a Whispering Gallery', 'In Church', 'In St Paul's a While Ago' and 'In Sherborne Abbey'.

Church restoration is a recurrent motif, featuring in *Under the Greenwood Tree*, *A Pair of Blue Eyes*, *A Laodicean* as well as in *Jude*. Writing in 1906 and looking back over the previous three-quarters of a century Hardy concluded that 'if all the mediaeval buildings of England had been left as they stood at that date, to incur whatever dilapidations might have befallen them at the hands of time, weather and general neglect, this country would be richer in specimens to-day than it finds itself to be after the expenditure of millions in a nominal preservation during that period'.[4] Though few knew better than Hardy that it was, as he acknowledged, easy to criticise with the benefit of hindsight, Hardy did at a considerably earlier stage express his reservations about restoration in his imaginative writing.

Most particularly it was the restoration of his native church of Stinsford that involved Hardy personally, and affected him emotionally. Hardy's family had been involved with the upkeep of Stinsford for many years. Though he was too young to remember the sweeping restoration of the early 1840s, its imaginative recreation forms a central part of the narrative of *Under the Greenwood Tree*; and he was probably deputed by Hicks to undertake the restoration work of 1868, involving a new roof, window alterations, and the addition of a vestry. In April 1909 Hardy joined the Stinsford Church restoration committee, advising that all works should be in accordance with 'the only legitimate principle for guidance', namely 'to limit all renewals to *repairs for preservation*, and never to indulge in alterations'.[5] In the subsequent decade, returning to the architectural notebook which he had used in the 1860s, he advised on the refurbishment of the font, and again in the next decade, two years before his death, advised the vicar on the restoration of the church bells.

The vicar of Stinsford, Arthur Shirley, who supervised both the nineteenth-century restorations of the church, sought to introduce to Stinsford the newest High Church practice – in fabric no less than in music or schooling. These changes are reflected in 'Afternoon Service at Mellstock (Circa 1850)':

> On afternoons of drowsy calm
> We stood in the panelled pew,

Singing one-voiced a Tate-and-Brady psalm
    To the tune of 'Cambridge New'.

We watched the elms, we watched the rooks,
    The clouds upon the breeze,
Between the whiles of glancing at our books,
    And swaying like the trees.

So mindless were those outpourings! –
    Though I am not aware
That I have gained by subtle thought on things
    Since we stood psalming there.

The poem, seemingly thrown-off, is precise in its frame of reference. It corresponds, for example, as does *Under the Greenwood Tree*, to an anonymous mid-century High Church architectural cartoon book, *Reformation and Deformation*, except that whereas the cartoon book applauds Puginesque tendencies, the novel and poem regret them. The musical point is a clear one: 'Cambridge New', the tune mentioned, was used at Stinsford for the Tate and Brady version of Psalm 78, which discusses a man's responsibility for passing his faith on to the next generation. The poem deals with a fabric and a set of customs (as much as with a viewpoint) now outmoded. Everywhere there is unwelcome alteration. The Victorian restorers preferred stained glass to the clear glass which once made the natural vistas of this poem possible; Tate and Brady were replaced by plainchant; and, in conformity with best High Church practice, Shirley removed the Stinsford box pews, replacing them with benches. The poem builds up a powerful feeling of vulnerable loneliness and erosion partly by an accumulation of precisely observed contemporary architectural detail.

What Hardy seems to have resented most in restoration work, as his fictional presentations of Mellstock Church make clear, is a concern with buildings at the expense of people. In two poems about new or restored churches, 'The Church and the Wedding' and 'Whispered at the Church Opening', new building work is associated with the dearth of historical and personal sentiment. The *locus classicus* is the barbed indictment of the architect of the new Marygreen church in *Jude*, an 'obliterator of historic records who had run down from London and back in a day'.[6] Hardy's own views on the relative merits of aesthetic elegance and memorial appeal are clear – indeed, they may partly explain how he came to desert architecture for a calling he felt had more human interest. The argument that '[t]he human interest in an edifice ranks before its architectural interest, however great the latter may be', is developed in 'Memories of Church Restoration' at some length: 'The protection of an edifice against renewal in fresh materials is, in fact, even more of a social – I may say a humane – duty than an aesthetic one. It is the preservation of memories, history, fellowship, fraternities.'[7] The report of this lecture in the *Life* records the particular satisfaction of the audience 'that Hardy had laid special emphasis on the value of the human associations of ancient buildings . . . since they were generally slighted in paying regard to artistic and architectural points only'.[8]

Hardy is predictably sensitive to suiting the style of his buildings to their occupants. 'Architectural Masks' explores the suggestion that different styles of building can provide indications of the moral nature of their occupants:

I

There is a house with ivied walls,
And mullioned windows worn and old,
And the long dwellers in those halls
Have souls that know but sordid calls,
    And daily dote on gold.

II

In blazing brick and plated show
Not far away a 'villa' gleams.
And here a family few may know,
With book and pencil, viol and bow,
    Lead inner lives of dreams.

III

The philosophic passers say,
'See that old mansion mossed and fair,
Poetic souls therein are they:
And O that gaudy box! Away,
    You vulgar people there.'

In this instance the 'philosophic passers' are mistaken, but such a hypothesis was central to Gothic theorists, for whom Gothic was not just an aesthetic preference, but a statement of ideological belief: 'it was always a principle that anything later than Henry the Eighth was anathema', Hardy recalled of his early grounding in taste.[9] Pugin's influential *Contrasts* set out to prove, by comparing medieval Gothic buildings with their later counterparts, the 'wonderful superiority' of the Gothic; Ruskin's essay on the nature of Gothic defined its 'moral elements'. Hardy's descriptions conform to these early prejudices far more frequently than might be expected: for him, as *A Laodicean* shows most plainly, architecture and morality remain deeply interfused. Those whose moral disposition is more likely to gain the reader's sympathy inhabit abodes which are either fully natural (Winterborne's hut, or, in still purer form, the shelter of his apple tree) or which have that architectural style (Gothic) which, according to Ruskin, had 'naturalism', a fidelity to the patterns and shapes of nature. (Hardy's poem 'The Abbey Mason' goes still further than Ruskin in making the link between Gothic and Nature; here, the rain falling on the architect's chalk drawing transforms his 'lame designs' into the beginnings of what we now know as 'Perpendicular Gothic'). Hardy's loose women, by contrast, frequently inhabit classical buildings. Bathsheba's manor is classical. Lucetta's house is Palladian and, 'like most architecture erected since the Gothic age', 'a compilation rather than a design'.[10] Fitzpiers's modishness shows in the Dutchness of his cottage and its garden: very much an adaptation of Nesfield and Shaw. The code is at its crudest – if also perhaps its most powerful – in *Tess*. Modern materials and an unnatural style characterise Alec's house at the Slopes in Chapter 5 and the housing estates of Sandbourne in Chapter 55 where he finally entertains Tess. The novel's final chapter is an entirely Puginesque contrast: a medieval town, with medieval systems of charity, compared, with an acute implicit disfavour, to the altered contemporary perspective over a red-brick prison which is preparing to execute an unnatural law. Angel and Liza-Lu look down from West Hill on

> the broad Cathedral tower, with its Norman windows, and immense length of aisle and nave, the spire of St Thomas's, the pinnacled tower of the College, and, more to the right, the tower and gables of the ancient hospice where to this day the pilgrim may receive his bread . . .
>
> Against these far stretches of country rose, in front of the other city edifices, a large red-brick building, with level grey roofs, and rows of short barred windows bespeaking captivity – the whole contrasting

greatly by its formalism with the quaint irregularities of the Gothic erections.

Examination of changes of wording in the manuscript version reinforces this point very clearly.[11]

As regards stylistic influence, a stress on the importance of function and a resultant emphasis on originality rather than uniformity or imitation lay at the centre of the views of the Gothic theorists. Pugin's *Contrasts* contended that 'the great test of Architectural beauty is the fitness of the design to the purpose of the building'.[12] H. H. Statham's 'Modern English Architecture', an article in *The Fortnightly Review* for 1 October 1876 which Hardy noted carefully, urged the architect to 'commence first from the basis of practical consideration'.[13] The principle is apparent in 'Heiress and Architect' and burlesqued in 'How I Built Myself a House': in the design of Max Gate, a house built from the inside out, it was, as Michael Millgate has noted, particularly respected.[14]

The resultant Gothic emphasis on originality sprang also from an ideological basis. Ruskin's view that the individual workman should express his unique personality, unhindered by any self-consciousness about that personality's shortcomings, was developed in *The Stones of Venice* into a 'universal law, that neither architecture nor any other noble work of man can be good unless it be imperfect'.[15] Ornament was viewed as one of the principal means by which the self-expression of such imperfection could be achieved. It was central to the profession of Gothic, as also to Hardy's involvement with it: the details of design were generally the responsibility of the architectural assistant, and Hardy's prize-winning essay had been on a means of ornament (polychromatic brick) recently introduced into the architect's repertoire.

Such theories are the background to Hardy's concept of the 'cunning irregularity' which, in a considered examination of his architectural training which is opaque but which repays careful study, he saw as the chief influence of his architectural past on his literary style.[16] Elsewhere, Hardy admitted that 'being, in fact, a little careless, or rather, seeming to be, here and there' was the considered method by which he sought to bring 'wonderful life' into his writing.[17] For critics, especially early critics of the poetry, such originality was problematic: in the reception of *Wessex Poems*, for example, the oddness of including illustrations (not to mention their varying quality), the dense stresses, inverted syntax, archaisms and strange coinages, all provoked adverse comment. When defending himself against such critical misunderstanding, both in the *Life* and in the stinging exchange of views with Robert Lynd, Hardy argued on Gothic lines in favour of originality employed for the production of effect, and based his defence on architectural analogy.[18] The critic who complained of the irregularity of the poems might, Hardy writes

> have gone to one of our cathedrals (to follow up the analogy of architecture), and on discovering that the carved leafage of some capital or spandrel in the best period of Gothic art strayed freakishly out of its bounds over the moulding, where by rule it had no business to be . . . have declared with equally merry conviction, 'This does not make for immortality.[19]

The moral implications of the aesthetic concept of imperfection also left a considerable mark, expressed for example in Hardy's admiration for, and choice of quotation from, Browning, for whom it was also a favourite idea: hence perhaps his choice of 'Rabbi Ben Ezra' as the last complete poem to be read to him.[20]

The concern with idiosyncrasy and with ornament was perhaps at the expense of an overall sense of proportion. Certainly, such criticism has consistently been directed at the architectural Rogue Goths, from contemporary times to the present. Hardy's defence of medieval Gothic makes it clear that he thought it might be a merit, not a defect, if the carved leafage of a capital or spandrel were allowed to stray 'freakishly' out of its bounds over the moulding, 'where by rule it had no business to be'. By comparison with a traditional Victorian practitioner such as Blomfield, however, Hardy exacerbated such a principle, as for example in his work on the conversion and expansion of an Early English church at Turnworth.[21] He defined his art as a disproportioning of realities and a Rogue Gothic influence may well be detectable here.[22] Architecturally as well as perhaps in his writing, there is some question as to how successfully Hardy is able to create a successful synthesis of the profusion of created ornament. The work of the Rogue Gothic architects possessed an emphasis on self-expression which in the view of many of its critics bordered on self-indulgence. A hostile assessment of Hardy, such as that of T. S. Eliot in *After Strange Gods* (1934) starts from a similar premise. Hardy the architect was not in many senses best suited for becoming Hardy the literary planner; for, if the best of Hardy's career as an architect was carried over into this second profession, so too were some of its quirkier characteristics.

Notes

1. *Jude the Obscure*, ed. Patricia Ingham (Oxford, 1985), p. 322.
2. Edmund Blunden, *Thomas Hardy* (1942: London, 1967), p. 35.
3. *The Return of the Native*, ed. Simon Gatrell (Oxford, 1985), p. 64; *The Mayor of Casterbridge*, ed. Dale Kramer (Oxford, 1987), p. 157; *Tess of the d'Urbervilles*, eds Juliet Grindle and Simon Gatrell (Oxford, 1988), p. 383; *Jude the Obscure*, p. 193.
4. 'Memories of Church Restoration', in *Thomas Hardy's Personal Writings*, ed. Harold Orel (1966; London, 1967), p. 203.
5. *Collected Letters*, IV. 18.
6. *Jude the Obscure*, p. 6
7. 'Memories of Church Restoration', edn cit., p. 215.
8. *Life and Work*, p. 356.
9. 'Memories of Church Restoration', edn cit., p. 208.
10. *The Mayor of Casterbridge*, p. 141.
11. *Tess of the d'Urbervilles*, p. 382. In the manuscript Hardy first wrote 'older streets', corrected to 'older erections', before settling on 'Gothic erections'.
12. A. N. W. Pugin, *Contrasts*, ed. H. R. Hitchcock (Leicester University Press, 1969), p. 1.
13. For Hardy's annotations, see *The Literary Notebooks of Thomas Hardy*, edited by Lennart Björk, 2 vols (London, 1985), I. 82 (entries 809–13), and the notes to these entries.
14. Michael Millgate, *Thomas Hardy: a Biography* (Oxford, 1982), p. 259.
15. *The Stones of Venice*, in *The Works of John Ruskin*, eds E. T. Cook and Alexander Wedderburn, 39 vols (London, 1903–12), X. 204.
16. *Life and Work*, p. 323.
17. *Life and Work*, p. 108.
18. For Hardy's letter to Lynd, dated 30 July 1919, see *Collected Letters*, 5. 318–19.
19. *Life and Work*, p. 323.
20. *Life and Work*, p. 480. See also the allusions to Browning's 'The Statue and the Bust', as for example in *Jude the Obscure*, edn cit., p. 249.
21. This is briefly described by Robert Gittings in his *Young Thomas Hardy* (London, 1975), pp. 115–16.
22. *Life and Work*, p. 239.

7
Wessex Poems, 1898

James Gibson

Hardy's first book of verse, *Wessex Poems*, was published in December 1898. In September 1798, almost exactly a century earlier, two little-known poets named Wordsworth and Coleridge had published a book of verse called *Lyrical Ballads*. Looking back now, a century after Hardy's *Wessex Poems* and two centuries after *Lyrical Ballads*, one is intrigued by the fact that the two books had at least one thing in common: they sounded a new note, a change of direction, in English poetry. *Lyrical Ballads* was an attempt to break away from the rigid rationalism of so much eighteenth-century poetry, a rigidity symbolised by the constant use of the heroic couplet and an artificial poetic diction which could result in lines like this:

> Say, shall we muse along yon arching shades,
> Whose awful gloom no brightening ray pervades;
> Or down these vales where vernal flowers display
> Their golden blossoms to the smiles of day . . .[1]

Wordsworth felt that poetry should come from the heart rather than the intellect. He had been in his youth a staunch supporter of the French Revolution and wanted to democratise poetry by simplifying it, and he agreed with Coleridge that his contribution to *Lyrical Ballads* should be poems about ordinary life. In the words of Coleridge, 'Mr Wordsworth . . . was to propose to himself as his object to give the charm of novelty to things of every day', to awaken 'the mind's attention from the lethargy of custom' and direct it 'to the loveliness and the wonders of the world before us: an inexhaustible treasure, but for which, in consequence of the film of familiarity and selfish solicitude, we have eyes yet see not, ears that hear not, and hearts that neither feel nor understand.'[2] Moreover, Wordsworth's poems were to be written in 'the real language of men',[3] a phrase so vague that it has resulted in endless discussion. Could it possibly be said, for example, that 'Behold her, single in the field,/ Yon solitary Highland Lass' was an example of the real language of men?

Hardy was so well acquainted with Wordsworth's work that before he was 20 he had written a poem called 'Domicilium' which described his Bockhampton cottage home in a style and with a vocabulary very much like that of Wordsworth; although much of Wordsworth's philosophy and love of Nature, expressed in such statements as that 'Nature never did betray the heart that loved her', would have been regarded by him as nonsense. He would have realised how much poetry in his time owed to *Lyrical Ballads* and would have seen his own poems as sharing much that Wordsworth and the Romantic poets believed in, not least that poetry was the supreme literary genre. He may have been sceptical about Shelley's claim that 'poets are the unacknowledged legislators of the world', or about Wordsworth's claim that 'Poetry is the breath and finer spirit of all knowledge', but he did believe that 'poetry and religion touch each other, or rather modulate into each other; are, indeed, often but different names for the same thing'.[4]

It is not surprising that Hardy, believing this, wanted to be a poet, and he tells us in the *Life* that while in London in the mid-1860s he

> had begun to write verses, and by 1866 to send his productions to magazines. That these were rejected by editors, and that he paid such respect to their judgement as scarcely ever to send out a MS. twice, was in one feature fortunate for him, since in years long after he was able to examine those poems of which he kept copies, and by the mere change of a few words or the rewriting of a line or two, to make them quite worthy of publication.[5]

In fact, 36 poems are dated in the 1860s, and 17 of these are included in *Wessex Poems*. It is difficult to understand why he did not include all 36 and why the remaining 19 were spread out over five of the following books, the last two not appearing until the posthumous *Winter Words* of 1928.

Why was it that 'Domicilium', that fine description of his cottage home at Bockhampton for so much of the first 34 years of his life, and a Wessex poem if ever there was one, was excluded from *Wessex Poems* and, apart from a small private printing, not made public until the first volume of his *Life* was published in 1928? Surely it couldn't be that in 1898 he was still shy of letting people know of his humble background? And where did he keep those poems of the 1860s and the many books he must have possessed during the peregrinatory years before he settled down in Max Gate in 1885?

Unable to get his poetry published he decided to try his hand at writing novels. Financial success and fame were slow in coming but when they did with the large sales resulting from the outcry caused by *Tess* (1891) and *Jude* (1895), he could at last think of returning to his first love, poetry, and some gave as his reasons for abandoning the novel that the vituperation which had been heaped on him by critics and the Establishment for writing such 'scandalous' books as *Tess* and *Jude* was too upsetting, and that he could express ideas in verse with impunity which would be viciously attacked if they were part of a novel. As he put it in the *Life*, 'Perhaps I can express more fully in verse ideas and emotions which run counter to the inert crystallized opinion – hard as a rock – which the vast body of men have vested interests in support-ing. . . . If Galileo had said in verse that the world moved, the Inquisi-tion might have let him alone.'[6] How right he was can be illustrated by how little criticism he evoked in writing poems like 'The Ruined Maid' and 'Panthera'.

There were other reasons for his obvious delight at the thought of returning to poetry and living on the income from his novels for the rest of his life. The writing of a novel was far more demanding than the writing of poetry, and, more important, the traditional novel was under-going a sea-change, and Hardy did not wish to follow it into the new realms of modernism. In his own words the novel was 'gradually losing artistic form, with a beginning, middle, and end, and becoming a spas-modic inventory of items, which has nothing to do with art'.[7] Even so, he must have realised that the novel had been a good milch-cow to him, and that those 25 years of writing it had been excellent preparation for becoming a poet. As Ezra Pound said on reading Hardy's *Collected Poems*, 'Now *there* is clarity. There *is* the harvest of having written 20 [sic] novels first.'[8] Hardy had, indeed, in writing his novels become an expert in the use of the English language, and he had outwitted Mrs Grundy by a remarkable use of imagery. Like Chekhov, he knew how to use prose poetically at moments of vision and high emotion. We are moved as if by poetry at such moments as Marty's lamentation on the grave of Giles and the discovery of Henchard's will. In writing his novels he had, he said, aimed at keeping his narratives 'as near to poetry in their subject as conditions would allow'.[9]

But from now on his first love, poetry, would dominate his profes-sional life. He tells us in the *Life* that before 1897 'he had already for some time been getting together the poems which made up the volume he was about to publish. In date,' he goes on, 'they range from 1865 intermittently onwards, the middle period of his novel-writing produc-ing very few or none, but of late years they had been added to with great rapidity.' At first, he said, there was some consternation because he 'found an awkwardness in getting back to an easy expression in numbers after abandoning it for so many years; but that soon wore off'.[10] Just why Hardy decided to publish his first book of verse in 1898 (was it because he remembered that it was the centenary of *Lyrical Ballads*?) and why he chose just those 51 poems when in addition to the 17 poems of the 1860s there were almost certainly several others he could have included, can be no more than a matter of conjecture. Was it, for example, the special autobiographical intensity of the poem, 'Wessex Heights', dated '1896', which meant that Hardy did not publish it until 1914? This is no poem recollected in tranquillity. It is particu-larly ironic that 'When I Set out for Lyonnesse', which celebrates the first fine careless rapture of Hardy's falling in love with Emma Gifford in 1870 and which must surely have been written then, was excluded from the new volume of verse. Why? Was it because the romance had died, the marriage had gone stale, and Hardy could not bring himself to publish it? Two years after her death in 1912 he included it in *Satires of Circumstance*. If she knew of its existence, and it is difficult to know how Hardy could have concealed it from her for all those years, it would have been another blow to her self-esteem that her husband left it out of *Wessex Poems*.

Hardy signed an agreement with his publishers, Harpers, in Septem-ber 1898, corrected the proofs in October, and the book was published during the week of 11 December at a price of six shillings. Hardy was obviously excited about the publication of his first book of verse but he suspected that it would have a bad reception and would not sell well, and he offered to 'take on his own shoulders the risk of producing the volume, so that if nobody bought it they should not be out of pocket'.[11] Harpers refused this generous offer but decided to print no more than 500 copies; this showed good business sense, as a second printing was not required until 1903. It says something for Hardy's determination to be a recognised poet that, regardless of the failure of *Wessex Poems*, he published his second book of verse in 1902. I wonder whether at the publication of his first book of verse he remembered how his first novel, *Desperate Remedies* – 27 years previously – had also had a print run of

500 copies and had not sold well. *Wessex Poems* was one of three of his eight books of verse which had a separate printing in America.

The title, *Wessex Poems*, seems to have been decided on as early as February of 1898. It is not a particularly appropriate title as fewer than half the poems have any connection with Wessex. Here we see Hardy the professional writer hoping to cash in on his reputation as the Wessex novelist, and failing to do so. But he was obviously delighted that he was now a published poet, and he proudly sent copies of his new book to a good many of his friends. Among them were Swinburne, 'whose genius', wrote Hardy in an inscription, 'has for more than thirty years been the charm of T. H'. Other copies went to his favourite sister, Mary, Leslie Stephen, Edmund Gosse and the poet William Watson. Watson's copy was inscribed 'with warm congratulations after reading the reprint of his deathless verse'. As a typical piece of Watson's 'deathless verse' is this, from his poem 'Song':

> April, April,
> Laugh thy girlish laughter;
> Then, the moment after,
> Weep thy girlish tears

One can only assume that Hardy was having his little laugh. Incidentally, in *The Oxford Book of Victorian Verse*, edited by Arthur Quiller-Couch and published in 1912, Hardy is represented by six pages of his Victorian verse and Watson by about the same. The modest editor published nearly five pages of his own verse. In *The New Oxford Book of Victorian Verse* edited by Christopher Ricks in 1987, Hardy has 14 pages, Watson's 'deathless verse' has been reduced to four lines, and Quiller-Couch has disappeared without trace.

Hardy wrote a short preface to *Wessex Poems* in which he mentioned that only four of the poems it contained had been published previously 'though many were written long ago, and others partly written'. Always anxious to hide the autobiographical nature of so much of his verse, he writes: 'The pieces are in a large degree dramatic or personative in conception, and this even where they are not obviously so.'[12] As 'personative ' in this context seems to mean no more than 'dramatic', this may be a case of the gentleman protesting too much, and, of course, Hardy who thought favourably of Leslie Stephen's dictum that 'The ultimate aim of the poet should be to touch our hearts by showing his own', was by that very belief committed to drawing on his own life for much of his material.[13]

In a final paragraph of the Preface Hardy refers to the illustrations which accompany the poems, telling the reader they 'have been recently made' and are 'inserted for personal and local reasons rather than for their intrinsic qualities'. Altogether, he made 32 drawings for *Wessex Poems*, but one, a tailpiece to 'The Casterbridge Captains', was not published. He had always enjoyed drawing and painting, but what was it that made him decide to share with the public drawings which are remarkable more for their personal interest than their artistic qualities? Writing to Edward Clodd at the time he said in that slightly self-denigratory way he so often adopted, that they 'had for me in preparing them a sort of illegitimate interest – that which arose from their being a novel amusement, and a wholly gratuitous performance which could not profit me anything, and probably would do me harm'.[14] In fact, the reviewers showed little interest in them. One who did was E. K. Chambers in the *Athenaeum* who, having pointed out that they would recall the fact that Hardy was originally apprenticed in an architect's office, then described them as being 'thoroughly in keeping with some of the most marked characteristics of the book itself. Primitive in execution, and frequently inspired by a somewhat grim mortuary imagination, they are still full of poetry, and show a real sense of the decorative values of architectural outline and nocturnal landscape.'[15]

Some of the more personal of Hardy's drawings have a special interest and deserve mention. The frontispiece illustration is of Stinsford church, viewed from the north, and linked to the poem, 'Friends Beyond', by a quotation: 'At mothy curfew-tide,/ They've a way of whispering to me.' His family had been closely connected with the church, *Under the Greenwood Tree* had been written about it, many of his relations were buried there, and for Hardy it was 'the most hallowed spot on earth'. Through the gate, on the extreme left of the drawing, can be seen the grave of his father, who had died in 1894. One strange touch is the two decorations on the urns which look like human faces. The illustration accompanying 'The Temporary the All' is of the eastern turret of Max Gate. Hardy had long meant to decorate it with a sundial, and one appears as a feature on the illustration, but it was not put there until after his death. The poem 'The Alarm' is about his grandfather being called out to defend the coast near Weymouth when there were fears one night of an invasion by Napoleon's forces. The accompanying illustration shows the grandfather standing on the Ridgeway with Weymouth and Portland stretched out before him. The illustration for 'The Impercipient' depicts a service taking place in Salisbury Cathedral. In August 1897 he and Emma, who had given him a Bible in the hope that he might purge himself of all that *Jude* nonsense, were present at a service there. Tryphena Sparks, as we shall see later, plays quite a part in *Wessex Poems*, and Hardy's biographers seem generally agreed that the poem 'In a Eweleaze near Weatherbury' is about his love for her. Weatherbury is of course Puddletown, where Tryphena lived in the 1860s during that period of the romance. Her death in 1890, when his own marriage to Emma was in difficulties, made him think, as he was to do again later when Emma died, of his lost love. Hardy's illustration for this poem is of a country-field with sheep, a gate and a ring of trees, and one is tempted to assume that this must have for Hardy some memories of his affair with Tryphena. Superimposed on the illustration is a crudely drawn pair of spectacles, placed in such a way that it could represent someone looking out of the field or someone looking in. There was something deeply personal and enigmatic about this experiment with illustrations, an experiment which he never repeated.

Hardy the one-time architect always thought in terms of structures, and novels like *The Mayor of Casterbridge* and *Tess* and nearly all his poems are full of structural interest. He more than once described the contents of *Wessex Poems* as 'miscellaneous', and in later volumes of verse he tried to find some way of dividing the contents under appropriate headings, something he found it impossible to do with *Wessex Poems*. Thus in his second volume of verse, *Poems of the Past and the Present*, he has the sub-headings 'Preface', 'War Poems', 'Poems of Pilgrimage', 'Miscellaneous' (by far the biggest category), 'Imitations' and 'Retrospect'. In *Time's Laughingstocks* the miscellaneous poems become 'Pieces Occasional and Various' and in *Satires of Circumstance* we have both 'Lyric Reveries' and 'Miscellaneous Pieces'. However, he realised by then that his poems ranged over such a wide variety of overlapping subjects and moods that it was almost impossible to divide them up into groups of like poems, except very occasionally where there was a number of poems about the Boer War or the Great War. Seeing that it was a futile exercise, he abandoned any attempt at categorisation in his last three books of verse and used catch-all titles such as *Late Lyrics and Earlier, Human Shows, Far Phantasies, Songs and Trifle*s, and *Winter Words in Various Moods and Metres*. Michael Millgate, in his biography of Hardy, draws attention to 'the trenchant simplicity of [Hardy's] assumption that poetry was an entirely natural medium of human expression and, as such, entirely appropriate to almost any human situation'. That being so, is it surprising that it was so difficult to categorise his poems into meaningful divisions? *Wessex Poems* is the first volume of what will finish up with *Winter Words*, 30 years later, as a great epic not just of Wessex life but of human life.

Hardy realised that because his kind of poetry was something new he must expect to have some bad reviews. He was not disappointed. The *Saturday Review* lashed him. It was a 'curious and wearisome volume', said the reviewer. It contained 'many slovenly, slipshod, uncouth verses, stilted in sentiment, poorly conceived and worse wrought. . . . It is impossible to understand why the bulk of this volume was published at all . . .'. Of some of the ballads, it went on, 'it can only be said that they are some of the most amazing balderdash that ever found its way into a book of verse'.[16] William Archer in *The Daily Chronicle* made his well-known comment that 'there are times when Mr Hardy seems to lose all sense of local and historical perspective in language, seeing all the words in the dictionary on one plane, so to speak, and regarding them all as equally available and appropriate for any and every literary purpose'.[17] Hardy took this to be a compliment. I am not sure that Archer meant it to be so. The *Westminster Gazette* thought that Hardy's poems 'have interest and poignancy as criticisms of life' but were often 'clumsy in execution and harsh in sound'. He 'chiefly fails when he is telling a story in verse'.[18] The *Pall Mall Gazette* thought Hardy's metres were characterised by 'rough hacking', that he was 'a poet of thought' rather than of 'sound and melody'.[19] But there were those who found something to praise, among whom the most sympathetic was Annie Macdonell who in 1894 had written one of the first critical studies of Hardy's novels.

Hardy, always sensitive to criticism of his books, as, of course, all writers are, soon showed that the reviews had got home. Writing to Edmund Gosse on 14 February 1899, he says: 'The truth is I have been out of conceit with the Poems ever since they were printed – owing to a sense of my inexcusable carelessness in revising them so perfunctorily. My interest lay so entirely in the novel occupation of making the drawings that I did not remove defects of form in the verses which lay quite on the surface, and might have been cured in a couple of hours.'[20] That he was much exercised in his mind about this first wave of criticism is shown by the six important pages he devotes to defending himself in Chapter 25 of the *Life*. He accuses his critics of being so obsessed with the idea that novel-writing was his trade that they lost the power 'of looking clearly and responsively into his poetry as form and content'. Note that he is probably using the word 'form' not just as meaning structure but as meaning everything that was not content. He then goes on to accuse the critics of failing to see 'the solidarity of all the arts', and of falsifying their attacks by selecting a few bad lines and quoting them as samples of the whole. *Wessex Poems* might have had a better reception if he had imitated Wordsworth, Tennyson and Browning but he hadn't. 'There is no new poetry,' he writes, but the new poet 'comes with a new note. And that new note it is that troubles the critical waters.' Then follows his important definition of poetry: 'Poetry is emotion put into measure. The emotion must come by nature, but the measure can be acquired by art.' The critics, he said, were guilty of 'the inevitable ascription to ignorance of what was really choice after full knowledge. That the author loved the art of concealing art was undiscerned.' There were, he maintained, similarities between poetry and architecture, each art having to carry a rational content inside an artistic form. From architecture he had learnt the value of 'cunning irregularity' and 'spontaneity'. He ends this apologia by pointing out that he 'had a born sense of humour' which because it was of a Swiftian rather than of a Dickensian character was completely misunderstood by the critics. As an example he took 'The Fire at Tranter Sweatley's'. One critic had completely failed to see it as humorous and 'deplored the painful nature of the bridegroom's end in leaving only a bone behind him'.[21]

Wessex Poems, with its 51 poems, was Hardy's shortest book of verse, but he was only in bottom gear. *Poems of the Past and the Present* had 99, and he reached top gear with *Moments of Vision* in 1917 which contained 159. But even with the 51 poems we have to consider in *Wessex Poems* it is difficult to know where to begin. There are seven or eight sonnets mostly about love, four of them making a sequence called 'She, to Him'. They show Hardy flexing his poetic muscles and revealing how competent he was in writing imitations of the Elizabethan sonnet, especially those which were dominated by the lover's despair. The most important and most genuinely felt of the sonnets is 'Hap' in which Hardy deplores the 'Crass Casualty' which seems to rule our lives. It is the first, of course, of those poems of his which one loosely calls 'philosophical', in which he questions the Christian view of a benevolent God, sometimes addressing the poem to the God in whom he does not believe. Another poem of this kind is 'Nature's Questioning' in which 'Field, flock, and lonely tree' wonder why they were created and get no answer. In 'A Sign-Seeker' he walks in churchyards hoping for some voice from the grave which will provide evidence of immortality but not a sound is heard. Strangely enough in 'Friends Beyond', one of the best poems in the book, the churchyard is full of voices speaking from the grave. Some of the weaker poems seem to me to be the story poems, but Jean Brooks in *Thomas Hardy: the Poetic Structure* believes that even here, in poems like 'Valenciennes', Hardy 'sets against the destructive interruptions of war the eternal values of human relationships linked closely to the cycle of life'.[22] Five of these narratives are about incidents in the Napoleonic war (he was just about to turn his mind to *The Dynasts*), four are about incidents at home, and finally, the best of the bunch, there is the farcical and very funny 'The Bride-Night Fire', later to be called 'The Fire at Tranter Sweatley's', which makes excellent use of the Dorset dialect and which because of its references to the girl, Barbree's 'cwold little buzzoms' and to her being 'horsed . . . by jerks' meant that Hardy, as so often in the novels, was forced in one printing of the poem to resort to bowdlerisation. Just how awful Hardy could be in these narrative poems where his emotions were not really involved can be seen in such stanzas as this from 'The Burghers':

> But something held my arm. 'A moment yet
> As pray-time ere you wantons die,' I said;
> And then they saw me. Swift her gaze was set
> With eye and cry of love illimited
> Upon her Heart-king. Never upon me
> Had she thrown look of love so thoroughsped.

Such writing as this does something to excuse some of the abuse Hardy had to endure from the reviewers.

His emotions are certainly involved where the women in his life are concerned, and the poems about them are markedly better. With their marriage in the doldrums, Emma gets short measure. The one poem that might have pleased her is 'Ditty' which has below the title 'E. L. G.' and which must have been written during the happy days of the courtship in the 1870s although it is undated. But poor E. L. G. was very much upset by the poem 'The Ivy-Wife', which describes a wife throttling her husband as the ivy does the tree. How could that sensitive man have been so insensitive? But there was worse. His early love, Tryphena Sparks, had died in 1890, and there are two very good poems about her which might have upset any wife. The first, 'Thoughts of Phena, at News of Her Death', which he claims to have begun writing in a train before he knew she had died, begins with the lilting rhythm of a train: 'Not a line of her writing have I,/Not a thread of her hair . . .'. The second is 'In a Eweleaze near Weatherbury'. It seems likely that 'To a Motherless Child', in which he wishes that issue could be from one parent alone, is again Tryphena-inspired. And then there is 'Neutral Tones', one of the treasures of this volume, which is thought be about the break-up of the Tryphena affair some 30 years earlier, and has been described by J. O. Bailey as 'an etching in steel'. Mary, his much-loved sister, is his partner in 'Middle-Age Enthusiasms', and yet another woman he had loved is the subject of the poem 'At an Inn'. That woman was Mrs Henniker, the aristocratic lady with whom Hardy had fallen in love in 1893. The poem almost certainly refers to an occasion when they visited Winchester together in August of that year, and she made it clear that her interest in him was entirely literary. She was a writer herself and was to benefit substantially from her literary friendship with the great novelist. 'At an Inn' is one of those enigmatic Hardy poems that are deeply personal and leave the reader wanting to know more. As a novelist Hardy had learnt the value of leaving something to the imagination of the reader, and the act of catharsis for him did not mean, as it means today, telling everything.

Wessex Poems may be Hardy's first book of verse but, as Dryden said of Chaucer and as one feels with every book of Hardy's verse, 'Here is God's plenty'. Among other of his best poems is 'In a Wood' with its final emphasis on 'life-loyalties', something very important to Hardy. Think of the loyalty of Tess, and of Gabriel, and so many more in his fiction and poetry. 'Lines' is an occasional poem of real quality written almost overnight in aid of Lady Jeune's Holiday Fund for City Children. Here is Hardy, every inch a professional poet, at his most compassionate, and this and many another excellent occasional poem leave one regretting that, because he had written that 'naughty' book, *Jude*, and that 'naughty' poem, 'The Ruined Maid', he was never appointed the Poet Laureate.

In a first book of verse, even one published at the age of 58 by a famous novelist, it is not surprising that the poems, written as they were over a period of some 30 years, range from the 'ridiculous' to the 'sublime'. This diversity is well illustrated by the first and last poems in the book. 'The Temporary the All' creaks along with its unusual vocabulary of archaisms and neologisms, unlike anything that had been presented to the public before. 'I Look into My Glass' with its largely monosyllabic and simple utterance is one of Hardy's greatest poems, and one of the most poignant and moving poems in our language about the sadness of growing old. And there are several more of his finest poems in this strange hotchpotch of a book, among them 'Hap', the 'She, to Him' poems, 'Unknowing', 'Friends Beyond', 'The Impercipient' and 'The Bride-Night Fire'.

To begin his first volume of verse with 'The Temporary the All' in all its awkwardness was heroic if foolhardy, but the title could not have been more appropriate as the introduction to a poet who was so much concerned with the passing of time, the nostalgia and regret over what has passed away, and the need to seize the day, a universal theme in poetry since its earliest times. For readers who were used to the mellifluous lines of Swinburne, and of Tennyson, and the saccharine inanities of Watson, this new book must have been a shock. A new note *was* being struck in English poetry. Hardy was doing, often very successfully, what Wordsworth and Coleridge had set out to do in *Lyrical Ballads* a century before.

Notes

1. From 'Studley Park' by John Langhorne (1735–79).
2. See *Biographia Literaria*, Chapter 14; quoted from *Wordsworth and Coleridge: Lyrical Ballads*, ed. Derek Roper (London and Glasgow, 1968), p. 409.
3. Wordsworth, Preface to *Lyrical Ballads* (1805), edn cit., p. 38.
4. P. B. Shelley, 'A Defence of Poetry', quoted from *Percy Bysshe Shelley: Selected Poetry and Prose*, ed. Alasdair D. F. Macrae (London and New York, 1991), p. 233; Wordsworth, Preface to *Lyrical Ballads*, edn cit., p. 35; Hardy, 'Apology' to *Late Lyrics and Earlier*, in *The Complete Poems*, p. 561.
5. *Life and Work*, p. 49.
6. *Life and Work*, p. 302.
7. *Life and Work*, p. 309.
8. *The Letters of Ezra Pound 1907–1941*, ed. D. D. Paige (New York, 1950), p. 294.
9. *Life and Work*, p. 309.
10. *Life and Work*, p. 310.
11. *Life and Work*, p. 325.
12. *The Complete Poems*, p. 6.
13. *Life and Work*, p. 131.
14. *Collected Letters*, II. 217.
15. *Athenaeum*, 14 January 1899, p. 41.
16. *Saturday Review*, 7 January 1899.
17. *Daily Chronicle*, 21 December 1898.
18. *Westminster Gazette*, 7 January 1899.
19. *Pall Mall Gazette*, 21 July 1890.
20. *Collected Letters*, II. 214.
21. *Life and Work*, pp. 319–25.
22. Jean Brooks, *Thomas Hardy: the Poetic Structure* (London, 1971), p. 131.

8
The Figure of the Singer in the Poetry of Thomas Hardy

Danny Karlin

My title suggests a particular interest in Hardy's poetry, but it is an interest which bears on the work of many other poets. I can best put it in the form of a question: why do poets continue to describe themselves as singers long after poetry ceased to be sung? Apollo's lyre functions as a figure of speech, a metonym for poetry, even in periods when the spectacle of a bard with his lyre, or minstrel with his lute, was ludicrously outdated. Metonymy, taking the part to describe the whole, ought to depend on there being some connection between the two, and when the connection is lost the metonym ought to disappear. But in the case of poetry the opposite seems to have happened. The *Oxford English Dictionary* records the first use of 'lyre' as a figure of speech for poetry in the late seventeenth century, in a poem by Dryden, 'To the Memory of Mr Oldham', dated 1683: 'One common note on either lyre did strike/ And knaves and fools we both abhorred alike'. In 1782 we have William Cowper, writing of 'The painter's pencil, and the poet's lyre'. The same two terms occur Robert Browning's 'A Likeness' (1864), in which two middle-aged artists are chatting about this and that:

> We turn round chairs to the fire,
> Chirp over days in a garret,
> Chuckle o'er increase of salary,
> Taste the good fruits of our leisure,
> Talk about pencil and lyre,
> And the National Portrait Gallery . . .

At least you can say of the term pencil that it still represents something painters actually use, whereas the thought of Browning – or even

Dryden – actually striking a lyre is just not sensible. Yet the stereotype of the poet as bard is deeply ingrained and has probably still not completely disappeared from our collective consciousness. Fans of Asterix the Gaul will recognise a parody of this figure in the tribal bard Cacofonix, who always has to be gagged at the feast lest he sing one of his dreadful compositions. But in fact there's a parody closer to home in Hardy's poem 'The Respectable Burgher on "The Higher Criticism"', in which King David, author of the Psalms, is described as a skilled 'banjo-player'.

To return to Dryden's poem – although the *OED*'s first citation is 1683, other evidence suggests that an earlier date is plausible, and my guess is that the term lyre starts to be used as a figure for poetry in the mid-seventeenth century, around the time of the Restoration. I think this date is significant. It represents a break with the past because of the Interregnum, which not only closed the theatres but brought to an end the last flowering of true lyric poetry in England – poetry, that is, intended from the first to be set to music and sung, rather than recited as speech, let alone printed and read. The Cavalier poets (Carew, Lovelace, Suckling, Herrick) were the last heirs of a tradition extending back through Elizabethan times, back to the troubadours of the Middle Ages and beyond, far past the invention of the printing press and the notion of a *reader* of poetry as opposed to a *listener*. I don't of course mean to suggest that at some fixed moment in literary history poets stopped writing verse to be sung. They continued to do so and are still doing it; arguably our own times are witnessing the return of poetry as song, not only in the work of poets such as Allen Ginsberg, but in that of modern minstrels such as Bob Dylan. What I am talking about is a way of thinking, a preconception about what poetry 'is'.

What is true of the term *lyre* is also true of *song* as meaning poetry or a particular poem, even where there is no question of a musical setting. The *OED*'s first citations here are to Milton, who speaks of his 'adventurous song' in *Paradise Lost* and his search for a fit subject of 'heroic song'. And the first lines of *Paradise Lost* tell us emphatically where this conception comes from:

> Of man' s first disobedience, and the fruit
> Of that forbidden tree, whose mortal taste
> Brought death into the world, and all our woe,
> With loss of Eden, till one greater man
> Restore us, and regain the blissful seat,
> Sing, heavenly muse . . .

Milton is alluding to a classical epic tradition: Virgil's *Arma virumque cano*, 'Arms and the man I sing', and before him, Homer's *Iliad* and *Odyssey*. We know that the earliest poems, like all forms of recorded language, were oral compositions, transmitted across generations and across tribal or national boundaries, mutating as they went so that, when they came eventually to be written down, they consisted of layer upon layer of composition and revision by successive poets. And we know that these early poems were sung, probably to the accompaniment of a musical instrument, but at any rate chanted rather than simply spoken. Poets were indeed bards – like Demodocus, the blind singer at the court of King Alcinous in Book 8 of the *Odyssey*, whom I like to think of as Homer's self-portrait, even though hateful modern scholarship tells us that Homer never existed. Demodocus is the earliest 'figure of the singer' in Western literature, and by being so he perfectly exemplifies one of the paradoxes which lies at the heart of my subject: the paradox of an oral tradition which we know about only because it has been written down.

The epic bard gives the notion of poetry as song tremendous prestige, a prestige which subsequent poets are reluctant to let go, even – or perhaps especially – when its original conditions have long since disappeared. Milton wants to be Demodocus, or Homer, or Virgil, and his poem to be a song, precisely because he was, so to speak, relegated to writing. From the mid-seventeenth century on, you can trace a division between lyric poetry, which is no longer truly lyric, no longer composed to be sung, and songs, which acquire, by another irony of vocabulary, what we call *lyrics* – a term which only came in towards the end of the nineteenth century. The lyrics of a song, as everyone would now confidently state, are not the same thing as a lyric poem, even if that poem can be set to music. Another crucial figure in my forthcoming book will be Robert Burns, because so many of his poems are songs, and in his work the dividing line between *lyric verse* and *song lyric* is revealingly uncertain. The mention of Burns, incidentally, suggests a connection to Hardy's particular interest in these matters, and I'll say more about this in a moment.

The prestige of the epic singer is to do with his divine inspiration. Milton's heavenly muse is a Christian type of the classical goddess, and his poetic ancestors are not just Homer and Virgil but Orpheus and King David. Such poetry is associated with prophecy, with oracles and visions, with divine and magical powers. The song of the poet charms wild beasts, gains him entry into the underworld, drives out evil spirits; it is a sacred art, an emanation of the divinity of nature and the universe.

It is also powerfully erotic, as the Song of Solomon bears witness, or Tennyson's Tithonus, when the lovemaking of a goddess recalls to him the building of the walls of Troy, a passage in which Tennyson manages to convey with Victorian finesse the pleasure of an erection:

> while I lay,
> Mouth, forehead, eyelids, growing dewy-warm
> With kisses balmier than half-opening buds
> Of April, and could hear the lips that kiss'd
> Whispering I knew not what of wild and sweet,
> Like that strange song I heard Apollo sing,
> While Ilion like a mist rose into towers.

I'm sure, incidentally, that Hardy remembered this legend of Apollo's singing, and possibly even Tennyson's lines, when he saw, within the 'very shade' of classical ruins in Rome, the 'singing workmen' building their 'frail new mansion' ('Rome: Building a Street in the Old Quarter'). At any rate the erotic power of song is not exclusively masculine; in 'A Singer Asleep', Hardy's elegy for Swinburne, the presiding genius of song is Sappho, whose art in turn invokes natural and cosmic forces with which female sexuality has traditionally been linked: the sea, the night, the world of spirits and the dead.

It is not surprising that poets should wish to keep hold of an association with song which goes back to the very origins of their art, and which carries with it such powerful connotations of divine authority, potency, and vision. My argument is that the wish became an anxiety during a period which begins, very roughly, with Milton, and ends with a group of poets who straddle the end of the nineteenth century and the beginning of the twentieth: among them Hardy, Yeats, Kipling, and T. S. Eliot. What happened in this period is that poetry lost its status as a dominant, if not *the* dominant literary form, and began the long journey to the margins of culture where it skulks today, alternately boastful, maudlin, and resentful, like the remnant of an aboriginal tribe on a government reservation. Why this loss of empire happened is a fascinating and complex story, far too complex to analyse here, and like all such stories it has several plot-lines twisting and turning around and against each other; there is even an argument that the outcome, far from being a tragedy, has been one of rescue by a *deus ex machina*, literally in this case, the god being Thomas Edison and mechanical salvation coming in the shape of the phonograph or speaking machine, a cylinder covered in tinfoil and turned by a hand-crank, whose patent he applied for in 1877 and which retailed at $18. Nevertheless I think it is no coincidence that poets insisted on identifying themselves – self-consciously, rhetorically – as *singers* at a historical moment of divergence between poetry and song; nor is it a coincidence that this divergence signalled the beginning of the end of poetry's long supremacy, as an art which could encompass every form of knowledge – history, philosophy, cosmology, religion, science – as well as the entire gamut of human emotion, an art which owed its status and its life to the breath of an inspiring god.

Where and how does Hardy fit in to this story? I mentioned just now 'A Singer Asleep', his elegy to Swinburne, and I also spoke of a line of thought suggested by the songs of Robert Burns. The first of these, the elegy, to which I shall return in more detail later on, deploys the 'figure of the singer' in a way which, I may say, gratifyingly conforms to my theory. I look for a fully metaphorical identification of the poet as a singer, and behold! I find him, and with all the classical trimmings. But what the case of Burns suggests does not belong to a theory of high culture, but to the social history of poetry, which is also a crucial element in my story.

The songs which Burns wrote, and I am thinking here both of his original compositions and those which he remade from traditional oral sources – ballads, folk songs, sentimental ditties, comic or satiric songs – had a vigorous, popular, non-textual life, in part because Burns attached them to known, familiar tunes. They became documents of high culture, but also circulated as real songs, to be sung on glee nights in parlours and pubs, at wedding breakfasts and corporation dinners; they went forth and multiplied in thousands of anonymous private drawing-room renditions. Dozens of these songs entered the standard repertoire of popular song in the nineteenth century and the first half of the twentieth. 'My Love is Like a Red, Red Rose' may be, and no doubt has been, the subject of protracted discussion by Formalists, New Critics, Structuralists, Post-Structuralists, New Historicists, and Cultural Materialists, but it has been performed by more singers than all the critics of all these schools put together have had hot dinners. Many of Burns's *poems* are truly, in this sense, *songs*. Now my point about Hardy is not that he wanted, or tried, to write such songs, or that he was 'influenced' by Burns in the way that, for example, he was influenced by Wordsworth, or by Browning. What influenced Hardy was not Burns himself so much as the cultural 'mode' which he so masterfully expounded. We know how much of Hardy's life, from childhood onwards, was spent listening to, and performing, a vast range of sacred and secular songs. Formal and semi-formal singing groups – church choirs, village clubs and musical societies – are only the fountainhead of a river of song which runs through his life and work into an estuary of singing voices, belonging to family, friends, lovers, strangers, some heard intensely and repeatedly during years of relationship, others heard, or overheard, only once in stray encounters. For Hardy, therefore, the figure of the singer is both a figure of speech and a living figure, a man or woman singing, often playing a musical instrument themselves or with a musical accompaniment. The Ballad-Singer at Casterbridge Fair, the Mellstock Quire, the singing girls Sitting on the Bridge who are chased home by their father, the Maid of Keinton Mandeville, the Lady Playing and Singing in the Morning, the Chapel-Organist who commits suicide after her swan-song, the Singing Lovers in the stern of the rowboat, the Prophetess who sings the song called 'The Mocking-Bird', the 'woman's muslined form/ Sing-songing airily' On Stinsford Hill at Midnight, Nell leading 'the songs of long-ago/ She'd learnt from never a book' at The Harvest-Supper, Lizbie Browne and Mad Judy and Julie-Jane, the Phantom Horsewoman in the 1912–13 elegies who 'Draws rein and sings to the swing of the tide', those who 'sing their dearest songs' During Wind and Rain, the convict At the Railway Station, Upway, who, when the little boy plays his violin for him, sings 'With grimfu! glee: "This life so free/ Is the thing for me!"', the unseen lady whose playing and singing the poet hears On the Esplanade, the two fiddlers and the singer who stand with their backs to the sea At the Aquatic Sports, the tramp who breaks into 'thin song' as he enters the workhouse at Christmastide . . . these singers, and there are dozens more of them, populate Hardy's poems at every level of significance, of narrative or dramatic importance; some are divas and movie stars, others no more than extras in a street-scene; sometimes the songs they sing are central to a plot or an epiphany, at other times they are just stock parts of the landscape. But if there is a theme which preponderates it is, as you might expect, that of human relationships, of friendship or sexual love, and particularly that most Hardyesque of associations between desire and memory – here, for example, in 'The Change':

> In that week there was heard a singing –
>   Who shall spell the years, the years! –
> In that week there was heard a singing,
>   And the white owl wondered why.
> In that week, yea, a voice was ringing,
>   And forth from the casement were candles flinging
> Radiance that fell on the deodar and lit up the path thereby.

> Could that song have a mocking note? –
>   Who shall unroll the years O! –
> Could that song have a mocking note
>   To the white owl's sense as it fell?
> Could that song have a mocking note
>   As it trilled out warm from the singer's throat,
> And who was the mocker and who the mocked when two felt
>   all was well?

This motif of remembered song, and of a friend's or a lover's singing as part of that which is forgone by separation, or loss of love, or death, comes in many other poems: in 'Molly Gone':

> No more singing by Molly to me
>   In the evenings when she
> Was in mood and in voice . . .

– in 'Lost Love':

> I sing my songs once more,
>   And presently hear
>   His footstep near
>   As if it would stay;
>   But he goes his way
> And shuts a distant door.

– again, in 'An Upbraiding':

> Now l am dead you sing to me
>   The songs we used to know,
> But while I lived you had no wish
>   Or care for doing so.

– and again in 'Seeing the Moon Rise':

> We used to go to Froom-hill Barrow
>   To see the round moon rise
>   Into the heath-rimmed skies,
> Trudging thither by plough and harrow
> Up the pathway steep and narrow,
>   Singing a song.
> Now we do not go there. Why?
>   Zest burns not so high!

– and one more example, from 'A Wet August':

> Nine drops of water bead the jessamine,
> And nine-and-ninety smear the stones and tiles:
> – 'Twas not so in that August – full-rayed, fine –
> When we lived out-of-doors, sang songs, strode miles.

That last instance (again, there are many more to choose from) is reveal-ing just because it is so brief, and takes its place in the line with such an unselfconscious air. And all these instances of singing draw atten-tion to the enormous change in social culture which has come about since Hardy's time: it is now an uncommon, and not an ordinary house-hold which sings to entertain itself or its neighbours, and though we may like to think we have a thriving amateur music scene, it has only a fraction of the social presence it had for Hardy and his readers. Need-less to say the decline in churchgoing, in the sung liturgy and the singing of hymns and psalms plays a part in this story. Hardy's sense of why such singing matters is acutely caught in 'Afternoon Service at Mellstock', where the speaker recalls not pleasure or devotion but soporific routine:

> On afternoons of drowsy calm
>   We stood in the panelled pew,
> Singing one-voiced a Tate-and-Brady psalm
>   To the tune of 'Cambridge New'.
>
> We watched the elms, we watched the rooks,
>   The clouds upon the breeze,
> Between the whiles of glancing at our books,
>   And swaying like the trees.
>
> So mindless were those outpourings! –
>   Though I am not aware
> That I have gained by subtle thought on things
>   Since we stood psalming there.

The poem turns on the distance between a remembered 'we', the choir which sang 'one-voiced' – the term suggests both harmony and mo-notony – and the solitary 'I', whose 'subtle thought' does not give him access to meanings which are embedded in the 'mindless outpourings' of the past. These meanings are not religious, or at any rate not doctrinal; they manifest themselves in the connection between the children singing and the natural world outside. A wonderfully acute 'moment of vision' catches the children swaying to and fro as they go through their mechanical exercise, a gesture which anyone who has been to a church or synagogue will immediately recognise, yet the gesture is also that of the trees swaying in the wind, an image not only of natural but spiritual grace, since the breeze is also the spirit which, as the scripture says, 'bloweth where it listeth' (John 3: 8).

The formative, profound, and pervasive influence of song in Hardy has another aspect, not that of subject matter but of form. The figure of the singer in this sense is that of a poet who thinks in lyric forms, whether religious or secular, classical or modern, from high or low culture. There is, as I have indicated, a long list of poems in which songs and singers appear, including 44 where the word 'song' appears in the title or subtitle, but these are a fraction of the poems where 'lyric' (in the strict sense of the term) is the keynote of the poem's form. The hymn, the popular ballad, the classical ode, the modern *Lied*, the comic or sentimental or drinking song, all contribute to the shape of his poetry – its utter devotion to rhyme, for example a tiny handful of blank verse or unrhymed poems outside *The Dynasts* – and not just to rhyme, but to the recurring metrical forms of stanzas and strophes, and to refrains and other stock devices of repetition.

Hardy's poetry, then, is impregnated with song – and I ought to add here that I haven't even mentioned the song of birds, which opens up a whole other line of literal and figurative meanings of song, some of them, as in the magnificent early poem 'Shelley's Skylark', directly to do with poetry. For the poet can be figured as a singing-bird, a 'proud songster' to use the title of another poem, or, as the poet's vulgar widow in 'I Rose Up as My Custom Is' dismissively terms her late husband, a 'romantic chanticleer', a cock crowing on an idealistic dunghill. The figure of the singer, the metaphorical persona of the poet, is therefore a figure in a crowd. The concept of poetry as *figurative* song is present in Hardy's work, but it has to take account of the lived experience of singing, so that for him to call a poem a song is more than conforming to a cultural stereotype; it is a more conscious, a more deliberate aesthetic choice.

If we look at the poems where Hardy does make this choice, several patterns become visible. To begin with there is a strong association with Romantic poetry. 'Shelley's Skylark' is part of this association, and Shelley and Keats are the 'matchless singers' whose graves Hardy visited in Rome, 'At the Pyramid of Cestius'. In a later poem 'At a House in

Hampstead', Hardy concludes that Keats's English home is, after all, a fitter place of pilgrimage than his Italian grave, because, although 'never a nightingale pours one/ Full-throated sound', still it is 'Pleasanter now . . . to hold/ That here, where sang he, more of him/ Remains than where he, tuneless, cold,/ Passed to the dim'.

Romantic poets are singers because their poetry is inspired, unconstrained, passionate, because it affirms, or reaffirms, the status of poetry as the highest form of artistic expression. Hardy is drawn to it, believing, as so many post-Romantic poets believed, that his own art was necessarily subordinate, alienated, and orphaned. I am not saying that Romantic poetry was in fact what Hardy believed it to be. Arguably Keats and Shelley were as anxious as Hardy, as embattled as he in their thinking about poetry. After all it was Shelley who was stung into writing a *Defence of Poetry* against his friend Thomas Love Peacock's stinging satire 'The Four Ages of Poetry', which argued that poetry was a relic of irrational, barbaric times, unfitted to deal with the modern world. The *Defence of Poetry*, by a pleasing coincidence, was not published until after Shelley's death, and first appeared in 1840 – the year Thomas Hardy was born. Hardy was well equipped to take up the cudgels for Shelley's flaming idealism, but there were also moments in which he saw the force of Peacock's argument. In a late poem, 'He Inadvertently Cures His Love-Pains', a title which strongly suggests that Hardy had been casting a beady eye over some of Yeats's early verse, the poet satirises his own Romantic art:

> I said: 'O let me sing the praise
> Of her who sweetly racks my days, –
>   Her I adore,
> Her lips, her eyes, her moods, her ways!'
>
> In miseries of pulse and pang
> I strung my harp, and straightway sang
>   As none before: –
> To wondrous words my quavers rang!

Clearly we're not asked to take the vocabulary seriously here: this poet is indeed a 'romantic chanticleer', and the image of him stringing his harp is burlesque. But that's not quite the whole story. The rest of the poem tells what happened as a result of all the wondrous quavering:

Thus I let heartaches lilt my verse,
Which suaged and soothed, and made disperse
    The smarts I bore
To stagnance like a sepulchre's.

But, eased, the days that thrilled ere then
Lost value; and I ask, O when,
    And how, restore
Those old sweet agonies again!

Romantic poetry plays a rather cruel practical joke on the lover here. It all turns on a shift of meaning in a small word, 'let'. The poem begins: 'I said "O let me sing the praise/ Of her who sweetly racks my days".' But it goes on 'Thus I let heartaches lilt my verse.' What began as a prayer, or a noble resolve, becomes a mistake which the lover doesn't realise he is committing until it is too late. 'Let me do this' implies power, or at least an active will; 'I let this happen to me' implies weakness. Poetry assuages, and in so doing cancels, the feelings which made him want to write in the first place. The irony of this process is emphasised by the fact that the poem, which is supposed to be about song, flatly opens with the words 'I said'. But if we go back to a much earlier poem, 'Her Initials', we find a different slant on this question:

Upon a poet's page I wrote
Of old two letters of her name;
Part seemed she of the effulgent thought
Whence that high singer's rapture came.
– When now I turn the leaf the same
Immortal light illumes the lay,
But from the letters of her name
The radiance has waned away!

This is a fiendishly complex little poem. To begin with it juxtaposes two kinds of writing: the printed words on the 'poet's page', and the initials which the lover adds to them. The woman's abbreviated name is, the lover believes, a sign of the 'effulgent thought' which inspired the 'high singer's rapture', as if she were the poet's Muse. But this can't be true, of course; it is a delusion, though different in kind from the delusion of the lover in 'He Inadvertently Cures His Love-Pains', because it is the

delusion of a reader and not a writer. In 'Her Initials' the lover associates his beloved with a quality which is, so to speak, both inside and
outside the poetry which he admires. When he uses the phrase 'that
high singer's rapture', does he mean the feeling with which the poet
composed his poem, or the feeling which it inspires in his readers? Similarly, the 'Immortal light' which 'illumes the lay' long after his love has
faded – is that a quality which belongs to the poem, or is it shed by the
'effulgent thought' which gave rise to it?

At the heart of this ambiguity is a question about what a poem is and
what it is for. The word 'rapture' is significant here because of a poem
which Hardy would have known well, Robert Browning's 'Home-
Thoughts, from Abroad'. The speaker of Browning's poem hears a 'wise
thrush' who 'sings each song twice over/ Lest you should think he never
could recapture/ The first fine careless rapture'. Again, the word 'rapture'
equivocates between different meanings: the pleasure the bird takes in
singing, the perfection of the song itself, the enrapturing effect it has
on the listener. Why is the thrush 'wise'? Because he has a lesson to
teach us, the lesson that he, at least, can perfectly imitate, perfectly
reproduce himself. His song is, to use the title of another Hardy poem,
the 'selfsame song':

> A bird sings the selfsame song,
> With never a fault in its flow,
> That we listened to here those long
>   Long years ago.
>
> A pleasing marvel is how
> A strain of such rapturous rote
> Should have gone on thus till now
>   Unchanged in a note!
>
> – But it's not the selfsame bird. –
> No: perished to dust is he. . . .
> As also are those who heard
>   That song with me.

The pathos of this poem shouldn't blind us to its sharp distinction
between the 'selfsame bird' and the 'selfsame song'. One partakes of
human fragility, the other (like the 'poet's page') is always immortal and
unchanging, a quality beautifully summed up in the phrase 'rapturous
rote', which glances again at the song of Browning's thrush. What the

thrush does instantaneously – singing each song twice over – is also what the bird does generically, across time, its individuality of no account in comparison with its art. It shouldn't surprise us to find the source of this idea in Romantic poetry, indeed in the most famous of all poems about the rapture of birdsong and the fleetingness of individual human life, Keats's 'Ode to a Nightingale':

> Thou wast not born for death, immortal Bird!
> No hungry generations tread thee down,
> The voice I hear this passing night was heard
> In ancient days by emperor and clown:
> Perhaps the self-same song that found a path
> Through the sad heart of Ruth, when, sick for home,
> She stood in tears amid the alien corn;
> The same that oft times hath
> Charmed magic casements, opening on the foam
> Of perilous seas, in faery lands forlorn.

> Forlorn! the very word is like a bell
> To toll me back from thee to my sole self!

This is the climax of Keats's poem – the descent, abrupt and terrible, from the bird's 'self-same song' to his own 'sole self'. The song of the nightingale sublimely encompasses classical and biblical history, embraces the extremes of the social scale, and makes its way to the heart of our imaginative life. The 'sad heart of Ruth' recalls the aching heart of the poet with which the ode famously begins ('My heart aches, and a drowsy numbness pains/My sense, as though of hemlock I had drunk'). Ruth is like the poet in her solitude and alienation; but we need also to think of the end of the biblical story. Ruth does not remain 'amid the alien corn'. Rescued by Boaz, she becomes the mother of a line which culminates in the house of David. The nightingale's song prophesies the birth of the greatest singer of all, the singer of the Psalms. Keats views himself, in relation to Ruth, with sublime self-pity, not foreseeing, or not admitting, that the prophecy of immortal fame might actually apply to him.

For Hardy, too, the prestige of a certain kind of poetry, the poetry which could be figured as song, lies in its immunity to time, its indifference to the 'self', even the self which produces it. But in the 'Ode to a Nightingale', indifference to human individuality is only one side of the story; the other is a revelation of the poet's all-too-human, passionate and sensuous self. The result is an extraordinary combination of passionate resistance and imaginative striving within a sublime equanimity of form. The great poised stanzas, classically flawless and graceful in the performance of their intricate metrical dance, are simultaneously the expression of a violent, anguished, rebellious, unaccommodated spirit. I believe that Hardy was incapable of such an aesthetic conciliation, and so the figure of the singer who is central to his thinking is not Keats but Swinburne, not a figure of poise but of continuing struggle. It is to this figure, as it appears in the poem 'A Singer Asleep', that I now turn.

> In this fair niche above the unslumbering sea,
> That sentrys up and down all night, all day,
> From cove to promontory, from ness to bay,
> The Fates have fitly bidden that he should be
> > Pillowed eternally.

cf Felicia Hemans's "The Last Song of Sappho"

> – It was as though a garland of red roses
> Had fallen about the hood of some smug nun
> When irresponsibly dropped as from the sun,
> In fulth of numbers freaked with musical closes,
> > Upon Victoria's formal middle time
> > His leaves of rhythm and rhyme.

> O that far morning of a summer day
> When, down a terraced street whose pavements lay
> Glassing the sunshine into my bent eyes,
> I walked and read with a quick glad surprise
> > New words, in classic guise, –

> The passionate pages of his earlier years,
> Fraught with hot sighs, sad laughters, kisses, tears;
> Fresh-fluted notes, yet from a minstrel who
> Blew them not naively, but as one who knew
> > Full well why thus he blew.

> I still can hear the brabble and the roar
> At those thy tunes, O still one, now passed through
> That fitful fire of tongues then entered new!
> Their power is spent like spindrift on this shore;
> > Thine swells yet more and more.

– His singing-mistress verily was no other
Than she the Lesbian, she the music-mother
Of all the tribe that feel in melodies;
Who leapt, love-anguished, from the Leucadian steep
Into the rambling world-encircling deep
      Which hides her where none sees.

And one can hold in thought that nightly here
His phantom may draw down to the water's brim,
And hers come up to meet it, as a dim
Lone shine upon the heaving hydrosphere,
And mariners wonder as they traverse near,
      Unknowing of her and him.

One dreams him sighing to her spectral form:
'O teacher, where lies hid thy burning line;
Where are those songs, O poetess divine
Whose very orts are love incarnadine?'
And her smile back: 'Disciple true and warm,
      Sufficient now are thine.' . . .

So here, beneath the waking constellations,
Where the waves peal their everlasting strains,
And their dull subterrene reverberations
Shake him when storms make mountains of their plains –
Him once their peer in sad improvisations,
And deft as wind to cleave their frothy manes –
I leave him, while the daylight gleam declines
      Upon the capes and chines.

If this poem is a masterpiece, as I believe it is, it is certainly not one of smooth and consistent workmanship. On the contrary, it is formally, thematically, and stylistically irregular, though not for that reason incoherent. The stanzas vary in length and rhyme scheme; the poet begins by speaking about Swinburne in the third person, turns to address him directly in the fifth stanza, then reverts to talking about him; stanza 6 signals an abrupt change of topic, in which Swinburne's place in contemporary literary history, and in Hardy's own emotional and intellectual life, is replaced by a meditation on his affiliation to Sappho and a vision of their ghostly colloquy; the last stanza grandly states 'So here . . . I leave him', which sounds consequential but isn't, and implies that the poet had the option of not leaving him, which he doesn't. The poem's verbal texture is rough even by Hardy's standards. Lytton Strachey, writing in 1914, shuddered at the word 'naively', in line 4 of the fourth stanza, complaining that it was 'a horrid hybrid . . . a neologism exactly calculated to make [Swinburne,] the classic author of *Atalanta* turn in his grave'; and he might have added that it sticks out like a metrical sore thumb. Then there are the spiky Saxon words ('ness', 'fulth', 'freaked', 'brabble', 'chines') battling it out with sonorous Latin and Greek ('hydrosphere', 'incarnadine', 'subterrene reverberations'). Although some of these words, such as 'freaked', which you might think of as peculiarly Hardyesque, actually turn up in Swinburne, and indeed come from poems thematically akin to 'A Singer Asleep', nevertheless, to any reader familiar with Swinburne's poetry the effect is bizarrely mixed. The poem pays him homage, borrowing in multiple ways from his own elegies for other poets such as Baudelaire, Walter Savage Landor, and Victor Hugo, invoking his beloved Sappho and his characteristic imagery of the sea, of flowers, and of music; yet the result remains Hardyesque, so that, for example, the line 'fulth of numbers freaked with musical closes' manages both to describe Swinburne's poetry with superb accuracy and yet to stand out as a line which an infinite number of Swinburnes pounding on typewriters for all eternity would never have produced.

What are we to make of all this? We ought to take note of the explicit warning in the fourth stanza. Like Swinburne, Hardy is not blowing these 'Fresh-fluted notes' naively, he knows what he is doing. If the poem is irregular, it is the 'cunning irregularity' which Hardy identified in his dictated biography as the essence of 'the Gothic art-principle in which he had been trained – the principle of spontaneity'.[1] Suppose we look again at the apparently haphazard structure of the poem. It is framed by a shift from the third person to the first, and this shift is accompanied by a dramatic change in the imagery of the sea. The opening stanza is impersonal, dogmatic, and lapidary, like an inscription on a tombstone:

> In this fair niche above the unslumbering sea,
> That sentrys up and down all night, all day,
> From cove to promontory, from ness to bay,
> The Fates have fitly bidden that he should be
>   Pillowed eternally.

Why is it fitting that Swinburne should fall asleep above the 'unslumbering sea'? The sea is like a sentry guarding his tomb, perhaps in honour of the many poems he wrote about it; but the image is of a routine, a perpetual recurrence and redundance, 'From cove to promontory, from ness to bay', where 'from ness to bay' just means 'and back again'. The tide, you might say, sings a selfsame song, 'all night, all day', rocking Swinburne in eternal passivity. It is the Fates who have bidden this, not Hardy; for the poem ends on a different note:

> So here, beneath the waking constellations,
> Where the waves peal their everlasting strains,
> And their dull subterrene reverberations
> Shake him when storms make mountains of their plains –
> Him once their peer in sad improvisations,
> And deft as wind to cleave their frothy manes –
> I leave him, while the daylight gleam declines
>   Upon the capes and chines.

How different a word *waking* is from *unslumbering*! And what a different image, both of the sea and Swinburne, do we get from these lines! Instead of the dull routine of a sentry, we have the peal of 'everlasting strains', the noise and physical violence of storms, the 'frothy manes' of the white horses of the waves; most important of all, the sea has become an element of freedom, of unexpectedness, and Swinburne's verse matches its 'sad improvisations'. The final image of the poet is not of sleep but of action, not 'pillowed' but 'cleaving' the waves like the wind. The Fates have disappeared from the scene, which closes with an image of personal and human transience: 'So here . . . I leave him, while the daylight gleam declines'. It is a gesture both of authority and humility, by which Hardy, unlike Keats in 'Ode to a Nightingale', leaves the singer instead of being left or abandoned. Keats, remember, closes his ode with the song of the nightingale fading from his grasp:

> Adieu! adieu! Thy plaintive anthem fades
>   Past the near meadows, over the still stream,
>   Up the hill-side; and now 'tis buried deep
>   In the next valley-glades:
>   Was it a vision, or a waking dream?
>   Fled is that music . . . Do I wake or sleep?

Whatever Hardy has lost in comparison to Keats, at any rate he chooses rather than accepts his fate, closes not with a question but an observation grounded in the natural world and bearing the hallmark of his precise notation of landscape: the 'capes' which project outwards and the 'chines' or fissures in the cliff which project inward. It is an observation different in focus and intensity from the way the tide is seen earlier sentrying to and fro. In every sense the last stanza revises and answers the first, so that the poem is itself a dynamic event, and not a static memorial.

This process begins in the second stanza with a movement away from the grand abstraction of 'the Fates' and the grand sonority of 'unslumbering' and 'Pillowed eternally', to historical circumstance and individual life. Hardy records a general historical moment, that of 'Victoria's formal middle time', the years 1865 and 1866 when Swinburne published his first 'leaves of rhythm and rhyme', the lyric drama *Atalanta in Calydon* and the first series of *Poems and Ballads*. But Hardy also records a moment of personal revelation, and here, along with the 'Ode to a Nightingale' I think he alludes to another poem by Keats, the sonnet 'On First Looking into Chapman's Homer'. Keats's poem, too, is about the first encounter with a great writer, and famously ends with the image of the astronomer and discoverer of new worlds:

> Then felt I like some watcher of the skies
>   When a new planet swims into his ken;
> Or like stout Cortez when with eagle eyes
>   He stared at the Pacific, and all his men
> Looked at each other with a wild surmise –
>   Silent, upon a peak in Darien.

The scene in Hardy's poem is different because the watcher is looking not up but down, and the light which dazzles him, metaphorically the light of the poet – remember the 'effulgent thought' and 'Immortal light' of 'Her Initials' – this light is reflected into his face off the pavement as he walks along, his head bent over the book. I think it is at least plausible that Hardy deliberately inverted Keats's imagery, and yet the affinity between the two poems is stronger than the difference. The explorer's 'wild surmise' becomes the 'quick glad surprise' of the reader who discovers, as Keats did with Chapman's translation, a world which had been there all the time but was new to him, 'new words in classic guise'.

What did this discovery mean to Hardy? In the fourth stanza he praises Swinburne for two apparently opposite qualities, passion and deliberation. He is referring specifically to the early poetry, emphasising that Swinburne's emotionalism was part of a radical poetic design; already the focus has widened from Hardy's close-up of himself walking and reading. In making a positive critical judgement about Swinburne, Hardy ranges himself against the Philistines, whose 'brabble' and 'roar' he remembers as vividly as the verse itself; but the retrospective vision of elegy comes into play here, because Hardy can cast himself forward in time, 40 years past the 'fitful fire of tongues' through which Swinburne had to pass in a kind of anti-Pentecostal ordeal. He celebrates not just the first appearance of Swinburne's poems, but their triumph through time, their overcoming in a human struggle, and it is this triumph which prompts him to address Swinburne directly, the only stanza of the poem in which he does so.

Then, at the moment of victory, Hardy turns from one kind of time to another – from contemporary history to a myth of literary origins. And the mode of the poem also changes, from personal memory and judgement to visionary speculation, in which the 'I' becomes 'one' – 'one can hold in thought' . . . 'One dreams him sighing'. This 'one' is neither Hardy alone, nor an impersonal third party, but a fusion of the two, an extension of the poet's 'sole self' into a kind of collective fantasy. In this fantasy, Sappho communes with Swinburne – ancient with modern, sea with land, female with male, hidden with revealed, frag-mentary and fugitive with fullness and permanence. Swinburne's rela-tionship to Sappho is that of a disciple, a son, a lover, but above all an inheritor and fulfiller. The 'leaves' of his poetry which 'irresponsibly dropped as from the sun' are now bound into books, his 'Fresh-fluted notes' are fixed in songs, whereas Sappho's verses are lost, and we have only 'orts', fragments of her poems, just as her body is lost in the 'world-encircling deep' while Swinburne's has been found a 'niche' on earth. Yet it is her 'burning line' which kindles the living, the 'true and warm' songs of her successor, and they meet on the shoreline, the threshold between their different worlds.

The dead are restless in Hardy's poetry, we know that well; but they are not 'unslumbering', not mechanically wakeful. The only way Hardy can 'leave' Swinburne at the end of the poem is not to leave him be, not to allow him to rest, but to imagine him shaken by the echo of the sea's 'everlasting strains', which are figuratively the sound of his own poems – the waves, the sea-swell, whose power 'swells yet more and more'. His death, unlike Sappho's suicide, is not a sign of tragic loss but of endless consummation.

Hardy safeguards himself from the charge of triumphalism by making the climactic scene of the poem a matter of speculation rather than assertion: it is something 'one can hold in thought' rather than a fact to which he bears personal witness, as he does with regard to the historical reception of Swinburne's poetry in the mid-century. Nevertheless I take the poem to be a gesture of faith in poetry as song; not that Hardy is unaware of the difficulty of making such a gesture, in the early years of the twentieth century, nor of the irony which might shadow it; but he doesn't shrink from it either. Swinburne embodies, with as much force as Hardy can summon, the 'figure of the singer' in his glory. But I remember also those other singers, with whom I began this discussion – not the high singers, or the matchless singers, or the proud songsters, or the singing-mistresses, but the ones who sing at fairs and on street corners, glimpsed from a doorway or at a lighted window; and among these singers is Hardy himself, as he appears in 'Song to an Old Burden':

> The voice is heard in the room no longer
> That trilled, none sweetlier,
> To gentle stops or stronger,
> Where now the dust-draped cobwebs stir:
> Shall I then sing again again again
> As once I sang with her!

We think the question in the last lines of the stanza is a rhetorical question, that the answer is obvious; but the poem, after all, is called a 'song', and the singer, though he can no longer sing the *selfsame song* as he sang in the past, is singing to us, if we have the ears to hear him.

Note

1. *The Life and Work of Thomas Hardy, by Thomas Hardy*, ed. Michael Millgate (London, 1984), p. 323.

9

Thomas Hardy's Narrative Art: the Poems and Short Stories

Douglas Dunn

Hardy was such a productive writer that I can hardly hope to do full and proper justice to my subject. *The Complete Stories,*[1] in Professor Page's edition, runs to some 839 pages of text, or about 50 tales, and I don't need to emphasise Hardy's plurality of poems. It's best summed up for me by Christopher Ricks in his essay 'A Note on Hardy's "A Spellbound Palace"', where he writes that, 'A friend of mine, when I recently presented him with "A Spellbound Palace", said, with simple truth, "There's *always* another Hardy poem"'.[2] There may even be a note of irritation in this constant discovery of '*another* Hardy poem'. However, for those of us who can't get enough of Hardy's poetry, the bottomlessness of *The Complete Poems* is a delight and fascination rather than an annoyance. It's when you find yourself having to write about them that the astonishing numerousness of his poems becomes – not irritating, but humbling, and perhaps even baffling.

Although not the first of his published stories, 'The Three Strangers'[3] is especially interesting in that it contains a poem, or, rather, a song, '*As sung by* MR CHARLES CHARRINGTON *in the play of "The Three Wayfarers"'*, indicated beneath the title of 'The Stranger's Song' in *The Complete Poems.*[4] So, this is a work that appeared in three ways. First, it was published as a tale in *Longman's Magazine* in March 1883, and reprinted in *Wessex Tales* (1888). At the suggestion of J. M. Barrie it was made into a one-act play and performed for a brief period at the Terry Theatre in London in 1893. Then the lyric parts of an otherwise balladic prose narrative appeared in *Wessex Poems*. While the presence of the song is in itself effective as a narrative device – through it Hardy reveals the second stranger at the Fennels' christening party as a hangman – its impact and effectiveness are increased by the delays in its distribution of episodes and revelations. Hardy was too traditional a storyteller, too much in tune with the people about whom and for whom he was writing, to permit the song to be sung all at once. Instead, the narrative insists on purposeful postponements and surprises. Here, though, is the song.

THE STRANGER'S SONG

(As sung by MR CHARLES CHARRINGTON *in the play of*
'The Three Wayfarers')

O my trade it is the rarest one,
      Simple shepherds all –
 My trade it is a sight to see;
For my customers I tie, and take 'em up on high,
 And waft 'em to a far countree!

My tools are but the common ones,
      Simple shepherds all –
 My tools are no sight to see:
A little hempen string, and a post whereon to swing
 Are implements enough for me!

Tomorrow is my working day,
      Simple shepherds all –
 Tomorrow is a working day for me:
For the farmer's sheep is slain, and the lad who did it ta'en,
 And on his soul may God ha' mer-cy!

It is artfully contrived as entirely appropriate for the mouth of who sings it in the story, and for the inhabitants of a remote and rural farm who listen to it; all the cleverness in the world would fail to achieve that naturalness without there being present in the writer a familiarity and loyalty to place and community so confirmed as to function at the level of instinct. And that's what I mean when I claim that Hardy was a traditional storyteller. In his essay 'The Storyteller', first published in 1936 as an introduction to a collection of the Russian writer, Leskov, Walter Benjamin found it possible to say: 'Familiar though his name may be to us, the storyteller in his living immediacy is by no means a present force. He has already become something remote from us and something that is getting even more distant.' A few pages later he becomes more pessimistic. 'The art of storytelling', he writes, 'is reaching its end because the epic side of truth, wisdom, is dying out.' And he continues:

This, however, is a process that has been going on for a long time. And nothing would be more fatuous than to want to see in it merely a 'symptom of decay', let alone a 'modern' symptom. It is, rather, only a concomitant symptom of the secular productive forces of history, a concomitant that has quite gradually removed narrative from the realm of living speech and at the same time is making it possible to see a new beauty in what is vanishing.[5]

It seems to me that in his earlier stories Hardy is very aware of 'the realm of living speech', and of 'the epic side of truth, wisdom'. He asserts his authority as a storyteller of that place, although looking backwards in time, through the use of dialect, but especially through the kind of narrative he is writing. It has the symmetry and inevitability of ballad – three strangers, three knockings on the door, the discovery that the second arrival is the hangman, the false assumption that the third is an escaped prisoner, and the surprise that it is the first stranger who is the escaped prisoner awaiting execution in Casterbridge jail and that the third stranger is, in fact, the brother of the first. The crime was sheep-stealing, so the story also carries, although lightly, a burden of social comment. Much of that authority is conveyed by phrasemaking and descriptive touches in the writing. But while it is 'living speech' in the sense that it is closely in touch with the community it evokes, Hardy's prose outside of dialogue is more written than spoken, or to use terms coined apparently by critics of African-American writing, more writerly than speakerly. Consider this extract, for example, where the first stranger is introduced, but some time before he enters Higher Crowstairs, so that the reader sees him before the Fennels and their friends:

It was nearly the time of the full moon, and on this account, though the sky was lined with a uniform sheet of dripping cloud, ordinary objects out of doors were readily visible. The sad wan light revealed the lonely pedestrian to be a man of supple frame; his gait suggested that he had somewhat passed the period of perfect and instinctive agility, though not so far as to be otherwise than rapid of motion when occasion required. At a rough guess he might have been about forty years of age. He appeared tall, but a recruiting sergeant, or other person accustomed to the judging of men's heights by the eye, would have discerned that this was chiefly owing to his gauntness, and that he was not more than five-feet-eight or nine.

Notwithstanding the regularity of his tread there was caution in it, as in that of one who mentally feels his way; and despite the fact that it was not a black coat nor a dark garment of any sort that he wore, there was something about him which suggested that he naturally belonged to the black-coated tribes of men. His clothes were of fustian, and his boots hobnailed, yet in his progress he showed not the mud-accustomed bearing of hobnailed and fustian peasantry.[6]

Hardy's prose here is wonderfully measured, and although we haven't yet met the hangman, the one who turns out to be the escaped prisoner is described as if *he* were the executioner. At the same time Hardy comes close to giving the game away. If the reader remembers that passage I've just quoted, then, along with other clues – he's a pipe-smoker, but doesn't have a pipe or tobacco, for example – as soon as the mead-swilling hangman reveals who he is, a slightly confused or agitated atmosphere of suspicion surely arises.

But the skill of that passage, and the story's date (late 1870s, early 1880s) should remind us that Hardy had been a professional novelist for around ten years, even if *The Mayor of Casterbridge, Jude the Obscure* and *Tess of the d'Urbervilles* were still to come. My point is that for Hardy the short story was not the site of apprentice work as it has been for many more modern writers (or as it was for R. L. Stevenson, for example, in Hardy's younger lifetime). Indeed, unless you take seriously such antics as sound poetry, concrete poetry, cyberpoetry, and so on, then the literary short story is the newest of literary forms. Sir Walter Scott's 'The Two Drovers' is credited with being the first, but that forgets Pushkin, although Pushkin was much influenced by Scott's narrative poems and novels. The form had been in existence for only 60 or so years when Hardy wrote 'The Three Strangers'. Its development in Europe and America was of course stimulated by the demands of a market in the form of the magazines from which writers like R. L. Stevenson and Hardy made much of their livelihood. Even more important, though, is that the short story in a sense had *always* existed except that it was expressed in verse, the chief medium of literature until the mid-to-late seventeenth century. I know of eighteenth-century chapbooks by Dugald Graham, the 'Skellit Bellman' of Glasgow – the Glasgow town-crier – and they are short prose tales, crudely written, but interesting enough for all that. There must be lots more from other parts of the island, waiting for a brass-bowelled scholar immune to book-dust to sift through and make a claim for the earlier, non-literary origins of the prose tale as a written form designed to be appropriated by the purchaser probably for spoken performance and adaptation.

Hardy came to the short story after considerable experience as a novelist and as a poet. This may not strike us as in any way remarkable, but there is at least one sense in which it is. 'What differentiates the novel from all other forms of prose literature', Walter Benjamin wrote in the essay from which I have already quoted,

> – the fairy tale, the legend, even the novella – is that it neither comes from oral tradition nor goes into it. This distinguishes it from storytelling in particular. The storyteller takes what he tells from experience – his own or that reported by others. And he in turn makes it the experience of those who are listening to his tale. The novelist has isolated himself. The birthplace of the novel is the solitary individual, who is no longer able to express himself by giving examples of his most important concerns, is himself uncounseled, and cannot counsel others.[7]

'Oral tradition' is quite clearly foregrounded in many of Hardy's stories. For example, the very last sentence of 'The Three Strangers' reads: 'But the arrival of the three strangers at the shepherd's that night, and the details connected therewith, is a story as well known as ever in the country about Higher Crowstairs.' And I feel convinced that Hardy really enjoyed the resonance of that sentence. Above all, he enjoyed forging that link, whether through invention or re-telling, with 'a story as well known as ever'. Indeed, one of the most fascinating aspects of Hardy's writing as a whole is his status as a 'tradition-carrier', as they say of traditional singers and storytellers in Scotland and Ireland, especially in Gaelic culture and the balladists of the travellers. Written literature, the expression of High Culture, has much room for tradition-carriers too, for chroniclers of place and community. Similarly, at the end of 'The Melancholy Hussar of the German Legion',[8] Hardy concludes with a nod to 'the epic side of truth, wisdom', to the invaluableness of communal epic, when he writes: 'The older villagers, however, who know of the episode from their parents, still recollect the place where the soldiers lie. Phyllis lies near.'[9] Also, it is Phyllis, cruelly thwarted in love, who has told the story to the narrator, presumably when she was very old and the narrator very young, a feature of Hardy's earlier tales shared by J. M. Barrie's of the 1880s which were founded on stories told to him by his mother. But the short story has always been much involved with memory. Part of its business has been the chronicles of the tribe, from Scott's 'The Two Drovers', James Hogg's and John Galt's stories, Hawthorne's, Turgenev's, Chekhov's, or Sherwood

Anderson's *Winesburg, Ohio*, William Faulkner's stories, Dylan Thomas's early stories of the Jarvis Valley (and also *Portrait of the Artist as a Young Dog*), and through to some more recent writers.

John Bayley once described poems by Hardy – he mentions 'The Frozen Greenhouse' – as 'sung short stories'. (Incidentally, I've quoted his delightful phrase so often that it's high time I sent Professor Bayley an acknowledgement.) While it can apply to a great many of Hardy's poems, though far from all, it makes especial sense when thinking about such poems as 'A Trampwoman's Tragedy', which like his poems of Wessex traditions and memories from far back, stems from the same source as his stories and fiction in general.

As storytelling, 'A Trampwoman's Tragedy' is masterly in its unfolding of one of Hardy's habitual concerns – mistakes in love and their consequences. There would seem to be little more to be said. Reading Hardy's notes to the poem (dated April 1902) suggests that it could be an example of his archaeological imagination playing over recollections of local materials and family memories. Blue Jimmy in the tenth stanza is said to have stolen a horse belonging to a neighbour of Hardy's grandfather. Any memory at all can result in a poem, but this particular memory seems a bit unimportant, although perhaps not to a writer like Hardy with his fascination for memories and for hangings. It's a haunted poem, with a haunting in it. Strangely, too, it permits Hardy to use balladic speech to an extent that he could never quite get into the narrative parts of his stories. He had too much prose experience for that to be entirely possible in his tales where his best touches are literary and outside the linguistic scope of the oral tradition from which his stories emerged. In 'The Withered Arm',[10] for example, he writes of Mrs Lodge's face being as pale as Rhoda Brook's seen against 'the sad dun shades of the upland's garniture'. A little later we're told that 'a story was whispered about the many-dairied lowland that winter'. Diction and phrasings of that kind would have been inappropriate to the trampwoman. But Hardy's notes also add to the poem. In its final sentence, for example, the location of Ilchester jail is said to be 'now an innocent-looking green meadow'. It adds considerably to the poem's effect. For one thing, it returns the reader to the present. As a result 'A Trampwoman's Tragedy', as well as being spoken by an underdog, one of those marginalised beings which the short story especially seems drawn to represent, leaves the reader – or this reader – with the sense of a curiously farsighted glimpse of that rugged, wilder past which Hardy was determined should not be forgotten. Even in the movement of the verse he seems doggedly obedient to what was current long before and which he seems to be asserting as tuneful and authentic. But his meaning is a contemporary one – the power of jealousy, and the reckoning that will have to be paid when its passion overwhelms reason.

If 'A Trampwoman's Tragedy' is a bold and brave poem in its encounter with the past, then the same can be said of 'The Withered Arm'. Unlike Stevenson, whose fondness for the supernatural was overdone, Hardy's tale hinges more on the impact of thoughts on another person, the intuitive transfer of hurt or disfigurement inflicted against the conscious wishes of the inflicter. It suggests dream as an active intermediary in human affairs. Rhoda Brook's vision of a withered arm materialises in Gertrude Lodge, who has just married the father of Rhoda's illegitimate son. There is something uncanny about Hardy's storytelling skill. 'Yes, mother,' said the boy. 'Is father married then?' In contemporary short fiction it is extremely difficult to get away with a sentence like this: 'Half a dozen years passed away, and Mr and Mrs Lodge's married experience sank into prosiness, and worse.' That is 'telling', not 'showing', and very unfashionable. However, the tale in Victorian times enjoyed a greater spaciousness of timescale than is nowadays preferred, just as a 'short' story then could be a great deal longer than is now the case, due to the generosity of page-space granted by magazines in response to what readers desired and expected. But even with such spaciousness at his command, there are some tricky moments in the narrative of 'The Withered Arm', where Hardy must have felt obliged to be both delicate and brief. After Rhoda and her son have left, due to the unbearable disclosure by Conjuror Trendle that Gertrude's withered arm has been inflicted by the power of an enemy, namely Rhoda, although it is not intentional, the childless Lodges are given this exchange followed by Hardy's necessary explanation. (And if there's one thing that story-writers detest, it's being obliged to explain.)

'Damned if you won't poison yourself with these apothecary messes and witch mixtures some time or other,' said her husband, when his eyes chanced to fall upon the multitudinous array.

She did not reply, but turned her sad, soft glance upon him in such heart-swollen reproach that he looked sorry for his words, and added, 'I only meant it for your good, you know, Gertrude.'

'I'll clear out the whole lot, and destroy them,' she said huskily, 'and try such remedies no more!'

'You want somebody to cheer you,' he observed. 'I once thought of adopting a boy; but he is too old now. And he is gone away I don't know where.'

And this is the moment which Hardy must have found obligatory, for although the reader knows, the reader also has to be told how Gertrude Lodge knows.

> She guessed to whom he alluded; for Rhoda Brook's story had in the course of years become known to her; though not a word had ever passed between her husband and herself on the subject. Neither had she ever spoken to him of her visit to Conjuror Trendle, and of what was revealed to her, or she thought was revealed to her, by that solitary heathman.[11]

Conjuror Trendle offers a cure. It is to touch the neck of a prisoner freshly cut down from the scaffold. 'It will turn the blood and change the constitution.' And you're dead right: it most certainly would. But during her conversation with the hangman the alert reader guesses who the unfortunate prisoner is – aged 18 and condemned to hang for burning a hayrick. It's Rhoda's son. Of course it is. High drama, of the kind in which Hardy revelled, is the result:

> Gertrude shrieked: 'the turn o' the blood', predicted by the conjuror, had taken place. But at that moment a second shriek rent the air of the enclosure: it was not Gertrude's, and its effect upon her was to make her start round.[12]

Quite probably, the reader won't be taken by surprise; but the reader will certainly be engrossed, with hair raised, by the sheer curiosity of the episode, the dead youth's neck already having been described as having on it 'a line the colour of an unripe blackberry', which Gertrude touches with her wasted arm.

> Immediately behind her stood Rhoda Brook, her face drawn, and her eyes red with weeping. Behind Rhoda stood Gertrude's own husband; his countenance lined, his eyes dim, but without a tear.
> 'D—n you! what are you doing here?' he said hoarsely.
> 'Hussy – to come between us and our child now!' cried Rhoda. 'This is the meaning of what Satan showed me in the vision! You are like her at last!' And clutching the bare arm of the younger woman, she pulled her unresistingly back against the wall. Immediately Brook had loosened her hold the fragile young Gertrude slid down against the feet of her husband. When he lifted her up she was unconscious.

The mere sight of the twain had been enough to suggest to her that the dead young man was Rhoda's son.[13]

No, they don't write them like that any more. They don't even try to. But Hardy was right in engaging so much with stories set in the past, before he was born, but whose survivors lived on into his own earlier days. It enabled him to write freely about enormous and destructive passions. Gertrude dies three days later and Lodge sells his farms, dying after two years of lonely life in lodgings elsewhere, and leaving his money to a reformatory for boys 'subject to the payment of a small annuity to Rhoda Brook, if she could be found to claim it'. Most writers would end there, but Hardy adds a final paragraph which discreetly and perhaps for Hardy necessarily connects the story to the oral tradition and history from which it grew:

> For some time she could not be found; but eventually she reappeared in her old parish, – absolutely refusing, however, to have anything to do with the provision made for her. Her monotonous milking at the dairy was resumed, and followed for many long years, till her form became bent, and her once abundant dark hair white and worn away at the forehead – perhaps by long pressure against the cows. Here, sometimes, those who knew her experiences would stand and observe her, and wonder what sombre thoughts were beating inside that impassive, wrinkled brow, to the rhythm of the alternating milk-streams.[14]

'The Withered Arm' is a better title, but it could as easily have been called 'The Milkmaid's Tragedy'. Hardy's poem, 'The Milkmaid', from *Poems of the Past and Present*, while serious, is also more light-hearted.

> The maid breathes words – to vent,
> It seems, her sense of Nature's scenery,
> Of whose life, sentiment,
> And essence, very part itself is she.

We can take that as the serious aspect of the poem, that association of the milkmaid with the landscape of a remote place. However, the poem continues,

> She bends a glance of pain,
> And, at a moment, lets escape a tear;
> Is it that passing train,
> Whose alien whirr offends her country ear? –
>
> Nay! Phyllis does not dwell
> On visual and familiar things like these;
> What moves her is the spell
> Of inner themes and inner poetries: . . .

– which fairly sets up the reader's expectations, as if anticipating a Wordsworthian flourish. But it finishes with:

> Could but by Sunday morn
> Her gay new gown come, meads might dry to dun,
> Trains shriek till ears were torn,
> If Fred would not prefer that Other One.

The seeds of tragedy are there, perhaps, as in any love story; but Hardy chooses to observe with worldly amusement. But he must have his story, too.

Particularly successful as a short-story poem is 'At the Railway Station, Upway', from *Late Lyrics and Earlier*.

> 'There is not much that I can do,
> For I've no money that's quite my own!'
> Spoke up the pitying child –
> A little boy with a violin
> At the station before the train came in, –
> But I can play my fiddle to you,
> And a nice one 'tis, and good in tone!'
>
> The man in the handcuffs smiled;
> The constable looked, and he smiled, too,
> As the fiddle began to twang;
> And the man in the handcuffs suddenly sang
> With grimful glee:
> 'This life so free
> Is the thing for me!'
> And the constable smiled, and said no word,
> As if unconscious of what he heard;

And so they went on till the train came in –
The convict, and boy with the violin.

In telling the story of this encounter on a station platform, Hardy or his narrator is a perceiving presence (as in 'The Milkmaid'), and protected by an unannounced or absent first-person singular. Convict, boy and constable, are more than ciphers or unnamed strangers, though. They're untold stories. I agree with Tom Paulin, in his book *Thomas Hardy: the Poetry of Perception* (1975)[15] when he claims that when Hardy is at his most perceptive and observational the result is a quality of seeing that becomes what Paulin calls 'visionary'. What I would add to that is this: Hardy's observational/visionary dynamic is the direct result, not just of uncannily perceptive powers – and is there a finer poet at sheer *naming* than Hardy? – playing through 'inner themes and inner poetries', but of highly developed narrative, storytelling skills. A fine example is another railway poem, 'Midnight on the Great Western', from *Moments of Vision* – but where do you draw the line? – there's always another poem by Hardy. Note, though, the directness of the two titles – 'At the Railway Station, Upway' and 'Midnight on the Great Western'. Each title asserts a fact of place and encounter. It is against the challenge of such a simplicity of statement that Hardy's tuneful skills are obliged to contest the real with the visionary. Note, too, the plainness of the opening lines of both poems. 'At the Railway Station, Upway', starts with the 'pitying child's' declaration of pennilessness, for which he compensates by playing his fiddle for the convict (and with innocent wisdom, for it leads the convict to break into ironic song: 'This life so free/Is the thing for me!'). 'Midnight on the Great Western' opens with plain statement: 'In the third class seat sat the journeying boy.' We could suppose that the phrase 'the journeying boy' (repeated four times in the poem) is poetic, but it could hardly be described as remarkable. What's peculiar about it is its timelessness: 'the journeying boy' could be from any place and age, and the fact that he's on a train is neither here nor there. Similarly, the descriptive purpose of the remaining lines of the first stanza seems to reach for a higher poetic level than the first line achieves (although I doubt if Hardy meant his first line to be in any way 'powerful'):

And the roof-lamp's oily flame
Played down on his listless form and face,
Bewrapt past knowing to what he was going,
Or whence he came.

So much of what is poetic in Hardy's poetry is a matter of narrative heightened by the vigour and delicacy of the tunes given to him by his venturesome, robust versification, flexible to the point of elasticity. The second stanza continues with a close-up, one of Hardy's best and most intuitive touches in his poetry. Readers at this point ought to be entranced by the commonplaceness of the objects evoked – the ticket, the key to the boy's box on a piece of string – and then the near-visionary leap of the play of light on the key. As a poem about vulnerable innocence then the key is surely significant, perhaps almost symbolic, but in too demotic, too real a manner for the concept of symbolism to be critically apt. (And this is a dimension of Hardy's poetry which I adore: the way he makes the commonplace proud of being what it is.)

> In the band of his hat the journeying boy
>   Had a ticket stuck; and a string
> Around his neck bore the key of his box,
> That twinkled gleams of the lamp's sad beams
>   Like a living thing.

Clearly, a poem by the author of 'Old Furniture'. But this, too, is a poem in which the story is that of an encounter. The story of 'the journeying boy' is untold, and if Hardy, poignantly, tries to guess, his speculation never gets beyond a question.

> What past can be yours, O journeying boy
>   Towards a world unknown,
> Who calmly, as if incurious quite
> On all at stake, can undertake
>   This plunge alone?

Strangely plain, and yet strangely soaring also, Hardy's question is primary to the narrative art of this poem. It invites the reader to make up the boy's story and yet because Hardy has himself refused to do so it also lays down the limits beyond which such guessing would be sentimental and condescending.

> Knows your soul a sphere, O journeying boy,
>   Our rude realms far above,
> Whence with spacious vision you mark and mete
> This region of sin that you find you in,
>   But are not of?

Presumably, 'region of sin' indicates that the train is approaching London, and for a reader of the present time the image evoked is of those runaway children of the North who somehow fetch up on the predatory concourses of King's Cross Station. 'But are not of' enforces the boy's innocence, perhaps with the rueful implication that it will not last for long in the Great Wen, or that his Dorsetshire origins (presumably) will help see him through. It could also suggest Hardy's conviction in the virtue of the district of the south-west of England from which the boy has come. But the boy has a box and round his neck on a piece of string the key to it. So someone has prepared him for his journey. Perhaps he's an orphan being sent to live with an aunt or other relative. Perhaps, perhaps. . . . Inevitably, the reader tries to make up a story, and Hardy encourages it while at the same time he forbids it. Indeed, it is not a story, but a lyrical anecdote that could become a story were more known by fact or provided by imagination. Or if it is a story then it is one of the poet's perception, the drama of compassion and speculation picked out on a verse melody from Hardy's immense and constantly plundered repertoire.

A poet's 'narrative art', especially that of a poet like Hardy, who excelled in the novel and shone in the short story, by itself introduces a constant possibility of fiction. Real persons and real events may well be changed to a lesser or greater extent by the poet's psychological momentum – 'inner themes and inner poetries' – and by a need to re-experience the lived, which may be, according to the fact, imperfectly re-created (from the point of view of the prosaic), but which turns into perfect poetry. For example, was Hardy an habitual railway passenger in the third class? I doubt it. Who *was* the boy? Was it Hardy himself re-observed in adulthood? Is it a poem about ambition and cutting loose from the ties of livelihood and trade? Was the boy one whom Hardy sat opposite on the train? Was it an encounter he experienced or one that was told to him by another? Did he make it up? Does it matter?

There are clues in Hardy's poetry which can help us to define his 'psychological momentum' as I've called it. Essentially, it has to do with the status of time. In a sonnet either of April 1887 or written then, when he was in Italy, 'Rome: On the Palatine', he concludes:

> When lo, swift hands, on strings nigh overhead,
> Began to melodize a waltz by Strauss:
> It stirred me as I stood, in Cæsar's house,
> Raised the old routs Imperial lyres had led,

>   And blended pulsing life with lives long done,
>   Till Time seemed fiction, Past and Present one.

'Till Time seemed fiction, Past and Present one' — it is a remarkable declaration of principle, and, of course, Hardy did not need to visit Rome
to find it. His work is pervaded by it. The past in the present, the present
in the past, time as fact and history, and time as stuff and substance of
fiction and of art and poetry – such themes are everywhere in his work
as a kind of pulse, and inform his versification, his obstinately creative
exercising of the possibilities of timeless song offered by the English language with a local or (in a good sense) provincial root. Hardy is the least
deracinated and, next to Chaucer, Shakespeare, Wordsworth, Crabbe,
and, more recently, Geoffrey Grigson, Ted Hughes and Philip Larkin,
the most English of poets – and maybe it takes a disinterested Scot to
see this exhilarating phenomenon.

When Hardy came to write his celebrated 'Poems of 1912–13', his
poems recollecting Emma Hardy, and other poems after these dates on
the same subject, he was already more than well-rehearsed in haunting
and being haunted. This time, though, the haunting was even more real
than those which had happened before. And the haunting was not fictitious, although the potency of fictitious hauntings is not one which I
would care to dismiss. A poet's 'narrative art' is just as likely to be as powerful, and probably more so, when speaking *in persona propria* as in poems
where the first-person singular is absent or observational merely. In
Hardy's case, the result was a melismatic and elegiac complicatedness, for
reasons which we all know about. It led to such a complex line as the last
of 'Your Last Drive' – 'You are past love, praise, indifference, blame',
perhaps the best earned and truest of all his lines. The poem is full of
minute give-aways, to such an extent that I would claim that a poet's
'narrative art' is not so very different from that of a novelist or a short-
story writer (although, as has often been said, the short story is closer to
the lyric poem than to the novel; and as a writer of both I find myself
increasingly doubtful of this critical commonplace). Outside of his poems
of first-person, haunted predicament, Hardy's work, it seems to me, is
pretty well all of a piece; but it's his first-person poems, no matter their
possible fictitiousness, that strike me as his masterpieces. 'Your Last
Drive', though, is a risky poem to the extent that it introduces dialogue
from his dead wife. In terms of fiction, an ethical hazard is undertaken
in that it reports speech the actuality of which can only be asserted by
the poet. Is it real? Did she say it? And then, once again, does it matter?

But more important, perhaps, is the question of how an accomplished versification can dulcify or change a real experience or set of emotions. Could the verse skills and narrative or storytelling skills of a writer like Hardy modify lived experience to a point where the result could be a kind of misrepresentation, or even mendacity? I think the answer is 'Of course, but does it matter, if the poet is also being honest to what we know of the biographical record?' And that's the case with these poems, especially when you consider the harshness of 'Without Ceremony', the last line of which is 'Good-bye is not worth while!', meaning what it did when Emma was alive and taking off without telling Hardy, and that her haunting of him would be permanent, and a reckoning which he would have to continue to meet until the day he died. Here, though, is 'Your Last Drive':

> Here by the moorway you returned,
> And saw the borough lights ahead
> That lit your face – all undiscerned
> To be in a week the face of the dead,
> And you told of the charm of that haloed view
> That never again would beam on you.
>
> And on your left you passed the spot
> Where eight days later you were to lie,
> And be spoken of as one who was not;
> Beholding it with a heedless eye
> As alien from you, though under its tree
> You soon would halt everlastingly.
>
> I drove not with you . . .

Already a reader's eyebrows may have risen in a tic of interior puzzlement or questioning at 'You told of the charm of that haloed view/ That never again would beam on you' after a reading of 'The Going', which precedes 'Your Last Drive', and which expresses the surprise of Emma's death. Also, 'I drove not with you . . .', followed as it is by three dramatic dots . . . well, the three dots are themselves an expression of remorse – punctuation as gasp, as breath withheld. Hardy, however, doesn't persevere with his absence but, instead, imagines his presence:

> Yet had I sat
> At your side that eve I should not have seen
> That the countenance I was glancing at
> Had a last-time look in the flickering sheen,
> Nor have read the writing upon your face,
> 'I go hence soon to my resting-place;
>
> 'You may miss me then.'

'You may miss me then' – is that not Hardy mounting a terrible indictment upon himself through speech directed at him from the wife whom he may have neglected and who could have been difficult and awkward towards him? From the biographical evidence, we think we know about this, but it's too easy to be prurient or decisive. Hardy's poem picks up the story – and it *is* a story, Hardy's own story, the story of his marriage, but as told by Hardy, even if part of it is told riskily and fictitiously through the words of his wife, Emma:

> 'But I shall not know
> How many times you visit me there,
> Or what your thoughts are, or if you go
> There never at all. And I shall not care.
> Should you censure me I shall take no heed,
> And even your praises no more shall need.'

Clearly, there's something rueful there – 'I shall not care/Should you censure me' . . . and 'even your praises no more shall need.' Death, then, is a sort of release from the demands of her husband, Thomas Hardy. It's honest of Hardy not to say so, precisely, but to implicate himself in the truth of the matter. However, it's Hardy who, inevitably, has the last word:

> True, you'll never know. And you will not mind.
> But shall I then slight you because of such?
> Dear ghost, in the past did you ever find
> The thought 'What profit,' move me much?
> Yet abides the fact, indeed, the same, –
> You are past love, praise, indifference, blame.

To be perfectly blunt about the matter, a poet's narrative art is the dynamic of thought, disclosure, description, and so on, that leads up to the conclusion of a poem, especially the last line. Much the same design can be experienced in Hardy's short or shorter fiction, or in his novels – the distribution of time, or events, or of thoughts. But it is when we read a poem like 'During Wind and Rain' that we really find ourselves faced with Hardy's 'narrative art' in verse and poetry at its most powerful, when his passion, versification and tunefulness meet the invisible but communicative and moving story he has to tell. Never mind that it is one of Hardy's greatest poems, it is one of the great poems of the world.

> They sing their dearest songs –
> He, she, all of them – yea,
> Treble and tenor and bass,
>   And one to play;
> With the candles mooning each face . . .
>   Ah, no; the years O!
> How the sick leaves reel down in throngs!
>
> They clear the creeping moss –
> Elders and juniors – aye,
> Making the pathways neat
>   And the garden gay;
> And they build a shady seat . . .
>   Ah, no; the years, the years;
> See, the white storm-birds wing across!
>
> They are blithely breakfasting all –
> Men and maidens – yea,
> Under the summer tree,
>   With a glimpse of the bay,
> While pet fowl come to the knee . . .
>   Ah, no; the years O!
> And the rotten rose is ript from the wall.
>
> They change to a high new house,
> He, she, all of them – aye,
> Clocks and carpets and chairs
>   On the lawn all day,
> And brightest things that are theirs. . . .
>   Ah, no; the years, the years;
> Down their carved names the rain-drop ploughs.

Notes

1. *Thomas Hardy: the Complete Stories*, ed. Norman Page (London, 1996).
2. Christopher Ricks, 'A Note on Hardy's "A Spellbound Palace"', in *Essays in Appreciation* (Oxford, 1998), p. 239.
3. *Complete Stories*, p. 7.
4. This is number 22 in *The Complete Poems*. Subsequent references are to this edition.
5. Walter Benjamin, *Illuminations*, ed. Hannah Arendt (London, 1970), pp. 83, 87.
6. *Complete Stories*, p. 10
7. Walter Benjamin, *Illuminations*, p. 87.
8. *Complete Stories*, pp. 32–47.
9. *Complete Stories*, p. 47.
10. *Complete Stories*, pp. 48–51.
11. *Complete Stories*, p. 61.
12. *Complete Stories*, p. 70.
13. *Complete Stories*, p. 70.
14. *Complete Stories*, p. 71.
15. Tom Paulin, *The Poetry of Perception* (London, 1975), p. 11 and passim.

10
Noticing Things:
Hardy and the Nature of 'Nature'

Phillip Mallett

In the first volume of *Modern Painters*, published in 1843, John Ruskin argued that the 'ceaseless and incomparable' complexity of the natural world would always elude the artist:

> The detail of a single weedy bank laughs the carving of the ages to scorn. Every leaf and stalk has a design and tracery upon it; every knot of grass and intricacy of shade which the labour of years could never imitate[.]

What the eye perceives is a 'beautiful incomprehensibility': beautiful, because the created world bears the impress of its Divine author; incomprehensible, because its complexity is a type or image of the infinite power of God:

> the Divine mind is as visible in its full energy of operation on every lowly bank and mouldering stone, as in the lifting of the pillars of heaven. . . . to the rightly perceiving mind, there is the same infinity, the same majesty, the same power, the same unity, the same perfection, manifest in the casting of the clay as in the scattering of the cloud, in the mouldering of the dust as in the kindling of the day-star.[1]

Infinity and unity are the key words in Ruskin's account of the natural world. Nature is infinite because it is filled with 'the exhaustless living energy' of God; it is coherent, or unified, because that energy reaches into its every part.[2] Unity, Ruskin insisted, was a given fact of the seen world, not something to be achieved by following academic rules and conventions. The artist's task was to go to Nature, selecting nothing, rejecting nothing, in the certainty that what he would find was the work of God.

In the closing paragraph of *The Origin of Species*, published in 1859, Charles Darwin turned his attention to another bank of earth and vegetation:

> It is interesting to contemplate a tangled bank, clothed with many plants of many kinds, with birds singing on the bushes, with various insects flitting about, and with worms crawling through the damp earth, and to reflect that these elaborately constructed forms, so different from each other, and dependent upon each other in so complex a manner, have all been produced by laws acting around us.[3]

He then lists these laws: Reproduction, Inheritance, Variability, Struggle for Life, Natural Selection, Divergence of Character, the Extinction of forms less well equipped to survive. Darwin could respond as enthusiastically as Ruskin to the abundance of the natural world, but not because it provided evidence of the infinite power or the eternal oneness of God.[4] Darwin's tangled bank is filled with energy – unlike Ruskin's, it includes birds, insects and worms, as well as vegetation – and there is unity of a sort, but only in the form of the complex interplay of a local economy. It is a world of process; it represents nothing but itself. What binds the part into the whole is to be explained by biology and geology, not by metaphysics. Where Ruskin had found evidence of a sacred bond between God and Man, Darwin detects the more literal bonds of descent from a common ancestor and subjection to the same set of laws.

There is a further, critical difference between the two passages. Ruskin had demanded that the artist efface his own personality in order to record the various truths of form and colour. Darwin's observer is apparently equally detached, equally intent on what is seen, but in reality he, or she, is ineluctably a part of the world observed. Darwin's study of the natural world led him to conclude that 'not one living species will transmit its unaltered likeness to a distant futurity. And of the species now living very few will transmit progeny of any kind to a far distant futurity.'[5] The laws acting 'around us', which the scientist can trace in the interplay of the life forms of the bank, also act *on* us. Darwin was too tactful to mention humanity, but his readers could draw their own conclusions.

Thomas Hardy, an early admirer of Darwin, certainly did so. In *A Pair of Blue Eyes*, Henry Knight conducts a small experiment on the air currents flowing over the Cliff without a Name. A few moments later, he finds himself hanging on the cliff-face, gazing into the eyes of a fossilised trilobite, apparently to be the victim of one of nature's 'experiments in killing'. The experimenter has become the experimented-upon. This is a fall in more than the literal sense of the word. In Knight's anguished discovery that 'the dignity of man' means nothing, that it cannot save him from being 'with the small in his death', we can find a crisis at the narrative level which mirrors the impact of Darwin's work on his readers in the 1860s and 1870s.[6]

Hardy has a number of passages which recall Darwin's entangled bank. We might think of the moment when Stephen Smith watches from the garden as Henry Knight and Elfride enter the summer house, or of Tess listening in the garden at Talbothays as Angel plays his harp, or of this, from *The Return of the Native*, where Clym, half-blind, is working as a furze-cutter:

> His daily life was of a curious microscopic sort, his whole world being limited to a circuit of a few feet from his person. His familiars were creeping and winged things, and they seemed to enroll him in their band. Bees hummed about his ears with an intimate air, and tugged at the heath and furze-flowers at his side in such numbers as to weigh them down to the sod. The strange amber-coloured butterflies which Egdon produced, and which were never seen elsewhere, quivered in the breath of his lips. . . . Tribes of emerald-green grasshoppers leaped over his feet, falling awkwardly on their backs, heads, or hips, like unskilful acrobats. . . . Huge flies, ignorant of larders and wire-netting, and quite in a savage state, buzzed about him without knowing that he was a man. . . . Litters of young rabbits came out from their forms to sun themselves upon hillocks, the hot beams blazing through the delicate tissue of each thin-fleshed ear, and firing it to a blood-red transparency in which the veins could be seen.[7]

The passage combines a Darwinian sense of the unceasing creative energies of the physical world with a Pre-Raphaelite intensity of observation, and both are important. In the first chapter we are told that in its monotony and uniformity Egdon suggests a satire on the human aspiration towards individuality; here Clym appears to be wholly absorbed into his environment, no more than 'a brown spot in the midst of the expanse of olive-green gorse'. To his mother, three chapters later, he resembles a green caterpillar on a leaf, 'an insect . . . a mere parasite of the heath, fretting its surface in his daily labour as a moth frets a

garment' (278–9). Implicitly, such descriptions mock his professed ambition to be an educator and agent of social change. The passage also tells
against Eustacia, whose beauty is compared in Chapter 10, not quite to
that of a rare butterfly, but to the tiger-beetle, which when seen in a
dull light seems to be of a neutral colour, 'but under a full illumination
blazes with dazzling splendour' (88).[8] Such illumination is denied to
Eustacia. Thwarted in her ambition to blaze among the bright lights of
Paris, she will never become the 'splendid woman' she longs to be (359).
Like the 'strange amber-coloured butterfly', the most she can hope for
is a brief, flickering glory. Neither will ever exist outside Egdon.

   And yet the effect of the passage is not simply to diminish either Clym
or Eustacia. We don't have to read it through Mrs Yeobright's eyes. Like
a Pre-Raphaelite painting, Hardy's account of Clym's microscopic world
is utterly convincing, yet we realise that we could never apprehend it
as a whole. The separate details press too hard on us; it is as if everything has become foreground, tantalising us with the sense of a reality
too vividly present for us to grasp.[9] It suggests how life might be if
we could be fully immersed in the particularities of touch, sound, sight,
temperature and movement, without thought or plan for the future. But
both Clym and Eustacia are conscious, thinking beings who necessarily
look before and after. What Hardy called 'the disease of feeling' has
'germed' in each of them.[10] Consciousness takes us out of the single
moment, into a world of choice, perspectives, the differentiation of far
and near. Gazing into Clym's world is both joyous and saddening,
because it reminds us that we are both enrolled into the natural world
and exiled from it. In the Wessex Edition of 1912, Hardy allowed himself
to dwell on this world one moment longer before turning away, by
adding, after the sentence about the rabbits, the words 'None of them
feared him.' There is a nostalgic impulse at work here, as well as a satirical one.[11]

Hardy insisted that his works offered 'impressions' and not 'convic-
tions', but when he is writing of Nature with upper case N, these impressions are engraved on steel rather than on wax, and they are, as a
number of critics have shown, deeply informed by the work of contemporary scientists, much to the frustration of those who looked to
him for pastoral or idyllic fiction.[12] 'The more we know of the laws &
nature of the Universe', Hardy wrote in 1902, 'the more ghastly a business we perceive it all to be.'[13] The Cliff without a Name is a reminder

of 'the immense lapses of time'; the 'voids and waste places of the sky', which Swithin St Cleeve describes to Viviette, are new forms of 'horror'.[14] The reaches of Time and Space seem to swallow up human life and meaning, but it is not only vastness which troubles the imagination. Change the telescope for the microscope, and there is the world of bacteria and parasites: *'A world of life within ours'*, as Hardy noted in 1876, existing with the same intensity as their human observers or hosts.[15] Everywhere there is evidence of the struggle for existence. The speaker in the poem 'In a Wood' (40) enters the woodlands in search of 'sylvan peace', only to find that the trees are 'Combatants all!' Hardy's city-dweller returns to the human world, since 'no grace I find/Taught me of trees'. Hardy's Nature, is, precisely, grace-less. In Wordsworth's 'Lines written in Early Spring', the 'budding twigs' spread out to 'catch the breezy air', and the birds which hop and play beneath them, testify to the 'pleasure' of their existence. Not so in Hardy. The birds which come to winter at Flintcomb-Ash are 'gaunt spectral creatures with tragical eyes', reeling witnesses to 'curdling temperatures' and 'colossal storms'.[16]

'Ghastly' seems an appropriate word for such a universe. The poetry of Wordsworth, and of a long line of sub-Wordsworthian poets throughout the Victorian period, found a human scale in landscape, together with a reassuring permanence, and a space for the 'ennobling interchange' of Man and Nature. Hardy's landscape, on the other hand, is full of violent shifts in scale;[17] it is permanent only in that it outlasts humanity, but is itself in constant process; and poem after poem emphasises that human or moral consciousness is an anomaly in an indifferent world. What Hardy calls 'the merely unconscious push of life' takes no account of human pain or joy; and since this is so far removed from what we wish, and from what so many of Hardy's contemporaries had grown up to believe, this indifference feels like hostility.[18]

But it's not hostility. In its relation to us, the action of the natural world is a matter of chance, or in Hardy's terms 'Hap' (4), where sun and rain are the means by which 'Crass Casualty' obstructs human intentions – and rain more often than sun: 'During Wind and Rain' (441) might serve as a general title for his work. Human action in Hardy almost always takes place in a densely given locale, with real weather. In his work, almost for the first time in English fiction, men and women get hot, cold, wet.[19] The rain features in some 60 of the poems, the wind in as many more. Sometimes the rain is merely a fact – it comes down indifferently on the merrymakers and the messengers, the busy and the idle, the live and the dead, in an autumn rain scene (569), or it forms part of the pattern of life, of snow, rain and shine, endured by the field women at Flintcomb-Ash (866), or it soaks the auctioneer and his book at a sheep fair (700). Sometimes it matches the mood of the occasion, as when it comes down drenchingly on the wives who gather to watch their husbands go off to war in South Africa (57), or descends dankly, drip, drip, drip, on the two lovers who pace beyond the last lamp (257). At times it generates an image: it falls like silken strings on Swithin's day, watched by a couple who are beginning to chafe at the cords that bind them to each other (355); it pierces the green rafters of a child's house among the ferns, an emblem of the inevitable coming of adult life (846); it slides down the pane like the colourless thoughts of a commonplace day, washing away the sense of possibility (78). Typically, it contributes to life's little and not so little ironies: it provides a chance, untaken, for the poet to kiss the woman sheltering beside him in a carriage (255); it compels another young woman, sheltering at Wynard's Gap, to kiss a man she has just met in order to preserve her reputation (718). It distorts the designs chalked on a mason's board, and in doing so suggests the forms of Perpendicular Gothic (332); it stains the sketch of the figure in the scene, marked across by rainfall, presaging her eventual death (416). It falls like arrows on Emma's grave, reminding Hardy of how she would in her lifetime shudder before it, though now it doesn't hurt her (280); it falls again as he looks back down the hill at Castle Boterel, to see her phantom figure shrinking from sight (292). It is both background and agent, literal and figurative. It destroys and creates. It ploughs down the names chiselled on the gravestones, obliterating memory and records (441); it loosens the earth so the starving birds can find food (117), then joins with particles of earth and air and grain to form the songsters of next year's growing (816).

But if Hardy was acutely aware of the chance of what happens to happen, he was as persuaded as any of his contemporaries that the natural world was governed by impersonal laws, acting 'by universal regular sequence, without partiality and without caprice'.[20] Cause is linked to effect. The air currents run upwards over a cliff face, and continue to do so whether trivially, as a fact which Knight wants (rather exasperatingly) to demonstrate to Elfride, or bizarrely, when causing the rain to fall upwards while he clings for his life to the rock, so that only his shoulders and the top of his head remain dry. Hardy's Nature, like Thomas Huxley's, resembles a game of chess:

The chess-board is the world, the pieces are the phenomena of the universe, the rules of the game are what we call the laws of Nature.

The player on the other side is hidden from us. We know that his play is always fair, just and patient. But we also know, to our cost, that he never overlooks a mistake, or makes the smallest allowance for ignorance . . . one who plays ill is checkmated – without haste, but without remorse.[21]

Those who understand the rules, and don't suppose that they will be put by for their own benefit, can at least keep the game going, as Gabriel Oak does when Nature provides him with somewhat of an overplus of clues about the coming storm.[22] Hardy's notion in his poem 'In Tenebris II' (137), that 'if way to the Better there be, it exacts a full look at the Worst', is entirely consonant with Huxley's emphasis on the importance to the scientist of 'veracity of thought and action', and a resolute willingness to face 'the world as it is', shorn of the garment of make-believe by which the pious and the fearful – in Huxley's view, these were often one and the same – have covered up its uglier features.[23] Appropriately, it was as a man of 'fearless mind' that Hardy recalled Huxley in the *Life*.[24]

The law that caused most disquiet was that everything was subject to change. Charles Lyell prefaced the second volume of his *Principles of Geology* (1830–33) with a quotation: 'The inhabitants of the globe, like all the other parts of it, are subject to change. It is not only the individual that perishes, but whole species.'[25] In the same vein, Hardy summarised Cotter Morison's *The Service of Man* in his Notebooks: 'Decay & death stamped not only on man & his works, but on all that surrounds him. Nature herself decays – Alps – Sun himself – from the animalcule to the galaxy.'[26] His reading in astronomy had taught him that the stars are not everlasting; the trilobite died out (the word 'dinosaur' entered the language in 1841, the year after Hardy's birth); Shelley's skylark is reduced to a pinch of dust in a field (66); and in the human world, skin wastes, and the human frame at eve is more fragile than it was at noon-tide (52). Like other natural laws, the law of change is indifferent to human wishes. Jude doesn't want to grow older, but he does; Tess wants to repress the life within her, but as the summer comes round at Talbothays, so too her vitality returns.

These three strands – the power of chance, the impersonal operation of natural laws, and the inevitability of change – come together in Darwinian argument: one reason, perhaps, why the theory established itself so quickly. (For all that his theories threatened to overturn orthodox Christian teaching, Darwin was buried in Westminster Abbey after his death in 1882.) It is a mere matter of luck whether one is born with a slight advantage in the pursuit of scarce resources. Herschel meant to be hostile when he attacked Darwin's theory of natural selection as 'the law of higgledy-piggledy', but he was right to recognise that the evolutionary process is driven by random, undirected variations. It is a law, as Darwin knew from his reading of Thomas Malthus's *Essay on the Principle of Population* (1798), that populations tend to outgrow the resources available, so that some will fail to achieve what they need, and die. And as the external environment changes, the qualities that were advantages become disadvantages; species that had once flourished are wiped out, for others to succeed in their place: as, in the human economy which in Hardy's fiction reflects the natural one, the prudent Farfrae succeeds the reckless Henchard, and the spiritualised Liza-Lu outlives her more incarnate sister Tess. Huxley's metaphor is, after all, in one sense misleading: as we play out our game on Nature's chess-board, the rules are ever so slowly being changed.

These arguments, in various inflections, underlie most of Hardy's work. Yet in so far as they suggest that Victorian science offered only grounds for despondency, they are not a sufficient account of Hardy's understanding of 'Nature'. But this brings me to a fork in my argument. One road forward would be to show how both the scientists, and Hardy, could treat these ideas in a much more positive manner. 'There is grandeur in this view of life', wrote Darwin, in the closing paragraph of the *Origin*; Huxley wrote of 'the wonder and the mystery of Nature'; John Tyndall, in his 'Belfast Address' of 1874, insisted that there was nothing to fear in the study of the material world, since here was to be found 'the promise and the potency of every form and quality of life'.[27] One might go on from here to suggest that Tyndall 's view, shared by Huxley, that matter was continuous with spirit, rather than simply opposed to it, has its echo in *The Dynasts*, in the push of the Will to become conscious. And one could find readily passages in such overtly 'philosophical' poems as 'Nature's Questioning' (43), 'The Mother Mourns' (76), or 'The Lacking Sense' (80), which similarly question how it might be if human consciousness was no longer an anomaly in the scheme of things.

The route I want to take is more tortuous, but I think more interesting. In brief, I want to suggest that Plot, in Hardy's fiction, operates as an analogue to Nature. Consider, say, Knight on the Cliff without a Name. The episode operates at a number of levels, but most immediately it reveals man in confrontation with the forces of nature disclosed by nineteenth-century geology. All that happens on the Cliff happens in accordance with the known laws of nature. Knight slips because the rain has wetted the surface, he falls only a certain distance because of the angle of the slope, and so on. Trapped on the cliff-face, Knight cannot help thinking that Nature has been 'treacherous' (209), is acting with 'lawless caprice', even a sense of 'feline fun' (210). Elfride seems to have been away longer than she has, the summer rain seems colder than it is, the sea appears black rather than a deep neutral blue. But the narrator is at pains to explain that everything is according to natural laws, even when Knight's world seems to have been turned upside down, the sea becomes a 'nether sky', and the rain ascends from below (212). The chess-game is being played impassively, but the closer Knight's opponent comes to mating him, the more he feels the game has been rigged.

In the moment of crisis, Knight's experience comes to resemble that of Henchard in *The Mayor of Casterbridge*. In Chapter 19, Henchard tells Elizabeth-Jane that she is his daughter, only to discover a few minutes later the letter from Susan telling him that she is not. Confronted by the defeat of his hopes, he wonders if 'some sinister intelligence [is] bent on punishing him'. Yet, says the narrator, events 'had developed naturally. If he had not revealed his past history to Elizabeth he would not have searched the drawer for papers, and so on.'[28] Like Nature, Plot operates 'naturally', according to cause and effect; it is modified by chance (if Farfrae had not overheard the discussion of Henchard's grown wheat, the story would never have been enacted (39)); and what happens is experienced as if directed by a personalised force – that force which, in 'Hap', Hardy had wished was there, so that at least he could shake his fist at it.

Here it might seem that my argument is threatening to collapse into a tautology: Plot, in Hardy's fiction, operates as a kind of analogue to Nature because both are according to the nature of things. To this I'd want to reply that the nature of things, and the perception of nature, need not come together, and indeed don't come together in most fiction. We might read back from the novels of George Eliot or Conrad to discover how these authors understood the physical world, but we could hardly do so with Dickens or Thackeray, Trollope or Charlotte Brontë, or only at the broadest level. There is a Megalosaurus on the first page of *Bleak House*, but the most we could make of that would be the inference that there are some institutions which, like the dinosaurs, have outlived their time; while there is nothing in *Vanity Fair* which would tell us if Thackeray thought the sun went round the earth, or the earth round the sun. In contrast, to see Plot and Nature in Hardy's fiction as parallel but distinct allows us to move more deeply into the novels.

The parallels can be complex and sustained. As Henry Knight hangs on the Cliff without a Name, Time closes up 'like a fan before him', bringing him, literally, face to face with the stages of life on earth. The 'numberless slaty layers' of rock record how each form is buried by those which succeed it: on one rib or flange of the fan is the trilobite; on another, the mammoths and the earliest human beings; on another, Knight himself. The confrontation parallels his discovery, later, that he is one of a succession of men who have loved Elfride, and his fear that he will come to exist as one layer in her memory, perhaps, like the fossils on a cave floor, irretrievably mingled with others – very much as Elfride, under his relentless interrogation, momentarily mixes up Stephen, whom she kissed while sitting on Jethway's tomb, with the not-so-Felix Jethway who lies buried beneath it.

In the event, however, it is Elfride's own identity which is blurred by the unfolding of the narrative. In Chapter 26, while preparing a tomb for Lady Luxellian, John Smith and Simeon have to move the coffin of another member of the family – Elfride's grandmother, also called Elfride – and recall the story of her elopement with the singing-master: 'That trick of running away seems to be handed down in families, like craziness or gout. And they two women be alike as peas.' Stephen, understandably confused, has to ask 'Which two?', even though he knows (as the other speakers don't) of the second Elfride's aborted elopement with him. This Elfride will of course repeat her grandmother's story in another way, by becoming the second Elfride to die in childbirth and be buried in the family vault. Where we might have expected the narrative line to shape and record her individuality, it absorbs it; the familiar pattern of character progressively revealed in action through the length of the novel is disrupted. Indeed, after her trip to London to see Knight (itself an echo of her near-elopement with Stephen), Elfride disappears from the story, to reappear only as the second late Lady Luxellian. What his confrontation with the natural world had suggested to Knight would be his fate – to be lost and forgotten among the layers of time – the narrative has inflicted on Elfride.[29]

I want to move towards another area where Hardy's sense of 'Nature' can be seen to have informed his decisions about narrative and plot. One of the more straightforward parallels we might note is that there is room for manoeuvre in both arenas. In Chapter 36 of *Far from the*

Madding Crowd Oak receives a series of 'direct message[s]' from Nature, warning of the impending storm: a toad on the path, a slug crawled indoors, sheep huddled together: 'Every voice in nature was unanimous in bespeaking change.'[30] There are opportunities, however limited, to intervene in the processes of nature, and Oak takes advantage of them. This can be paralleled by Elizabeth-Jane's actions at the level of plot and event. She too is a patient reader of situations, who has learned to make the best of what chances she has by the 'cunning enlargement . . . of those minute forms of satisfaction' open to everyone not in absolute pain.[31] Like Oak, she has what Clym in *The Return of the Native* is said not to have: a 'well-proportioned mind', which allows her to recover from her early setbacks and enter on a life of unbroken happiness. The processes of plot, like those of Nature, leave room for negotiation.

Oak and Elizabeth-Jane are, however, at odds with Nature in one key respect. They are frugal, Nature is generous and wasteful. Perhaps the strongest impression left on a reader of the novels is of the extraordinary local life and energy of the natural world. This sense of inexhaustibility is what Lawrence takes away from Egdon Heath in *The Study of Thomas Hardy*. The individual life is short, but Egdon survives. It is, says Lawrence, 'very good': which is not quite Hardy's emphasis, since his narrative follows the arc of the individual life, and with the end of that comes the end of the novel, as if to affirm the validity and meaning of the life span of a single man or woman.[32] I've commented on one example of this local life; among others we might think of the hiss and fermentation at Talbothays, or the profusion of life in the garden in which Tess hears Angel playing on his harp; or the thick floor of vegetation beneath the densely planted trees in *The Woodlanders*; or of the wonderful passage in *The Well-Beloved*, when Pierston returns to the Isle of Slingers for Avice's funeral, and Hardy makes us aware simultaneously of the hum of saws working in the quarry, the sunlight flashing on a school of mackerel glimpsed beyond the coffin as it is carried into the cemetery, the 'vast spread of watery babble and unrest' which is the sea, the warmth of the sun on the stone in the churchyard. . . .[33] But every reader will find her own examples. Hardy's work constantly reminds us that the world – to borrow words from Louis MacNeice – is various, and more of it than we think.

Read in Darwinian terms, the variety and profusion of nature have both a positive and a negative aspect. It is both the sign that not everything will survive, since within the variety some creatures will lose out in the battle for resources, and the assurance that some other creatures will. The abundance of the natural world, its endless coming into life, is echoed in the plots of the novels. As Lawrence put it in his *Study of Thomas Hardy*: 'These people of Wessex are always bursting suddenly out of bud and taking a wild flight into flower.'[34] In Hardy's fiction, the most vital, the most richly endowed, generally fail to survive, or to leave any progeny – Eustacia, Henchard, Tess. But alongside their defeat, and making it all the more painful, is the sense of what might have been: those shadowy other plots, in which Elizabeth-Jane was indeed Henchard's daughter, in which Angel did stop to dance with the girl in the white dress and the red ribbon, in which a passer-by did aid Jude as he struggled with his grammar books, and it was not true that 'Nobody did come, because nobody does'.[35] Hardy, like Egdon, had one of those natures which become vocal at tragedy, and for the most part he leaves these other, happier stories to be told elsewhere; but he would not have forgotten that a happy outcome in one place is no answer to the question of pain.[36] Resources will be wasted in a busy and active universe, as one individual or species survives and another does not; or in the fictional world as we follow the line of plot which takes one story to its conclusion, and as it does so sheds those other possible stories which might have been.[37] What Gillian Beer has called Hardy's 'shadow-plots of achievement and joy' return us all too sadly to the single plot which has become a reality.[38]

The parallel I want to suggest here is between the abundance of the natural world, conceived in Darwinian terms as a struggle for survival in which for every success there are necessarily many failures, and the presence of those unrealised possibilities in the plot, the roads not taken, or travelled too late. To none of Hardy's novels does this argument apply better than to *Tess*. Nature, in the garden at Talbothays, seems to have run riot; Darwin's entangled bank is tame in comparison. This brings us near to the centre of the novel. The garden suggests the unstoppable proliferation of energies of the natural world; these are energies which make 'offensive smells', leave stains on the skin and the clothes, dazzle the eyes with 'red and yellow and purple hues'. Moving like a cat through the garden, almost literally enthralled by the sensuous richness around her, Tess is simultaneously fully herself – a woman whose will to live, to enjoy, to desire is returning – and 'an almost standard woman', a representative of a desire to reproduce which is stronger than any one individual.[39] There is no distinction here, as there is in the social world, between the pure and the impure: simply the sense that every available space has been filled with life. The passage does not diminish Tess. Rather, it places her, as it were, in two dimensions. In the line of the narrative, she will live and die, and her doings will be like the doings of thousands of others; but within the moment, as we apprehend the garden as an image of her living awareness, her incarnate selfhood, what we dwell on is her vitality.

Like the paragraph describing Clym cutting furze on the heath, the garden passage in *Tess* briefly suspends our awareness of time and space, and offers to our imagination a world in which experience is fuller, more immediate, and it seems there is nothing to resist 'the appetite for joy'. But of all Hardy's novels, *Tess* is the one most saturated in time, as the division into Phases suggests: 'The Maiden', followed by 'Maiden No More'; 'The Rally', followed by 'The Consequence', and, at the end of the novel, 'Fulfilment'. In Darwinian fashion, the local economy has to subsist within the larger one. Here, as elsewhere, only those forms will survive which find a niche to which they are perfectly adapted; and Tess, as both Alec and Angel tell her, is not adapted to the niche which society has prepared for her. She is not allowed to remain Tess Durbeyfield, but neither can she become Mrs Angel Clare. What she might have been able to offer will be squandered. In its place Hardy offers us the most ironic of his shadow plots: the possibility that Angel Clare, finally escaping from the conventions that have crippled him, will leave to find a world elsewhere with Liza-Lu – spiritualised, slighter, younger, but impelled by her own appetite for joy to move into the space made vacant for her by the death of her sister.

It was Herbert Spencer who thrust the phrase 'survival of the fittest' into evolutionary debate. Hardy thought well of Spencer, but did not share his optimism. He recognised that the survival of the fittest did not mean that the best would come through, only that those who survived were those who fitted best into their environment: '*Science tells us that*, in the struggle for life, the surviving organism is not necessarily that which is absolutely the best in an ideal sense, though it must be that which is most in harmony with the surrounding conditions.'[40] As the environment changed, so some forms were lost forever, though different ones would rise to take their place. In one context, this might be a dialect word, which the Oxford English Dictionary would then list as 'archaic', though it might find a last burst of life in one of Hardy's poems or novels; in another, it might be an amber butterfly, which the naturalists would describe as extinct, though Hardy hoped to be remembered as 'one who strove that such innocent creatures should come to no harm' (511); and in another, it might be a young dairymaid, with whom the President of the Immortals had finally finished his sport.

Notes

1. *The Works of John Ruskin*, ed. E. T. Cook and Alexander Wedderburn, 39 vols (London, 1903–12), III. 338, 493.
2. Ruskin, *Works*, III. 383.
3. Charles Darwin, *The Origin of Species*, in *Darwin. Norton Critical Edition*, ed. Philip Appleman, 2nd edn (New York and London, 1979), p. 131.
4. The tropical landscape left his mind 'a chaos of delight'. See *Charles Darwin's Diary of the Voyage of H.M.S. Beagle*, edited by Nora Barlow (London, 1933), p. 39.
5. *The Origin of Species*, edn cit., p. 131.
6. *A Pair of Blue Eyes*, ed. Alan Manford (Oxford and New York, 1985), pp. 212, 209.
7. *The Return to the Native*, ed. Simon Gatrell (Oxford and New York, 1990), pp. 253–4.
8. In 1876 Hardy was reading J. G. Woods's *Insects at Home*; he owned two other books by Woods, *Common British Beetles* and *The Common Moths of England*. See *The Literary Notebooks of Thomas Hardy*, ed. Lennart Björk, 2 vols (London, 1985), I. 32–5, and notes to these pages.
9. The detail of the rabbits' ears caught against the sun strongly recalls a similar and much-discussed effect in Holman Hunt's 1852 picture *Strayed Sheep (Our English Coasts)*.
10. See the poem 'Before Life and After', number 230 in *The Complete Poems of Thomas Hardy*, ed. James Gibson (London, 1976). All subsequent references to the poetry are to this edition, with the number given in brackets in the text.
11. Gillian Beer, in *Darwin's Plots* (London, 1983), discusses the scene in terms of plenitude and liberty; see pp. 254–6.
12. See, in addition to Gillian Beer, Tess Cosslett, *The 'Scientific Movement' and Victorian Literature* (Brighton, 1982), Peter Allan Dale, *In Pursuit of a Scientific Culture* (London and Wisconsin, 1989), and George Levine, *Darwin and the Novelists* (Chicago, 1991).
13. *The Collected Letters of Thomas Hardy*, ed. Richard L. Purdy and Michael Millgate, 7 vols (Oxford, 1978–88), 3, 5.
14. *Two on a Tower*, ed. Suleiman Ahmad (Oxford and New York, 1993), pp. 33–4; *A Pair of Blue Eyes*, edn cit., p. 209.
15. *Literary Notebooks*, I. 86. The passage is commented on by Brian Green in his *Hardy's Lyrics: Pearls of Pity* (London, 1996), p. 20.
16. *Tess of the d'Urbervilles*, edited by Juliet Grindle and Simon Gatrell (Oxford and New York, 1988), pp. 279–80.
17. There is a moving example in *Tess* when, after her confession to Angel, Tess sees the stars reflected in the puddles: 'the vastest things of the universe imaged in objects so mean' (edn cit., p. 228).
18. *The Life and Work of Thomas Hardy, by Thomas Hardy*, ed. Michael Millgate (London, 1984), p. 489; cf. also pp. 399–400.
19. In part of course this is because so many scenes take place outdoors; more significantly, it's an aspect of the way Hardy always sees his characters as bodied, and life as a physical fact as well as a moral or intellectual one.

20. The words are George Eliot's, in 'The Influence of Rationalism: Lecky's *History*' (1865); quoted from *Essays and Leaves from a Notebook*, 2nd edn (London and Edinburgh, 1884), p. 228.

21. T. H. Huxley, 'A Liberal Education' (1868), quoted from Tess Cosslett, *The 'Scientific Movement' and Victorian Literature*, p. 17.

22. In *The Woodlanders*, Marty South and Giles understand 'the origin, continuance, and laws' of the sights and sounds of the woods, which seem 'uncanny' to Grace. They are able to hold 'intelligent intercourse' with nature: a phrase which contrasts usefully with Wordsworth's 'ennobling interchange'. See *The Woodlanders*, ed. Dale Kramer (Oxford, 1985), pp. 248–9.

23. T. H. Huxley, 'Autobiography', in *Autobiographies of Charles Darwin and Thomas Henry Huxley*, ed. Gavin de Beer (London, 1974), p. 109. The emphasis on fidelity to the facts of the natural world, however unpalatable, tended to shift the notion of the ugly; what was fitted to its life could be seen as beautiful, or – more ambiguously – as fascinating: the sublime on a minute scale. The new scientific world suggested a need for new aesthetic categories.

24. *Life and Work of Thomas Hardy*, p. 125.

25. Charles Lyell, *Principles of Geology*, edited by James A. Secord (London, 1997), p. 181.

26. *Literary Notebooks*, I. 189.

27. Darwin, *Origin*, edn cit., p. 131; Huxley, in his leading article in the first issue of the journal *Nature* (1869); John Tyndall, 'Belfast Address', quoted from *Science and Religion in the Nineteenth Century*, ed. Tess Cosslett (Cambridge, 1984), p. 183.

28. *The Mayor of Casterbridge*, ed. Dale Kramer (Oxford and New York, 1987), p. 127. All subsequent references are to this edition.

29. See *A Pair of Blue Eyes*, pp. 271–2, 312. My discussion builds on Sophie Gilmartin's account of the novel in her *Ancestry and Narrative in Nineteenth-Century British Literature* (Cambridge, 1998), pp. 216–21; see also her essay in this volume. The parallels with Tess's fear that her identity will be swallowed up in the long line of d'Urberville stories hardly need to be noted.

30. *Far from the Madding Crowd*, ed. Suzanne B. Falck-Yi (Oxford and New York, 1993), p. 254.

31. *The Mayor of Casterbridge*, p. 334.

32. The 'Sixth Book' of *The Return of the Native* is the obvious exception, to which we might add the off-stage reunion of Grace and Fitzpiers at the end of *The Woodlanders*.

33. *The Well-Beloved*, ed. Tom Hetherington (Oxford, 1986), p. 76.

34. See *Lawrence on Hardy & Painting*, ed. J. V. Davies (London, 1973), p. 22.

35. *Jude the Obscure*, ed. Patricia Ingham (Oxford and New York, 1985), p. 27.

36. 'Pain has been, and pain is: no new sort of morals in Nature can remove pain from the past and make it pleasure for those who are . . . the bearers thereof.' See *Life and Work of Thomas Hardy*, pp. 338–9.

37. *Middlemarch* offers the extreme example of the shadow plot. In uniting what she had thought of as two stories, the Lydgate story and the one about 'Miss Brooke', George Eliot inevitably invited the reader to speculate on that

unwritten story in which they married each other. In this case, however, the sense of loss is mitigated by the death of Casaubon and the arrival in Dorothea's life of Will Ladislaw. Hardy's protest in *Tess*, against a universe which allows the wrong man to take the wrong woman, is implicitly set aside by George Eliot's second chance plot.

38. *Darwin's Plots*, p. 249.
39. One of the many ironies of *Tess* is that just as the dairymaids at Talbothays have begun to differentiate themselves in Clare's mind, 'as in a chemical process' (edn cit., p. 122), and to appear as the unique centres of experience that lie beneath the generalised Hodge, they are again subsumed into a group, this time by a biological process, as they each fall in love with him.
40. Hardy copied this passage from Theodore Watts in a notebook entry of 1876; see *Literary Notebooks*, I. 40.

11
Rediscovering Thomas Hardy's 'Facts' Notebook

William Greenslade

From his early twenties, until his death, Thomas Hardy was an habitual – even obsessive – note-taker. As far as we can tell, he began in 1863 with the 'Schools of Painting Notebook'. He kept notebooks, some of pocket-size, from early on in his career, only to destroy most of them or leave instructions that the remainder should be destroyed. Of those which did survive all have been edited, with the exception of 'Poetical Matter' (surviving only on microfilm), and the subject of this essay, described by Hardy as 'Facts: from Newspapers, Histories, Biographies, & other chronicles (mainly Local)'.[1] The history of the composition and make-up of this notebook is, as we shall see, full of puzzles, but in essence we can say that it belongs broadly to the period 1882–1913, but with a special concentration in its compilation in the year 1884. 'Facts', as I shall refer to it, is a substantial and stoutly-bound manuscript volume suggesting in its physical characteristics a deliberate and sustained enterprise, but one whose nature changed during the course of compilation.

This notebook, together with others, was preserved from destruction by Florence Hardy's co-executor, Irene Cooper Willis, who listed it as 'Literary Notes III', after Florence's death in 1937. It was deposited in the Dorset County Museum, becoming publicly available in 1962.[2] Since then, perception of the notebook's attributes and significance has developed slowly, perhaps fitfully, but in recent years decisively. In 1961 Samuel Hynes referred to all the surviving notebooks as 'full of Dorset gossip of dead lovers and bastards and wronged maidens'.[3] But with Christine Winfield's article 'Factual Sources of Two Episodes in *The Mayor of Casterbridge*' (1970), serious study of the creative potential of 'Facts' began.[4] Here the major contribution has been Michael Millgate's *Thomas Hardy: His Career as Novelist* (1971).[5] Millgate's intensive reading of 'Facts' in the light of Hardy's novels and stories was a benchmark for all future consideration of the notebook. His judgement of the status and utility of the notebook was confirmed 11 years later in his *Thomas Hardy: a Biography* (1982), where he sums up the purpose of 'Facts' as 'to record material which might prove usable in the writing of future stories or poems', and where with particular reference to the composition of *The Mayor of Casterbridge* he sees 'Facts' as 'part of a preconceived intention' by Hardy 'to establish the fictional Casterbridge as a densely and concretely realised image of a busy market town, and to base that image firmly upon whatever research, imagination, and personal memory could recover of the historical Dorchester of the second quarter of the nineteenth century'.[6] Millgate's groundbreaking work on 'Facts' has been variously followed by Norman Page, Kristin Brady, Frank Giordano, Simon Gatrell, Pamela Dalziel and Martin Ray.[7]

As has been noted by several of these critics, a major source on which Hardy drew in compiling 'Facts' was, as he put it, 'old DCC' – the *Dorset County Chronicle and Somersetshire Gazette*, especially for the years 1826–30.[8] If a bald summary of what Hardy found to interest him in these papers were to be made, it might run as follows: all kinds of crime, including thieving at fairs and highway robbery; confidence tricksters, theft, fraud, horse-stealing; smuggling, body-snatching; incendiarism; domestic accidents; abductions, elopements and impromptu marriages; suicides – more women than men; coach and waggon accidents; pugilism and wrestling; current fashions; advertisements for coach services, auctions, schools; balls, dinners, theatre, race meetings; county news of assizes and grand juries; trials, transportations and executions. All this, repeatedly, and more, is to be found in 'Facts', in excess, indeed, of what 'might prove useable in the writing of future stories or poems', or of realising the 'image of a busy market town'. Millgate himself, in effect, recognises this 'excess', a little later in the same discussion. He quotes Hardy on his striving for historical authenticity – 'I have instituted inquiries to correct tricks of memory . . . in order to preserve for my own satisfaction a fairly true record of a vanishing life' [9] – and comments that 'as the phrase "for my own satisfaction" suggests, the self-imposed demand for accuracy accorded with his own deeply personal need to preserve the local past, to keep it alive in memory if not in fact'.[10] The further exploration of the subtle, part-unconscious 'satisfactions' which Hardy sought in his reading of 'old DCC', remains one of the most necessary tasks to be undertaken by an editor of 'Facts'.

Yet the phrase 'old DCC' is a long way from representing Hardy's work in 'Facts'. His sources were by no means exclusively newspaper reports, but extended to material more familiar to readers of the editions of other surviving notebooks.[11] Hardy extracted items from some 35 separate sources which, taken together, comprise the 'Histories, Biographies and other chronicles (mainly Local)' of the full title. Particularly notable were the *Letters* of Horace Walpole and his *Journals*, dealing with court life of the mid–late eighteenth century, John Hutchins's *The History and Antiquities of the County of Dorset* (Hardy owned and annotated the four-volume third edition of 1861–73), Mary Frampton's *Journal from 1774–1846* (1885), and *Holland House* (1874) by Princess Liechtenstein, the adopted daughter of Henry Fox, 4th Lord Holland.

With these, and more, the expectation of 'Local' interest is as confidently answered as in Hardy's extracting of items from the local press. George III and his family, the Walpole connection through their ownership of Ilsington House in Puddletown, the long-remembered presence at Stinsford of Lady Susan O'Brien (a Fox-Strangways of Melbury), together with the fact of Hardy's grandfather making the vault for Lady Susan's Stinsford tomb – all this threads through the subtle filiations, entered so deliberately in 'Facts', which bind familial tradition and memory with the historical and national record.

Hardy had known about Walpole's letters as early as the 1860s.[12] A note from this source was copied into 'Literary Notes 1' some time between July 1878 and May 1879.[13] Cuttings from Walpole were first entered into what must be described as an 'ur-notebook' (items 20i–23h, 23j–24f), probably in 1881, were pasted into 'Facts', with additional items entered in 1885 or 1886 (151a) and, again, much later, in or about 1910 (211a–212a).[14] Hutchins is noted both in 'Literary Notes 1' in 1876[15] and in 'Facts' (19a–19f, 20i) again from pasted-in material from another notebook, probably of 1881. There are additional items (188a–189f) from Hutchins in 'Facts' from 1888. Extracts from *Holland House* were copied into 'Facts' (items 180a–183a) while others were entered in 'Literary Notes 1' in 1887.[16] In this case, as in several others, entries were made more or less simultaneously into the different notebooks.[17]

Hardy's own interest in facts about the local past was as developed a faculty as one might expect to find in an imaginative writer; he had certainly been soaked in stories about his family, their friends and immediate neighbours, as well as famous – sometimes infamous – local figures of eminence, be they titled women, smugglers or horse-stealers.

Moreover, there is abundant evidence that from an early age Hardy willingly assimilated and later encouraged stories told to him by his parents, particularly by his mother, Jemima (1813–1904), and by his paternal grandmother, Mary Head (1772–1857) whose memories, dating back to the French Revolution, were shared with her grandson, and commemorated in his poem 'One We Knew' (1902).[18] This facility for immersion in the local past was put to use, in a particularly direct way, in *Under the Greenwood Tree* (1872), in which the way of life of his father and grandfather in and around his birthplace of Upper Bockhampton and the parish of Stinsford was affectionately recaptured. In other novels less closely linked to his family background, such as *The Return of the Native* (1878), Hardy showed a similar ability to imagine the local past and recreate its lineaments from evidence periodically recorded in 'Memoranda of Customs, Dates, &c', begun in 1867.

By the mid-1870s Hardy was formally recording the widening of his range of his interest in the past. 'Literary Notes 1' intermittently records items from local written sources, such as newspapers, but in so far as it also contains several items from Hutchins, the note-taking suggests to Millgate a significant development as a 'resource of the first importance for Hardy's gradual evolution of Wessex as a total imaginative world with a solid, complex, comprehensively realised existence in space and time'.[19] The full flowering of this imaginative world was still a decade away, but in the meantime his next novel, *The Trumpet-Major* (1880), and the research which it would entail, signalled another important shift in his approach to documenting the local past. 'I am wishing to consult the "Sherborne Journal", or the old "Sherborne Mercury" mentioned in Hutchins, for the early part of the present century', he wrote to the Rev. Charles Bingham of Sturminster Newton, in September 1877. 'Can you tell me where . . . I could see any county records, notes, or memoranda relating to that time?'[20] Sensing, perhaps, that the past with which he had been so imaginatively familiar was now seeming to him increasingly remote in time, Hardy turned to the period of the Napoleonic wars, and to that period of it in which Dorset personalities and Dorset itself appeared particularly, even intimately, involved in a national emergency. The results of research conducted at the British Museum during 1878–79 were entered into what became the 'Trumpet-Major Notebook' and the novel followed. Hardy's need to recapture the past increasingly required the support of hard evidence – of battles, dress, style, habits of speech, leading personalities, significant events.

This fact-finding enterprise is in itself significant: the 'precision and range' of Hardy's note-taking, as Richard H. Taylor puts it, is certainly formidable.[21] Unlike 'Memoranda' and 'Literary Notes', the 'Trumpet-Major Notebook' has a practical focus; the facts assembled relate essentially to the public and verifable matter of the story, rather than to characters and incidents suggested by local or even family reminiscence. Nevertheless (and this is always the case with Hardy) the fact-finding was built upon deep reservoirs of emotional and intellectual identification, derived from childhood fascination with stories of the Napoleonic Wars and after, conveyed through powerful and still active memories and encounters.[22] And this also holds good for 'Facts'.

The Hardys moved to Wimborne Minster in June 1881, but by the autumn of that year it seems to have become a 'temporary' staging-post *en route* for Dorchester.[23] As early as March 1882, Hardy was enquiring about a freehold site to build on and by the end of June 1883 the move to Dorchester (Shire-Hall Place) had been made.[24] Construction of Max Gate was underway, and the Hardys' move into it followed two years later in 1885. It is significant that in 1882 Hardy joined the Dorset Natural History and Antiquarian Field Club, at which he would give a paper at Dorchester in May 1884.[25] Hardy's contribution to local culture was formally modest, but in a more private, intimate way he was committing himself with 'Facts' to an alternative archaeology of the local past more thoroughly than might have been apparent to his fellow-members.

The Club opened in new premises, the newly built Dorset County Museum, in January 1884.[26] While it is certainly possible that Hardy consulted the newspaper and other holdings of the Museum, it is more probable that he found a means of consulting the old newspapers he needed at home in Shire-Hall Place. The house which the Hardys had chosen was only a few minutes' walk away from the Museum, but it was also very conveniently placed for the newspaper office of the *Dorset County Chronicle*, from which – to judge from two of his letters to the proprietor Charles Lacey, written in 1917 and 1927 – he appears to have borrowed old copies of the *DCC*, quite possibly for the period in question (1826–30).[27]

Whatever the location of the note-taking from the *DCC* and other newspaper sources, the choice of Shire-Hall Place could not have been more fortunate; but then Hardy's return to Dorchester had the stamp of genius to it. He had found the trick of willing into shape what, at this time in his life, was best suited to harmonise his unconscious, imaginative life with his instincts as a writer and his curiosity as an intellectual. Millgate expresses the process well as an 'orderly falling back upon his oldest, deepest, and surest creative resources. Bockhampton was now within daily reach, an hour's walk away along those same roads and paths he had travelled daily as a boy and youth.'[28]

And the balance in his creative life which this new phase seemed to secure and to express, was echoed, as Millgate reminds us, in the relationship he struck between the life of a country town and that of London 'to which . . . he remained a constant visitor'.[29] Max Gate, on the south side of town, was, after all, handy for the station to London. His regular access to the society of the metropolis underlined Hardy's continuing intellectual development. London reaffirmed him as, in Raymond Williams's phrase, the 'educated observer';[30] for it was as a knowledgeable rather than as a naive reader that, within nine months of settling in Dorchester in 1883, he embarked on the archival adventure recorded in 'Facts'. Hardy was seeking out a social landscape with which, mediated through story and narrated memory, he was familiar as with a species of fiction, but which now required confirmation as public event in the discourse of the best available historical record – the local newspaper.

The genesis of the 'Facts' notebook is complicated, but a reliable account of the date of its composition is an important precondition for an assessment of its significance for Hardy's development as a writer in the early–middle 1880s, and thus of its critical significance. Yet from the outset there is a difficulty. Because of the erratic sequencing of entries over the first 11 pages of the notebook, it is not possible to establish for certain when its composition began; neither can the date of the final sequence of entries be firmly established. Michael Millgate believes that it was begun 'in late 1882'.[31] While Millgate is right to emphasise the early density of 1882 items, the actual process of entering material in the notebook cannot have begun earlier than July 1883. The fact is that the first entry in the notebook comes from a review of Thorold Rogers's *History of Agriculture and Prices in England* in the *Spectator* for 21 July 1883.[32] On, or shortly after that date, Hardy initiated the notebook with the entry on Rogers from the *Spectator*. He then handed the notebook over to Emma who, until November 1883, entered, in no apparent order, contemporary items from newspapers and magazines alongside a backlog of items which had been accumulating in one form or another, from as early as 1876, as cuttings, separate notes or entries in an existing notebook or notebooks.

There was a precedent for such division of labour early on in the composition of a notebook. Björk notes that Hardy may have wanted to show Emma the way, since at the outset of 'Literary Notes 1' Hardy 'wrote the first entry of the notebook proper . . . only to show how he wanted the material copied; his wife then penned the next 228 entries'.[33] Among the more suggestive of the 28 'Facts' items entered by Emma in this early phase were extracts from J. F. Pennie's *The Tale of Modern Genius* (1827) (2a–4c). Hardy had borrowed Pennie from a friend in Wimborne, returning it in December 1882, but not before Emma, it is reasonable to assume, took notes from it.[34] Emma also wrote up items taken from newspapers and magazines – the *Daily News*, the *Times*, the *Saturday Review*, the *Pall Mall Gazette* and *Harper's Bazaar* from December 1882 to November 1883, punctuated by an item from Hutchins, and one from Debrett's Peerage. Hardy reassumed the note-taking in late November 1883 (11c) and established thereafter a reasonably consistent forward momentum.

With the entry headed 'Dog-fighting', with its source given as 'Old DCC Jan 5 1826' (27c), we enter the most sustained and critically important sequence in the notebook, the point at which the first 1826 edition of *DCC* was consulted and items from it noted. The most likely date of entry is March 1884, since there is an adjacent entry (item 26c) from a contemporary newspaper dated '14.3.84'. There is no reason to dispute Millgate's verdict that 'it was with the notebook beside him and *The Mayor of Casterbridge* specifically in mind that Hardy sat down, in or about March 1884, to read his way systematically through the files of the local newspaper, the *Dorset County Chronicle*, for the period beginning January 1826'.[35]

It was an exercise undertaken with thoroughness and discipline. Even when interrupted by the appearance of other fascinating sources – whether a volume of memoirs, an autobiography, a volume of correspondence, or unexpected contemporary newspaper reports too intriguing to ignore – he hardly deviated from what appears to have been a pre-conceived plan of recording as much as he could, in as short a time as he could, from each of five years from 1826 to 1830. Starting at the beginning of each calendar year of the files the procedure was to work through to, more or less, the end of the year, before moving on to the next. The sequence running through 1826 was the most sustained of all, consisting of 146 items taken from January–November 1826 (items

27c–60b). With one exception (a jump between 50f and 51a), all months of the year were covered. Then began the file for 1827 which accounted for 65 items; after a jump forward of nine weeks between early May and June (65a and 65b), there was a brief return to February (65f) before moving ahead to December where, with the insertion of one item of Emma's from April (71a) the remaining entries coalesced (to 77b). Thereafter followed 75 items from 1828 papers, with no deviations, and a further 61 from papers of 1829. The entering of a formidable nine-page summary of a 1826 divorce case, mainly by Emma (120e), marks a convenient staging-post: the break in the sequence is reinforced by two entries (132a and 132b) from contemporary papers from May and June 1884.

This by now rather unexpected intrusion of the contemporary makes it possible to date this point of the note-taking with some precision. It appears that by the middle of May 1884 Hardy, with occasional help from Emma, had covered the files for four out of the five years – 1826–29 – which had been planned: it had taken about two months for Hardy and Emma to enter 350 reports from the *Dorchester County Chronicle* of these years. And although far from complete, the bulk of the immediate work had been done, sufficient at least to provide necessary source material for the novel, *The Mayor of Casterbridge*, which Hardy had been actively planning since January, and to which he now turned in earnest.

The 60 items from 1830 fall into a new phase of the note-taking, as the enterprise gives way to the pressures and demands of manuscript composition of *The Mayor*. The now frequent punctuation of the sequence by some of the 'Histories, Biographies and other chronicles' mentioned above is one characteristic of the notebook from this point on. A concomitant feature, as might be anticipated, is the slowing-down of the rate of entry of the 1830 *DCC* items: 16 entries between May and July 1884, only 17 between August and November 1884, a further six items to late December. By the beginning of 1885 Hardy had worked through to May 1830. He then entered a further 23 items to take the coverage up to July (153a) but this was carried out over 14 months (January 1885–March 1886), during which time he was both completing *The Mayor* and writing *The Woodlanders*.[36] A further batch of 40 entries was taken from July–October 1830 issues, in late 1886 or 1887.[37] Eight final *DCC* entries from November and December 1830 (192a–192h, 193c) follow some time between March 1888 and September 1890. And at this point Hardy enters the final *DCC* item (194b) from a contemporary issue (11 September 1890).

In its marked miscellaneous character, the final phase of the notebook (items 194c–221), entered very sporadically over a further two decades between 1890 and 1913, would appear to resemble the opening pages. But while these are also extremely miscellaneous, the earlier entries were being made within a period only of months, July 1883–March 1884. By contrast, this latter phase extended over a protracted period, of years, as if the existence of the notebook had been from time to time forgotten.[38] This last phase combines the characteristics of both commonplace book and scrapbook. There are entries for *DCC* of the 1880s as well as the 1830s, and there are many extracts from late-century and Edwardian memoirs, alongside reports taken from *Annual Registers* and the *Monthly Review* of the Napoleonic period. A new feature is the pasting-in of cuttings from journals and newspaper sources. The miscellaneous character of this phase is emphasised by a pasted-in section (204b) of 20 pages from a notebook of a third and as yet unidentified hand, containing passages from Basnage's *History of the Jews* (1708), Ernest Crawley's *The Tree of Life: a Story of Religion* (1905) and an as yet unidentified narrative (some of it in Latin) which describes the story of an alternative lineage for Christ – his descent from a Greek soldier, Jacob Panthera and Miriam – and included both in the Jewish *Talmud* and the medieval *Sepher Toldoth Jesu*. There is no available evidence about how Hardy obtained this copy, nor why he chose to paste it into 'Facts'. But taken together along with a further entry, a translation of Origen versus Celsus (trans. Bellamy) (205a–206c) and an interesting editorial aside: 'Vide also Haeckel, Strauss etc.', these sources point to a particular interest of Hardy's (probably in the middle-1900s) in revisionary studies of Christ's origins and significance.[39]

A second anomalous feature of this final phase is the uncertain chronology of these final entries and cuttings. 194b is entered, probably about 1890, on what is the last numbered page of the notebook. Hardy had consistently numbered the recto page, but henceforward all recto pages lack numbering. However, the items are recorded, albeit with decreasing frequency, in a forward-moving sequence into the middle–late 1900s ending with Walpole's *Last Journals* (1910) (211a–212a), entered about 1910, and *My Recollections* by the Countess of Cardigan (1909) (211b–215a), entered about the same time. Thereafter, the sequence is more indeterminate, for the next entry is an extract from a work of 1901, Bishop Walsham How's *A Memoir* (Hardy includes How's notorious letter condemning the 'insolence & indecency' of *Jude the Obscure*), and the notebook ends with a clutch of pasted-in articles from 1902 and 1912 on the subject of Dorchester's old theatres (ff.217–19) and a final cutting about Porphyry, Bishop of Gaza, from the *Periodical* of April 1913 (f.221). Since it is inconceivable that Hardy did not come across the How volume soon after its publication in 1901, the most likely sequence would appear to be that about 1912, Hardy, for whatever reason, returned to How's book, noted it, or copied it from other notes, then proceeded to paste in major items in the debate surrounding Dorchester theatres which surfaced in the *Dorset County Chronicle* in 1902 and again in 1912. An undated cutting on Paganini (f.220) and the *Periodical* article were pasted in shortly afterwards.

Emma's role in the compilation of 'Facts' can be inferred only from internal evidence resting on a discrimination between her hand and that of Hardy, which, while not beyond dispute, is reasonably certain.[40] As we have seen, Emma had made a significant contribution to the note-taking for 'Literary Notes' from spring 1876. Millgate suggests from this that 'the Hardys, during these early years of their marriage, saw themselves as a "team", sharing the same interests and activities, working together in the common project which was Hardy's career'.[41] Simon Gatrell notes that Emma had made a fair copy of the manuscript of *Desperate Remedies* and later wrote some leaves of *The Return of the Native* manuscript. Their co-operation survived well into the 1880s: there was her (later censored) work on the manuscript of *The Mayor of Casterbridge*,[42] followed by 'the frequent appearance of Emma's hand in the manuscript' of *The Woodlanders*; yet, as Millgate remarks, 'neither this nor any other surviving manuscript provides evidence of her participating in the actual process of literary creation'.[43] In the case of 'Facts' Emma may have been free to enter summaries of items which caught her attention, but there was probably little entered which did not secure Hardy's prior agreement.

Emma plays a minor but significant role in the preparation of the notebook, being responsible for copying altogether 59 items out of the 600-odd which are entered into 'Facts', a relatively modest number. The bulk of these (47) were copied in the early pre-'Old DCC' phase – that is, before the notebook assumed its primary focus. Of the 11 entries from the *Dorset County Chronicle* for which Emma is responsible, either mainly or entirely, there are some distinguishing features. Her contributions are habitually of greater length than an average Hardy entry: 34b, the report of a parliamentary election (with comic touches reminiscent of Dickens's Eatanswill election in *The Pickwick Papers*) is over a page long; 71a, 'Coach Robbery', the report of a court case, occupies three pages; 97c, the case of William Kennedy, occupies about eight pages; 120e, the divorce case Bligh vs Wellesley, is 11 pages long and is shared with Hardy; 134a, 'Chaise at Sea' occupies two pages, as does 168a, 'Wreckers' (after which there is virtually no further evidence of her involvement in the notebook). In four cases she and Hardy share the work (34b, 69c, 97c and 120e – the longest entry in the notebook).

While Emma's assistance might have been valuable to Hardy in transcribing the lengthier and more tedious items (such as 97a or 120e) he presumably knew from experience that Emma would invariably tend towards a fuller, word-for-word (rather than selective) form of transcription. Such a consideration doubtless meant that her role in transcribing the *Dorset County Chronicle* was kept to modest proportions, given the intensive regimen which Hardy appears to have set himself from March to May 1884.

If 'Facts' had gone the way of other papers in one of Hardy's or Cockerell's bonfires,[44] Hardy's devotion to its compilation and Emma's contribution to it during the years 1883–85 would have remained quite unknown. For no explicit mention or record of the notebook has yet been found anywhere in Hardy's published writings. The nearest we get to that is a note added by Hardy to his poem 'The Beauty' in *Late Lyrics and Earlier* (1922) where the wording of the note is virtually identical with an entry in 'Facts' (90a), from *DCC*, 16 October 1828, itself taken from a London newspaper, which is the only source Hardy here acknowledges. Hardy also refers to his 'papers', which must have been 'Facts', when corresponding, in 1911, about allusions to smuggling in 'The Distracted Preacher'.[45] It is likely that all the copying was done privately at home, at Shire-Hall Place, and later at Max Gate, using old copies borrowed from the editor.

Hardy's desire for privacy needs no particular defence. But while this is not the place to reflect at length on his title-page injunction, in pencil: 'to be destroyed uncopied', it cannot be overlooked. One aspect of this reticence was his disinclination to have the outside world aware that in the writing of his novels a certain amount of team-work was involved – Emma's participation as amanuensis. More significant was his anxiety to be valued as a writer endowed with powers of invention and creative imagination, not disparaged as a mere rural Naturalist. In his 1888 essay

'The Profitable Reading of Fiction' he had sought to place aesthetic limits on the significance of incidents derived from factual record. Such material – the 'trifles of useful knowledge, statistics, queer historical fact' – was of use in so far as it provided 'the accidents and appendages of narrative', and was to be distinguished from those 'essential literary elements which offer intellectual and moral profit to active and undulled spirits'.[46] Elsewhere Hardy would underpin this aesthetic hierarchy by relegating accounts based closely on verifiable fact to the status of a 'record', as opposed to a 'story'. This was the deliberate distinction he used to recommend 'Blue Jimmy: the Horse Stealer', the story published in 1911 which with Hardy's support Florence Dugdale published in 1911, in which she stuck carefully to reports of the trial of one James Clace, in two contemporary local newspapers.[47]

Yet at the very time of writing this essay, and in the years leading up to it, Hardy had been intensely devoted to accumulating such 'trifles', some of which (at least 30) do provide established sources for 'accidents and appendages of narrative' in his novels, stories and poems. But what Hardy does not acknowledge, and what still needs further recognition, is that the larger purpose of 'Facts', for him, was to assist the genealogical project of penetrating and recapturing a culture, alive in the imagination, but badly in need of verification from the public record and private chronicle, and to initiate a new and key development in the creative life of a writer in his maturity. For 'Facts' marks not an 'innocent' quest after authentication, but witnesses to an extended record of recovery of what he already knew, and had known for years.

Notes

1. The microfilm of 'Poetical Matter' is in the Beinecke Rare Book and Manuscript Library, Yale University, the original having been lost or destroyed. The 'Architectural' notebook is edited by C. J. P. Beatty as *The Architectural Notebook of Thomas Hardy* (Dorchester: Dorset Natural History and Archaeological Society, 1966); the 'School of Painting Notebook', 'Memoranda Notebook' and the 'Trumpet-Major Notebook' are gathered in *The Personal Notebooks of Thomas Hardy*, ed. Richard H. Taylor (London: Macmillan, 1978; hereafter cited as *Personal Notebooks*); *Thomas Hardy's 'Studies, Specimens &c' Notebook* is edited by Pamela Dalziel and Michael Millgate (Oxford: Clarendon Press, 1994); 'Literary Notes' is edited by Lennart A. Björk as *The Literary Notebooks of Thomas Hardy*, 2 vols (London: Macmillan, 1985; here-

after cited as *Literary Notebooks*). 'Facts' is in the Hardy Memorial Collection, Dorset County Museum. For access to the notebook and for permission to quote from it I am indebted to the Trustees of the Memorial Collection, and to the Curator, Richard de Peyer. Research towards an edition of the 'Facts' Notebook to which this essay is a contribution, has been supported by the British Academy, Humanities Research Board. I am very grateful to the staff of the Dorset County Library, Dorchester, to Richard de Peyer and Lillian Swindall at the DCM, and to Michael Millgate, James Gibson and Phillip Mallett for their valuable comments.

2. Björk, 'Textual Introduction' to *Literary Notebooks*, I. xxxi; Michael Millgate, 'The Max Gate Library', in Phillip. V. Mallett and R. P. Draper (eds), *A Spacious Vision: Essays on Hardy* (Newmill: Patten Press, 1994), p. 143.

3. Samuel Hynes, *The Pattern of Hardy's Poetry* (London: Oxford University Press, 1961), p. 6.

4. Christine Winfield, 'Factual Sources of Two Episodes in *The Mayor of Casterbridge*', *Nineteenth-Century Fiction* 25 (2) (September 1970):, pp. 224–31.

5. See Michael Millgate, *Thomas Hardy: His Career as Novelist* (London: Macmillan, 1971), pp. 237–41, 396–7, 400–1.

6. Michael Millgate, *Thomas Hardy: a Biography* (Oxford: Oxford University Press, 1982; 1985), p. 248.

7. Norman Page, *Thomas Hardy* (London: Routledge, 1977); Kristin Brady, *The Short Stories of Thomas Hardy* (London: Macmillan, 1982); Frank Giordano, *'I'd Have My Life Unbe': Thomas Hardy's Self-Destructive Characters* (Alabama: University of Alabama Press, 1984); Simon Gatrell, 'The Early Stages of Hardy's Fiction' in *Thomas Hardy Annual* No. 2, ed. Norman Page (London: Macmillan, 1984), pp. 3–29; *Thomas Hardy: the Excluded and Collaborative Stories*, ed. Pamela Dalziel (Oxford: Clarendon Press, 1992); Martin Ray, *Thomas Hardy: a Textual Study of the Short Stories* (Aldershot: Ashgate Press, 1997).

8. Hardy's use of the *Dorset County Chronicle* was not confined to 'Facts'; entries from it appear sporadically in other notebooks before the inception of 'Facts'. An item entered into 'Literary Notes 1' in 1877, 'A Shorthorn Cow – the highest price ever given was for "The Duchess of Geneva" – 7000 guineas', came from the *Dorset County Chronicle* (13 September 1877, p. 14) (*Literary Notebooks*, I. 116, 353n). Another item entered into 'Literary Notes 1' was a report of a speech on India by a Capt. Digby (*DCC* 8 November 1877, pp. 4–5), (*Literary Notebooks*, I. 116, 354n). The 'Trumpet-Major Notebook' contains a reference to a trial report from an 1829 *DCC* newspaper, 'Trial of Kennedy for shooting at Rev. H. Willoughby' (*Personal Notebooks*, p. 168), an episode later followed up extensively in 'Facts' (item 97c). Later, in 1888, long after the bulk of the work for 'Facts' had been completed, Hardy spotted a *DCC* report of the suicide of an Army Officer in 1888 (*DCC*, 2 August 1888, p. 12) which furnished him with details of the sensational murder of Alec d'Urberville by Tess, and which was pasted into a copy of *Tess* presented to Florence Dugdale in 1911. (See Millgate, *Thomas Hardy: His Career as Novelist*, p. 265, p. 401n).

9. Millgate, *Thomas Hardy: a Biography*, p. 252. Millgate cites this famous passage from Hardy's 'General Preface to the Novels and Poems' for the Wessex edition of 1912; it is reprinted in *Thomas Hardy's Personal Writings*, ed. Harold Orel (London: Macmillan, 1967), p. 46.

10. Millgate, *Thomas Hardy: a Biography*, p. 252.
11. *Literary Notebooks*, I. 396, 397 (notes to items 1454 and 1464).
12. Millgate, *Thomas Hardy: a Biography*, p. 112.
13. *Literary Notebooks*, I. 118 (item 1097).
14. This notebook ran to at least 80 pages, some of which, for the years 1876–81, were included in 'Facts', ff.19–24, by a process of cutting and glueing at which Hardy was adept.
15. *Literary Notebooks*, I. 60–2, 308–10n (items 584, 586–601).
16. *Literary Notebooks*, I. 187, 396n (item 1454).
17. Other important sources entered both in 'Literary Notes' and 'Facts', and appearing to be entered at more or less the same time, are: Cotter Morison's *The Service of Man* (1887), entered in 'Literary Notes 1' in the winter of 1887–88 (items 1464, 1466–1471, *Literary Notebooks*, I. 189–92, 396–7n) and in 'Facts' (items 185a–185b) at the same period; W. P. Frith's *My Autobiography and Reminiscences* (1887) recorded in 'Literary Notes 1' (items 1475–81, *Literary Notebooks*, I. 193, 397–8n) and in 'Facts' (items 187b, 190a–191b) in January 1888. Among other less significant items are an article on the German poet Nikolaus Lenau, entered into 'Literary Notes 1' (item 1232, *Literary Notebooks*, I. 141, 374n, autumn 1881, and into 'Facts' (items 24f–24g); and an item from Louis de Bourienne's *Mémoires de Napoleon*, copied into 'Literary Notes 1' (item 1528, *Literary Notebooks*, I. 203, 400–1n) and into 'Facts' (item 191c) in February or early March 1888.
18. Millgate, *Thomas Hardy: a Biography*, p. 18.
19. Millgate, *Thomas Hardy: a Biography*, p. 189.
20. *The Collected Letters of Thomas Hardy*, eds Richard Little Purdy and Michael Millgate, 7 vols (Oxford: Clarendon Press, 1978–1988), I. 51.
21. *Personal Notebooks*, p. xxii.
22. *Personal Notebooks*, p. xxi–xxii.
23. *Collected Letters*, I. 91, 95.
24. *Collected Letters*, I. 105.
25. See Millgate, *Thomas Hardy: a Biography*, p. 244; James Gibson, *Thomas Hardy: a Literary Life* (London: Macmillan, 1996), p. 98.
26. Jo Draper, 'The Founding of the Dorset County Museum', *Dorset Year Book* (1997): 59–63 (p. 62).
27. In a letter of 1917 to Lacey (who attended Isaac Last's British School in Dorchester at the same time as Hardy (*Collected Letters*, II. 237n)) Hardy writes that he is returning 'old papers', 'numbers of the Dorset County Chronicle', which 'must have been borrowed I think from a former editor for reference to something or other connected with the first Reform Bill', and which had been kept in a cupboard which he has turned out (*Collected Letters*, V. 210). Ten years later, in a further letter to Lacey (17 March 1927) Hardy refers to another 'bundle of old Chronicles lent me many years ago' which he is about to return (*Collected Letters*, VII. 62). My thanks to Michael Millgate for referring me to these letters.
28. Millgate, *Thomas Hardy: a Biography*, p. 247. The shift in interest towards material with a specific reference to the locality is reflected in the decline in the rate of entry of Hardy's entries into 'Literary Notes', used actively by Hardy since 1876. While nearly 80 entries are recorded in the period 1881–83, the year of 1883 itself shows a modest 24 or 25 items. But then in

the six months from September 1883 to April 1884 'Literary Notes' has virtually ceased to be active, with only two items entered. After a short spurt of nine entries from periodicals in April, there are no further entries until August and only another three entries to November. No further items are recorded until March or April 1885. Between January 1884, when he began serious planning of *The Mayor*, and September 1885, on the point of beginning *The Woodlanders*, Hardy records only 32 items from 16 sources. Thereafter the rate of entry picks up with nine entries in the period September–December 1885, approximately 38 in 1886 and 56 entries in 1887 (there are also some anomalous entries).

29. Millgate, *Thomas Hardy: a Biography*, p. 247.
30. Williams, *The Country and the City*, p. 206.
31. Millgate, *Thomas Hardy: a Biography*, p. 248.
32. Rogers's *History of Agriculture and Prices* clearly touched on matters of interest raised in Hardy's own 'Dorsetshire Labourer' essay, published in *Longman's Magazine* on 25 June 1883, only a month before the review of Rogers appeared. Although the extract deals with rural England under Henry VIII, the title given to it by Hardy – 'Condition of Rural England' – suggests that he is likely to have been tempted to enter the item fairly soon after reading it. It is possible that Hardy's essay for *Longman's* was discussed with Edmund Gosse when Hardy dined with him at the Savile Club, on the day it appeared – 25 June 1883 (*Life and Work*, p. 166). Both Hardy's article and the review of Rogers in the *Spectator* may have been further alluded to by the two men the following month, when Gosse, the Hardys' first guest at Shire-Hall Place, arrived in Dorchester on Saturday, 21 July, the very day of the issue of the *Spectator* containing the review of Rogers's book (Millgate, *Thomas Hardy: a Biography*, p. 248).
33. *Literary Notebooks*, I. xxxv.
34. *Collected Letters*, I. 111.
35. Millgate, *Thomas Hardy: a Biography*, p. 248.
36. On 17 April 1885 a diary entry recorded: 'Wrote the last page of 'The Mayor of Casterbridge', begun at least a year ago. . . .' By November Hardy was well advanced with the planning of *The Woodlanders*, at this stage entitled 'Fitzpiers at Hintock' (Millgate, *Thomas Hardy: a Biography*, p. 269). Since May 1884, the strategic utility of the *DCC* entries had shifted away from supplying Hardy with materials for *The Mayor*.
37. Extracts from Mary Frampton's *Journal* (1885) are entered after these items; one *DCC* item (177b) is sandwiched between the Frampton entries.
38. Hardy did in fact put the notebook to use in these years, drawing on a lengthy entry he had made in Facts', 163a 'Lulworth Smugglers', for revisions to 'The Distracted Preacher' for the 1912 Wessex edition of *Wessex Tales*. Never acknowledging the existence of the notebook, he referred only to 'the notes I made', in a letter of 1911. (See Martin Ray, *Thomas Hardy: a Textual Study of the Short Stories*, pp. 56–7.)
39. These materials provide the sources for Hardy's poem, 'Panthera', which he acknowledges in a note to the poem; see *The Variorum Edition of the Complete Poems of Thomas Hardy*, edited by James Gibson (London: Macmillan, 1976), pp. 280–6. My thanks to James Gibson for pointing out this reference.

40. For discussions of the characteristics of Hardy's and Emma's handwriting, see Christine Winfield, 'The Manuscript of Hardy's *Mayor of Casterbridge*', *Papers of the Bibliographical Society of America* 67 (1973), pp. 357–60; Björk, *Literary Notebooks*, I. xxxv–xxxvi; Alan Manford, 'Hardy's Helping Hand' in *Critical Essays on Thomas Hardy: The Novels*, ed. Dale Kramer (Boston: G. K. Hall, 1990), pp. 100–21.
41. Millgate, *Thomas Hardy: a Biography*, pp. 189–90.
42. Simon Gatrell, *Hardy the Creator: a Textual Biography* (Oxford: Clarendon Press, 1988), pp. 47–8.
43. Millgate, *Thomas Hardy: a Biography*, p. 269.
44. Michael Millgate, *Testamentary Acts* (Oxford: Clarendon Press, 1992), pp. 159–60.
45. See note 38. Pamela Dalziel has drawn attention to the existence of another reference to 'Facts' – a manuscript note, in Hardy's hand, preserved in the DCM; see *Excluded and Collaborative Stories*, ed. Dalziel, p. 345.
46. 'The Profitable Reading of Fiction', in *Thomas Hardy's Personal Writings*, ed. Harold Orel, pp. 112–13.
47. See *Collected Letters*, IV. 114, cited by Pamela Dalziel, Introduction to *An Indiscretion in the Life of an Heiress and Other Stories* (Oxford: Oxford University Press, 1994), p. xxxv.

Index

'Abbey Mason, The', 101, 160
Abercrombie, Lascelles, 2
Academy, 14n
'After a Journey', 10
'Afternoon Service at Mellstock (Circa 1850)', 98–9, 124–5
'Afterwards', 167
Ainsworth, Harrison, 59
'Alarm, The', 110
Anderson, Sherwood, 141–2
Archer, William, xii, 112
'Architectural Masks', 100
Arnold, Matthew, ix, xi, xiv, 70n
Art Journal, 28–9
'At a House in Hampstead', 125–6
'At an Inn', 115
'At Castle Boterel', 160
'At the Aquatic Sports', 122
'At the Pyramid of Cestus', 125
'At the Railway Station, Upway', 122, 146–7
'At the Wicket Gate', 98
'At Wynard's Gap', 160
Athenaeum, 4, 110
Austen, Jane, 7
'Autumn Rain-Scene, An', 159

Bailey, J. O., 115
'Ballad-Singer, The', 122
Barham, R. H., 86
Barnes, William, 78
Barrie, J. M., 137, 141
Barth, John, 83, 84, 85
Baudelaire, Charles, 132
Bayley, John, 142
Beatty, Claudius, 97
Beautiful Thoughts from Latin Authors, 60
'Beauty, The', 181
'Beeny Cliff', 10
Beer, Gillian, 166
'Before Life and After', 158
Belgravia, 65, 66

Benjamin, Walter, xiii, 138–9, 141
'Beyond the Last Lamp', 160
Bingham, Rev. Charles, 174
Björk, Lennart A., 177
Blomfield, Arthur, 31–2, 96, 103
Blunden, Edmund, 97
Bowler, Henry Alexander, 26–31
Brady, Kirstin, 172
Brandon, Raphael, 96
'Bride-Night Fire, The' ('The Fire at Tranter Sweatley's'), 113, 114, 115
Brontë, Charlotte, 163
Brooks, Jean, 114
Browning, Robert, x, 77, 78, 79, 80, 103, 113, 117, 128
Builder, The, 97
'Burghers, The', 114
Burns, Robert, 77, 80, 119, 121
Butler, Samuel, 78
Butterfield, William, 95
Byatt, A. S., 61
Byron, Lord, 65, 77, 78, 80

Campbell, Thomas, 77, 78, 79, 81–2
Cardigan, Countess of, 179
Carew, Thomas, 118
'Casterbridge Captains, The', 110
'Cathedral Facade at Midnight, A', 98
Cézanne, Paul, 41
Chambers, E. K., 110
'Change, The', 122–3
'Chapel-Organist, The', 122
Chapman, Raymond, 58, 69n
Chatterton, Thomas, 78, 85, 86
Chaucer, Geoffrey, 47, 115, 150
Chekhov, Anton, 107, 141
'Childhood among the Ferns', 160
'Christmastide', 122
'Church and the Wedding, The', 99
'Church Romance, A', 98
'Clock-Winder, The', 98
Clodd, Edward, 110
Cockerell, Sydney, 181

Coleridge, Samuel Taylor, 105–6, 116
Collins, Wilkie, viii, 59
'Commonplace Day, A', 160
Conrad, Joseph, 163
Constable, John, 41
'Copying Architecture in an Old Minster', 97
Cornhill Magazine, xiv, 1
Correggio, Antonio da, 7
Cosslett, Tess, 168n
Cowper, William, 117
Crabbe, George, 150
Crashaw, Thomas, 78, 80, 81
Crawley, Earnest, 179
Crickmay, G. R., 96

Daily Chronicle, The, 112
Daily News, The, 177
Dale, Peter Allan, 168n
Dalziel, Pamela, 20n, 172
Darwin, Charles, 156–7, 161, 162, 165, 166
David (the Psalmist), 118, 119, 129
Davie, Donald, ix
Defoe, Daniel, xii, 62, 64, 65
Desperate Remedies, viii, xiii, 2, 5, 11, 14, 61, 76, 77, 78, 92, 97, 108, 180
Dickens, Charles, 7, 163, 180
'Distracted Preacher, The', 181
'Ditty', 114
'Domicilium', 106
Dorset County Chronicle, 172–82 passim
'Drawing Details in an Old Church', 97
Drayton, Michael, 78
Droz, Jacquet, 61
Drummond, William, 78
'During Wind and Rain', 122, 153, 159, 160
Dryden, John, 78, 80, 115, 117, 118, 123
Dylan, Bob, 118
Dynasts, The, 114, 162

Edison, Thomas, 120–1

Elgar, Edward, 5
Eliot, George, viii, ix, x, xi, 3, 45, 160, 163, 169–70n
Eliot, T. S., viii, 70n, 103, 120

Far from the Madding Crowd, viii, xiv, 1–19, 30–1, 44–5, 59, 61, 86, 97, 101, 161, 164–5
Faulkner, William, 142
Fielding, Henry, 45, 83–4, 85
'Figure in the Scene, The', 160
Forster, E. M., 18
Fortnightly Review, 102
'Friends Beyond', 110, 113, 115
'Frozen Greenhouse, The', 142

Galt, John, 141
Gatrell, Simon, 20n, 172, 180
Gay, John, 80
Gibson, James, xv
Gilmartin, Sophie, 169n
Ginsberg, Allan, 118
Giordano, Frank, 172
Gittings, Robert, 80–1, 104n
Gleanings from Popular Authors, 4
'Going of the Battery, The', 160
'Going, The', 151
Golden Treasury, The, ix, 60
Goode, John, 69
Gosse, Edmund, 78, 109, 112
Graham, Dugald, 140
Graphic, 3, 7
Graves, Robert, 51–4
Gray, Thomas, 24, 29, 80
Green, Brian, 168n
Greuze, Jean Baptiste, 61
Grigson, Geoffrey, 150
Group of Noble Dames, A, 32

Haggard, Henry Rider, 39n
Hand of Ethelberta, The, xiii, 1, 64–5, 70n, 78
'Hap', 113, 115, 159, 163
Hardy, Emma (*née* Gifford), 8–9, 33, 108, 110–11, 114, 150, 151, 152, 160, 176, 177, 178, 180–1
Hardy, Florence Emily (*née* Dugdale), 171, 182

Hardy, Jemima, 174
Hardy, Mary, 109, 115
Harper's Bazaar, 177
'Harvest-Supper, The', 122
Hawkins, Desmond, xv
Hawthorne, Nathaniel, 22, 141
'He Inadvertently Cures His Love-Pains', 126–8
'He Resolves to Say No More', xiii
Head, Mary, 174
Heine, Heinrich, 78
'Heiress and Architect', 102
Henley, W. E., 4
Henniker, Florence, 115
'Her Dilemma', 98
'Her Initials', 127–8
Herrick, Robert, 118
Herschel, J. F. W., 162
Hicks, John, 96, 98
Hillis Miller, J., 50
Hogg, James, 141
Holder, Caddell, 9
Homer, 61, 78, 119
Horace, 63, 77, 78
Hoskins, John, 78
How, Bishop Walsham, 179
'How I Built Myself a House', 102
Hughes, Ted, 150
Hugo, Victor, 132
Human Shows, 111
Hutchins, John, 173, 179
Hutton, Richard, viii
Huxley, Thomas, 160–1, 162

'I Found Her Out There', 33
'I Look into My Glass', 115, 161
'I Rose Up as My Custom Is', 125
'Impercipient, The', 97, 110, 114, 115
'In a Eweleaze Near Weatherbury', 111
'In a Whispering Gallery', 98
'In a Wood', 115, 159
'In Church', 98
'In Death Divided', 30
'In Sherborne Abbey', 98
'In St Paul's a While Ago', 98
'In Tenebris II', 161

'Indiscretion in the Life of an Heiress, An', 80
'Ivy-Wife, The', 114

James, G. P. R., 59
James, Henry, ix, 22–3
Janacek, Leon, 52
Jeune, Lady Mary, 115
John Bull, 4
Johnson, Lionel, 5
Johnson, S. F., 69n
Jude the Obscure, 38, 39, 61, 78, 81–2, 95, 97, 98, 99, 107, 111, 115, 140, 161, 166, 179
'Julie-Jane', 122

Keats, John, 77, 78, 80, 125–6, 129–30, 133–4
Keble, John, 78
Keeling, E. Bassett, 95
Ken, Bishop, 78
Kipling, Rudyard, viii, 120

Lacey, Charles, 175
'Lacking Sense, The', 162
Lamb, E. B., 95
Landor, Walter Savage, 132
Langbaum, Robert, 6
Langhorne, John, 105, 116n
Laodicean, A, 78, 87, 97, 98, 101
Larkin, Philip, viii, 150
Late Lyrics and Earlier, viii, 111, 146, 181
Lawrence, D. H., viii, 165, 166
Lecercle, Jean Jacques, 59
Leskov, Nikolai, xiii, 139
'Levelled Churchyard, The', 33
Levine, George, 168n
Liechtenstein, Princess, 173
Life of Thomas Hardy, The, xi, xii, xiv, 31–2, 39n, 46, 48, 59, 60, 62, 72–3, 92, 98, 100, 102, 103, 106, 107, 108, 112–13, 132, 159, 161, 169n
'Lines', 115
Lock, Charles, 59
Longman's Magazine, 137
'Lost Love', 123
Lovelace, Richard, 118

Lyell, Charles, 103, 161
Lynd, Robert, 103, 104n
Lyrical Ballads, ix, 105–6, 108, 116

Macdonnell, Annie, 112
Macmillan, Alexander, xiii, 62
MacNiece, Louis, 165
'Mad Judy', 121
'Maid of Keinton Mandeville, The',
    122
Mallett, Phillip, 21n
Malthus, Thomas, 162
Marie Antoinette, 65
Marlowe, Christopher, 80
Mayor of Casterbridge, The, 4, 5, 76,
    87–8, 89–90, 101, 111, 140, 163,
    165, 166, 172, 178
'Melancholy Hussar of the German
    Legion, The', 141
'Memories of Church Restoration',
    97, 98, 100, 101
'Middle-Age Enthusiasms', 115
'Midnight on the Great Western',
    147–9
'Milkmaid, The', 145–6
Millgate, Michael, xv, 6, 102, 111,
    171–2, 174, 175–6, 180
Milton, John, 64, 76–7, 78, 79, 80,
    118–19
'Molly Gone', 123
Moments of Vision, 73, 113, 147
Moore, Thomas, 77
Morgan, Rosemarie, 59, 94n
Morison, Cotter, 161
Morley, John, xiii, 62
Morris, William, 96
'Mother Mourns, The', 162
Moule, Horace, 19n
Mrs Grundy, 43, 107

'Nature's Questioning', 113, 162
Nesfield, W. E., 96, 101
'Neutral Tones', 115
Newman, John Henry, 77, 79

O'Brien, Lady Susan, 173
'Old Furniture', 148
'On an Invitation to the United
    States', 22–3

'On Stinsford Hill at Midnight', 122
'On the Esplanade', 122
'One We Knew', 174
Orpheus, 119
'Oxen, The', 73, 92

Page, Norman, xiv, 137, 172
Pair of Blue Eyes, A, ix, x, 1–19, 31,
    33–7, 38, 44, 63–4, 76–7, 80, 96,
    97, 98, 156–7, 158–9, 160, 162–3,
    164
Pall Mall Gazette, 2, 112, 177
'Panthera', 107, 185n
Patmore, Coventry, 5
Paulin, Tom, 147
Peacock, Thomas Love, 126
Pennie, J. F., 177
Periodical, 180
Pettit, Charles P. C., 21n
'Phantom Horsewoman, The', 122
Picasso, Pablo, 52
Pilkington, F. T., 95
Poe, Edgar Allan, 77
Poems of the Past and Present, 111,
    113, 145
'Poems of 1912–13', xi, 9, 33, 73,
    122, 150
'Poor Man and a Lady, A', 98
Poor Man and the Lady, The, xiii, 62,
    97
Pope, Alexander, 43
Post Office Directory of Devonshire
    and Cornwall, 9
Pound, Ezra, 107
'Profitable Reading of Fiction, The',
    182
'Prophetess, The', 122
'Proud Songsters', 125, 160
Pugin, A. W. N., 95, 101, 102
Purdy, Richard Little, 21n
Pushkin, Alexander, 140

Quarterly Review, 25
Quiller-Couch, Arthur, 109

'Rain on a Grave', 160
Raphael (Raffaello Sanzio), 7
Ray, Martin, 172
Reformation and Deformation, 99

'Respectable Burgher on the "Higher Criticism", The', 118
Return of the Native, The, 4, 5, 15, 65–8, 76, 157–8, 165
Ricks, Christopher, viii, 109, 137
Rogers, Thorold, 176
'Rome: Building a Street in the Old Quarter', 119
'Rome: On the Palatine', 149–50
Rossetti, Dante Gabriel, 77, 78
Rubens, Peter Paul, 7
'Ruined, Maid, The', 107, 115
Ruskin, John, 95, 101, 102, 155–6
Rutland, William R., 19n

Said, Edward, 38
Sappho, 65, 80, 94n, 119, 131, 132, 135, 136
Satires of Circumstance, 73, 108, 111
Saturday Review, 3, 4, 112, 177
Scott, George Gilbert, xii, 96
Scott, Walter, 78, 80, 140
Scrutiny, ix
'Seeing the Moon Rise', 123
'Selfsame Song, The', 128–9, 136
Shakespeare, William, 58, 61, 77, 79, 87, 150
Shaw, Norman, 96, 101
'She, to Him', 113, 115
'Sheep Fair, A', 160
'Shelley's Skylark', 125, 161
Shelley, Percy Bysshe, 38, 76, 77, 79, 106, 125, 126
Sheridan, Richard Brinsley, 78
Shirley, Arthur, 98–9
'Shut Out That Moon', xii
Siddons, Mrs, 65
'Sign-Seeker, A', 113
'Singer Asleep, A', 49, 120, 121, 130–6
'Singing Lovers', 122
'Sitting on the Bridge', 122
Smith, T. Roger, 96
Snell, Keith, 39n
'Son's Veto, The', 26
'Song to an Old Burden', 136
Sparks, Tryphena, 111, 114–15
Spectator, viii, 2, 176
'Spellbound Place, A', viii, 137
Spencer, Herbert, 167

Springer, Marlene, 58–9, 70n
Statham, H. H., 102
Steig, Michael, 19n
Stephen, Leslie, ix, xiv, 1, 21n, 109
Stevenson, Robert Louis, 5, 140, 143
Stinsford Church, 98–9, 110
Strachey, Lytton, 132
'Stranger's Song, The', 137–8
Suckling, John, 118
Swinburne, Algernon Charles, 46, 77, 78, 80, 89, 116, 120, 121, 130–6
Swindall, Lilian, 19n

Taylor, Dennis, xi, 62–3
Taylor, Richard H., 174–5
'Temporary the All, The', xii, 110, 115, 116
Tennyson, Alfred Lord, 5, 29, 78, 79, 80, 81, 88, 113, 116, 120
Terence, 78
Tess of the d'Urbervilles, x, 5, 15, 16, 23, 24, 38, 45, 73, 78, 86, 88–9, 90–1, 92, 97, 101–2, 107, 111, 140, 159, 161, 166–7, 168n
Teulon, S. S., 95
Thackeray, William, 163
Thomas, Dylan, 142
'Thoughts of Phena', 114
'Three Strangers, The', 137–41
'Thunderstorm in Town, A', 160
Time's Laughingstocks, 111
Times, The, 4, 20n, 177
Tinsley, William, 1, 3, 5
Tinsleys' Magazine, 10, 18
'To a Lady Playing and Singing in the Morning', 122
'To a Motherless Child', 114–15
'Trampwoman's Tragedy, A', 142–3
Trollope, Anthony, viii, 6, 7–8, 163
Trumpet-Major, The, 174–5
Turgenev, Ivan, 141
Two on a Tower, 76, 158
Tyndall, John, 162

Under the Greenwood Tree, 4, 8, 75, 76, 98, 99, 110, 174
'Unknowing', 115
'Upbraiding, An', 123

'Valenciennes', 114
Virgil, 61, 70n, 78, 80, 119
'Voice, The', xii

'Waiting Supper, The', 77
Walker, G. A., 25–6, 29
Waller, Edmund, 80
Walpole, Horace, 173, 179
Watson, T., 78
Watson, William, 109, 116
Watts, Theodore, 167, 170n
'We Field-Women', 160
'We Sat at the Window', 160
Well-Beloved, The, viii, x–xi, 31, 37, 41–57, 165
Wentworth, Sir Thomas, 1st Earl of Strafford, 68, 71n
'Wessex Heights', xii, 73, 108
Wessex Poems, viii, xii, 74, 97, 102, 105–16, 138
Wessex Tales, 137
Westminster Gazette, 112
Westminster Review, 13
'Wet August, A', 124

Wheeler, Michael, 26, 28, 60
'When I Set Out for Lyonnesse', 9, 108
'While Drawing in a Churchyard', 97
'Whispered at a Church Opening', 99
White, W. W., 95
Whitman, Walt, 78, 86
Widdowson, Peter, 59
Williams, Raymond, xiv, 59, 176
Willis, Irene Cooper, 171
Winfield, Christine, 171
'Winter in Durnover Field', 160
Winter Words, xiii, 106, 111, 112
'Withered Arm, The', 143–5
'Without Ceremony', 151
Woodlanders, The, 5, 23, 45, 64, 76, 79, 85, 101, 165, 169n, 178, 180
Wordsworth, William, viii, ix, 10, 24–5, 28, 29, 31, 80, 105–6, 113, 116, 121, 146, 150, 159
Wyatt, Thomas, 80

Yeats, W. B., viii, 52, 120, 126
'Your Last Drive', 150–2